Taste Britain
First published in the United Kingdom in 2010 by
Punk Publishing Ltd
3 The Yard
Pegasus Place
London
SE11 5SD

www.punkpublishing.co.uk

A catalogue record of this book is available from the British Library.

ISBN: 978-1-906889-05-0

10 9 8 7 6 5 4 3 2 1

Taste
Britain

A food-lover's guide

Contents

Introduction by Alex James

We live in a global culture. In the 2010s, it's almost as if, before anyone can consider themselves a successful musician, they need to have been number one in about 36 countries.

But artistic success can be measured in many different ways and when it comes to our specialist food producers the best of them are artists. They're not necessarily out to make as much of something as possible but they are all motivated by a desire to create something outstanding. They might not get rich, they probably won't be famous, but they're taking pride in making exceptional food. This goes further than the romance of knowing

"artisan producers pour their heart and soul into their products – just like musicians do with their music"

who makes the food we eat or where ingredients come from. People are beginning to realise that artisan producers pour their heart and soul into their products – just like musicians do with their music – and that the benefits of this are delicious.

My love of good food goes back to my childhood but, like many people my age, it really began in France on holidays and exchange trips. That's where I discovered cheese, pâtés, soufflés, pastries and how to cook chips and countless other delights. Back then British cuisine and food culture was practically non-existent. Nowadays, though, the best of British is as good as the best anywhere in the world.

When my wife and I got married a few years ago, we swapped Covent Garden for the Oxfordshire countryside where we now keep livestock, grow cereals and invent cheeses. It seemed like quite a reckless thing to do at the time and if we hadn't done it then, we probably would never have done it. But I'm really, really glad we did. We haven't looked back. Not least it has completely changed the way I look at food. It's hard to believe I was a vegetarian for 20 years.

Since I've lived here, I've really enjoyed discovering local producers and many excellent farm shops and food businesses. I've met people with passion for what they do, a dedication that is reflected in welfare standards and ultimately the quality and flavour of the food they produce. And this is happening all over the country: amazing food is being created up and down the land by devoted specialists, proud farmers, small-scale growers and innovative artisans. Independent shopkeepers, market stall-holders and local chefs are rallying to the cause, and an ever more discerning customer is recognising that the food itself – and the whole experience of visiting these local food destinations – is Britain's best-kept secret.

And this is where *Taste Britain* comes in. The book guides you to some of the most worthwhile food destinations in the country, a gastronome's mystery tour of Britain's tastiest places. As you would expect, there's an emphasis on artisan producers, independent shops and local and regional food. But here great food is included wherever it is found, whether that's a family pasty shop in Cornwall, a cheesemaker in Somerset, fish sheds in Suffolk or Fortnum & Mason in Piccadilly, where they've been championing high-quality independent British food for more than three centuries. But let there be no food snobbery! Manze's pie

How to use this book

- To find out what's near you, head to the regional maps on pages 14, 56, 98, 160, 216 and 250.
- To get straight to the cheeses, ice creams, farm shops or any other category, use the index on page 286.
- Or just dip in randomly to see what looks good and use the green map numbers to locate your finds.

The Lizard Pasty Shop **8**
See page 20

Cheddar Gorge Cheese Company **52**
See page 48

Sole Bay Fish Co **207**
See page 138

Fortnum & Mason **82**
See page 65

M Manze **88**
See page 65

Hound of the Basket Meals **25**
See page 36

and mash shop in London and a roadside snack van in a lay-by in Dartmoor both make an appearance simply because they serve up excellent food.

Use this book for inspiration: to try these places and to make more discoveries of your own. The customer is the most important person in the whole food chain and these tiny shops and little restaurants can't exist without you. Get an organic vegetable box delivery, pop into the farm shop down the road, pay a visit to the smelly cheesemaker or that weird smokery you've vaguely heard about, and your taste buds will thank you for it.

South-west England

Atlantic Ocean

Bideford

Exeter

Padstow

Plymouth

St Ives

Penzance

Falmouth

Isles of Scilly

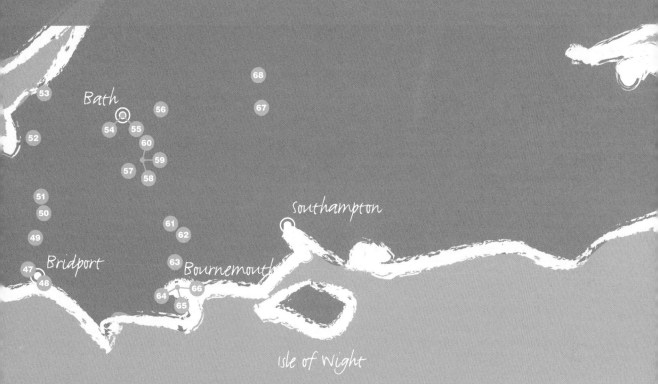

Guests at the Star Castle Hotel may be bemused to see the proprietor heading out to sea at the helm of his own fishing boat early in the morning, but this is just one side of this multi-talented man. Robert Francis, owner of the ancient star-shaped fortress protecting the harbour approaches at St Mary's in the Isles of Scilly, is so passionate about providing fresh food that he sails out every day and catches it himself.

'Captain Robert', as some of the guests call him, has 250 lobster- and crab-pots dotted around the island and uses nets to catch fish as well. On returning to port, he tramps back into the kitchens in his oilskins to deliver the crayfish, rays, monkfish, turbot and brill. The crabs are boiled, then delivered to a local farmer's wife who picks out the meat, which is all gratefully received by the hotel's chef.

But Robert's hotel guests can't eat all of his top-quality Scillonian lobsters, so the surplus is flown to fish markets in Newlyn and Paignton as well as to the luxury Devonshire hotel Combe House. His lobsters even travel as far as London; in fact, President Obama was served one at a dinner in 2009.

Star Castle Hotel 1
Garrison Hill, Hugh Town, St Mary's,
Isles of Scilly TR21 0TA
01720 422317
www.star-castle.co.uk

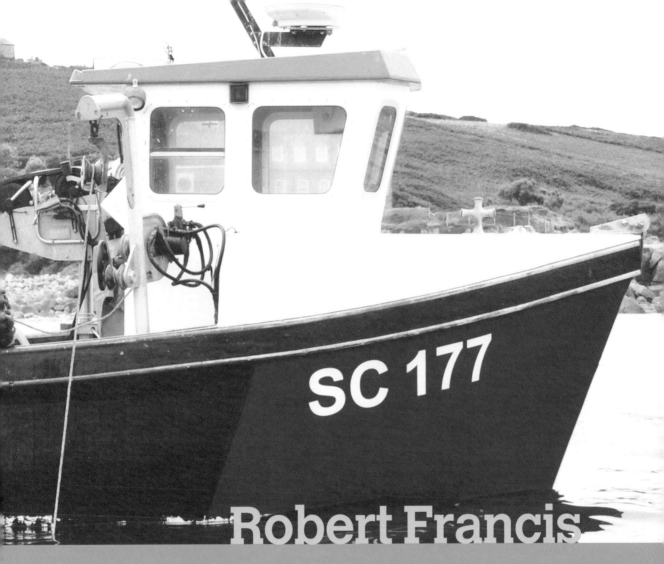

Robert Francis

"Robert is so passionate about fresh food that he sails out and catches it himself."

That would be enough for most busy hotel bosses but Robert is an eco-warrior of extraordinary energy. He has now taken over a two-acre plot on a local farm where he invites hotel guests to browse the bountiful market garden. A wide assortment of its home-grown vegetables feature on the hotel menu, including six types of lettuces, four of beans, four of onions, chicory, endives and cucumbers.

Yet still Robert is not satisfied. Any guest at the Star Castle Hotel soon realises their patron is a serious and generous wine expert; he visits vineyards around the world to select wines for his cellar. Some of his favourites, often from little-known producers, are offered with just a tiny mark-up. 'I'm not making much but I want people to enjoy these good wines. I'm trying to make them more affordable.'

His latest and perhaps most ambitious plan yet is to make his own wine. Robert has planted eight acres of south-facing, well-drained land near the hotel with 7,000 vines. The grapes are already fruiting and Robert is busy planning to build his winery with advice from his international vineyard contacts. 'I want to learn to make it myself and there's no point doing it unless it's really good stuff.'

St Martin's Bakery

Welcome to what must be one of the most remote bakeries in Europe: a small family-run bread shop tucked away on a one-by-two-mile island 28 miles out in the Atlantic Ocean. The 30 households on St Martin's in the Isles of Scilly far to the west of Land's End are certainly lucky to have a food shop as good as this on their doorstep.

St Martin's Bakery
Moo Green, Higher Town, St Martin's,
Isles of Scilly TR25 0QL
01720 423444
www.stmartinsbakery.co.uk
www.theislandingredient.co.uk
Open mid March–early October
9am–5.30pm Monday–Saturday and
9am–2pm Sunday.

The island baker Toby Tobin-Dougan arrived on St Martin's having made a lifestyle leap in 1992. He had had enough of commuting to his photography job in London and moved to the Isles of Scilly where he decided to farm flowers and fish, and where he met Louise, another escapee but from Bristol. Somewhere along the way they taught themselves to bake. Then, after restoring a lobster-pot-maker's granite barn, Toby used it to launch his second career…as a baker.

Thanks to the quality of their food, word soon spread to other islands and business boomed. So, the bakery has grown, taking over the converted fire station next door. Toby and Louise now live in a cottage just a field's-length away and they've taken over the island's pub, too.

The bakery is still the core of the operation, though. Expect to find shelves full of English loaves, continental sticks, pastries, tarts, cakes, pies and puddings (including Toby's 'croissant bread and butter pudding') all hand-made using largely organic local produce. Look out for his Lawrence Loaf – this speciality is flavoured with seaweed gathered in nearby Lawrence Bay, with home-dried tomatoes and feta cheese also popped into the dough.

Tourists can pick up picnic treats such as pizza (topped with home-smoked ham, chicken or fish), home-grown organic salads and, of course, Cornish pasties – made using beef from the Limousin herd on neighbouring Tresco and potatoes from St Martin's. Toby also catches and smokes his own Atlantic salmon and grey mullet, which you can sample in a roll or a quiche, or even on pizza.

The couple have become a mini food-factory: they bake using eggs from their free-range ducks and chickens; they keep free-range pigs; they produce pork joints, chops and salami; they turn grey mullet roe into a glorious taramasalata; plus, they grow their own salads, tomatoes, herbs, garlic and strawberries.

Toby somehow also finds time to run holiday baking courses, write cookery books and hunt for woodcock, pigeon, snipe, partridge and rabbit.

The bakery doesn't just sell to the lucky islanders and visitors on St Martin's. A daily boat whisks their delights across the waters to the other islands and from there to the mainland where they grace many a restaurant's menu. Diners can find Toby's gravadlaxed and cold-oak-smoked grey mullet, for example, at Rick Stein's seafood restaurant in Padstow (see page 23).

The Lizard Pasty Shop

It's hard to miss Ann Muller's roadside shop – it's bright yellow. Visitors heading for the lighthouse at England's most southerly point may stop at this tiny shop in Lizard village to grab a quick snack without thinking. But to locals this is one of the best-known shops in Cornwall…and Ann is renowned as a champion of the Duchy's most famous product: the pasty.

As with many a traditional craft, Ann first learnt pasty-making from her mother, Hettie Merrick. An expert at the great Cornish culinary art, Hettie also wrote *The Pasty Book* – a combination of historical story and recipes. 'Making pasties is something all the women in my mother's family did,' says Ann. Ann began making pasties for neighbours 'who'd bring round fish they'd caught or vegetables they'd grown. They treated my living room like a waiting room, sitting around gossiping waiting for pasties to come out of the oven.'

Soon word spread and, to cope with demand, Ann converted her garage into a pasty kitchen. Since then, she has won awards and appeared on TV and radio as well as in newspapers and food magazines. 'I've got a good reputation,' she says proudly, 'because I pay attention to seasoning. Too little and it's not interesting enough, too much and it's horrible. It's my gift on this planet – to be able to season a pasty just right.'

Her pasties are irresistibly tasty classics – a million miles from the cellophane-wrapped offerings of a supermarket's cold cabinet. She bakes up to 400 of these bulging packages of golden flaky pastry each day to her family recipe. Ann uses lean beef skirt or chuck from Retallack's Butchers in the village. Strong organic flour (kneaded to make it slightly stretchy so the filling doesn't burst out) comes from Truro Granary, swede (they call it turnip in Cornwall) comes from Falmouth and the potatoes and onions hail from Helston.

The 'oggie' – as it's known to many a local – is a cornerstone of the history, culture and sense of sheer Cornishness. Pasties may be eaten all over the world but the Cornish feel they own the rights to the original. Ann has often spoken out in the campaign to win regional accreditation from the European Commission, to stop producers outside Cornwall labelling pasties as 'Cornish'.

Yet the defining characteristic of any pasty isn't what's inside – it's the 'handle' of pastry on the outside. Legend tells that this hand-crimped crust enabled miners to eat their lunch while their hands were covered in poisonous dirt, such as arsenic or lead; they didn't eat the thick pastry strip. Hand-crimping the pastry crust together remains a symbol of traditionalism rather than of any actual benefit to the eater.

Dilettante experts practically come to blows about the ingredients of a true Cornish pasty but, historically, any old scraps could be bunged inside and baked. In fishing ports it was most likely bits of fish, and in really hard times ash was

The Lizard Pasty Shop
Beacon Terrace, The Lizard,
Helston, Cornwall TR12 7PB
01326 290889
www.connexions.co.uk/lizardpasty
Open 9.30am–2pm Monday–Saturday in winter or till 4pm in summer or 'when the pasties run out'.
Closed on Sundays always and closed on Mondays as well between the end of October and Easter.

JH & M Choak 10
30 Killigrew Street, Falmouth,
Cornwall TR11 3PN
01326 312426
Open 8am–2.30pm Monday–Saturday.

"The 'oggie' – as it's known to many a local – is a cornerstone of the history, culture and sense of sheer Cornishness."

added for cheap flavour. Some areas produced pasties that contained a main course and a fruity sweet section baked within the one pasty. Nevertheless, today's gourmet Cornish pasty generally involves chunks of steak (not mince), potato, swede and onion. The filling goes in raw and is baked for an hour creating the unique blend of flavours that soak into the pastry.

Other classic pasty makers favoured by locals include the Choak family who have made and sold pasties at their little stone terrace house-cum-shop just up from the ferry jetty in Falmouth for three generations. And if you're visiting the Isles of Scilly, head for St Martin's Bakery where the pasties are made with meat and vegetables from the islands (see page 18).

Newlyn Seafood Café

This diminutive diner could be Britain's smallest restaurant. Former fisherman and pasty-maker Kevin Hanley set up his eatery, which is little more than the size of a small greenhouse, across the road from the town's harbour. In fact, the Newlyn Seafood Café can hold only 20 people at a squeeze, and opens only between Easter and September; but what it lacks in grandeur it makes up for with an unpretentious menu of ultra-fresh seafood, served simply but enthusiastically.

Whatever the fishermen haul in from over the road goes on the daily specials board. You could be tucking into line-caught sea bass hooked an hour earlier or a raw steak of white tuna (served with olive oil and a slice of lime) caught with a line trailing from one of the bigger boats. Mackerel caught by 'one of the lads after work' is served with blackberries from nearby hedgerows and St Ives prawns turn up with a partner of deep-fried courgette flowers.

Kevin's first choice for super-fresh fish is the day-boat or rod catches, but 'these blokes have no social graces,' he says. 'One comes in here with whatever he's caught on Sennen Beach in an old blue Ikea bag. People just arrived from London can't believe what they're seeing.'

Newlyn Seafood Café 4
The Bridge, Newlyn, Penzance,
Cornwall TR18 5PZ
01736 367199
www.newlynseafoodcafe.co.uk
Open daily 6.30pm–late Easter–September.

Cornish Ice Cream

Made with local clotted cream and full-cream milk from herds grazing on lush pastures within 30 miles of their Bodmin factory, Kelly's Cornish ice cream has a distinctive yellowy colour, velvety smoothness and ultra-creamy taste. Sample it from one of their fleet of 30 traditional ice cream vans at beaches and beauty spots around Cornwall or at their flagship parlour on The Wharf at St Ives. Philip Kelly, who started working in his family's ice cream vans at an early age, now runs the company set up by his great grandfather more than 100 years ago.

Get up close and personal with the ice cream making process thanks to the viewing gallery at Callestick Farm near Truro, where Angela Parker and her team make an exotic range of flavours from traditional clotted cream vanilla to mango and sticky rice. Gaze upon the dairy cows grazing outside before tucking into the finished ice cream at the farm's very own parlour.

For a taste of Cornish home-made ice cream stop at the tiny family shop on the main road through Newlyn. Jelberts was started by proprietor Jim Glover's grandfather and still makes only vanilla ice cream to a closely guarded recipe served with a delightful dollop of clotted cream on top.

Kelly's Ice Cream Parlour 5
The Wharf, St Ives, Cornwall TR26 1LP
01736 797894
www.kellysofcornwall.co.uk

Callestick Farm Cornish Dairy 14
Ice Cream
Callestick, Truro, Cornwall TR4 9LL
01872 573126
www.callestickfarm.co.uk

Jelberts Ice Cream Shop 3
New Road, Newlyn, Cornwall TR18 5PZ

Cream Tea on a Farm

Farmer's wife Jill Brake starts the day by baking about 100 scones for the tea shop housed in her converted stables. Then she makes breakfasts using her own free-range eggs for Bre-Pen Farm B&B guests before she opens up the farm shop in the old barn. Jill also serves her home-made jams (made using fruit from nearby Mitchell Fruit Gardens) with scones rewarmed before serving. Her clotted cream hails from Delabole and other breakfast ingredients come from local farms.

Bre-Pen farm shop sells lamb raised on the family farm, including lamb burgers and lamb and mint sausages, naturally made by Jill. Being a Cornish housewife, Jill makes her own pasties, which are also for sale. And if there's any time left she'll make cakes, pies or chutneys for the shop.

At the end of each day, Jill can at last relax and enjoy the astonishing views from her house, which overlooks a wide sandy beach in an unspoilt bay.

Further down Cornwall's north coast there's a cracking home-made cream tea available at Trevaskis Farm near Hayle. While you're there, choose from the 80 or so different crops that farmer Paul Eustace grows on a pick-your-own basis. Plus, his family has been rearing rare-breed British Lop pigs for more than 100 years, so be sure to buy some delicious pork joints while you're there.

Bre-Pen Farm
Mawgan Porth, Newquay, Cornwall TR8 4AL
01637 860420
www.bre-penfarm.co.uk
Open daily 10am–6pm in summer,
10am–5.30pm in winter.

Trevaskis Farm
Gwinear, Hayle, Cornwall TR27 5JQ
01209 713931
www.trevaskisfarm.co.uk
Farm shop open daily 9am–6pm in summer,
9am–5pm in winter.

The Cornish Arms

Where can you enjoy a two-course Rick Stein meal for less than a tenner? In his local pub, of course. The chef and TV presenter lives in the village of St Merryn just outside the much-visited harbour town of Padstow, where his famous eateries and shops are based. It's less well known that Rick and ex-wife and business partner Jill have taken over the tenancy of their village's old white-washed pub, the Cornish Arms.

Rick has installed one of his long-standing chefs from Padstow in the pub kitchen and now it's a wonderfully relaxed spot to enjoy dishes such as grilled sardines with rock salt and lime, pork and garlic sausages from Tywardreath on the south coast and perfect mussels and chips at normal pub-grub prices.

Rick has been a regular at the pub for years and is a fan of local St Austell Brewery beers, such as Tribute, Tinners, HSD and Proper Job. He now says he is 'working on a couple of recipes to go with their beer. I'm keen to develop the matching of good beer with food'.

For the full Rick Stein experience, travel two miles down the road to what locals affectionately call 'Padstein', where Rick's empire includes four restaurants, three shops and a cookery school.

The Cornish Arms 16
Churchtown, St Merryn, Padstow,
Cornwall PL28 8ND
01841 520288
www.rickstein.com

The Seafood Restaurant 17
Riverside, Padstow, Cornwall PL28 8BY
01841 532700

Miles Lavers' Foodswild

Dinner might start with a plate of seaweed. The next course could be wild flowers and meadow cap fungi. And all washed down with stinging nettle cider. This meal like no other, in the company of Cornish foraging expert Miles Lavers, could totally change your perception of British food.

His encyclopedic knowledge of the natural wild food larder available around our coast and countryside is inspiring – even if some of the products seem bizarre. 'This is awesome,' he says enthusiastically grabbing brown leathery belts of oarweed (kelp) at the beach. 'Try drying them and eating them instead of crisps.'

Traditional gourmands may write this off as hippy nonsense as they reach for expensive ingredients flown in from around the world. Yet former Marine Commando Miles often finds his ingredients for free, within walking distance of his farm. And the word about the quality of these unfamiliar ingredients is spreading fast. Already more than 80 Cornish restaurants buy from Miles' range of about 30 foraged ingredients every week.

At the acclaimed Saffron restaurant in Truro you can sample Miles' wild leaves, such as pennywort, wood sorrel and garlic flowers, and puddings of 'Alexanders' (angelica stems). And chef Matthew Poultin at the Idle Rocks Hotel in St Mawes regularly stocks his two-rosette kitchen with Miles' edible seaweeds and wild herbs.

Check out the Foodswild operation in person at Miles' farm near Helston. Contact him to book a time first, as he is often out foraging. You may also bump into him on his fairly random schedule of food markets and shows around the county with a stall selling typical products like rabbit burgers and wild mustard. And if you fancy trying kelp crisps at home, then you can buy ingredients from his website too.

The best way to get close to what Miles does, however, is to join one of his regular guided foraging walks, either along beaches or through creekside woods. He'll show you how to find edible plants, seaweeds, flowers and fruits, all the time explaining about seasonal wild food. These foraging courses are no dainty trip to a deli. His advice to budding foragers is: 'take to the woods with a stout walking stick that can be used to pull down laden branches or to fight off brambles, plus tough gloves for picking nettles or sloes'.

If you fancy the food but are less of a forager, book one of the indulgent food experiences at Miles' Wild Food Feasts, held sporadically across Cornwall, often in innovative restaurants such as the Driftwood Spars in St Agnes. A typical menu might include dishes such as nettle ravioli with wild mustard pesto, squirrel rissoles, Falmouth spider-crab with steamed wild greens infused with a wild garlic oil, dandelion and ox tongue salad with wild green sauce or halibut wrapped in sea lettuce with mermaid hair seaweed.

Miles Lavers' Foodswild
Seworgan, Near Constantine,
Cornwall TR11 5QN
07988 796743
www.foodswild.com
Regular forays and wild food walks run from late June–end September. But mostly Miles takes out groups (minimum of four people) who simply phone up to book a three-hour forage, which costs £20 per person.

Saffron
5 Quay Street, Truro. Cornwall TR1 2HB
01872 263771
www.saffronrestauranttruro.co.uk

The Idle Rocks Hotel
Harbourside, St Mawes, Cornwall TR2 5AN
01326 270771
www.idlerocks.co.uk

Driftwood Spars
Trevaunance Cove. St Agnes,
Cornwall TR5 0RT
01872 552428
www.driftwoodspars.com

Miles insists: 'Wild food is not a gimmick. It is ancient common knowledge that has been largely lost since the Second World War when mass production of food became the norm. Rediscovering the vista of ultra-fresh, seasonally abundant produce is akin to discovering the cuisine of a whole new country.'

Miles and his Foodswild team also concoct a tangy brew that's a cross between beer and cider made purely from nettles – Cornish Stingers – at his own 'wild brewery' on the farm. Barrels are available for parties and Foodswild can cater for dinners or events at homes and holiday homes across the county. What you eat depends on the season but one thing is guaranteed – it will be a truly wild party.

The Ferryboat Inn

The Wright Brothers are renowned as one of the UK's top oyster merchants who supply many of London's fine restaurants; they also run their own acclaimed oyster bar in London's Borough Market (see page 70). In 2005 they won the rights to the centuries-old Duchy of Cornwall oyster beds on the picturesque Helford river in South Cornwall. These had been left uncared-for since a destructive attack by a parasite in the early 1980s. But it didn't take long for the brothers (well, they're not actually brothers but business partners Robin Hancock and Ben Wright) to regenerate the beds and cultivate oysters once more.

The Ferryboat Inn ⑨
Helford Passage, Near Falmouth,
Cornwall TR11 5LB
01326 250625
www.wrightbros.eu.com

This ancient fishery, part of the private estate of the Duke of Cornwall, The Prince of Wales, once produced what many revered as Britain's finest oysters. By 2008 these once-prized Helford Natives had regained their place on menus around the world. The Duchy of Cornwall Oyster Farm, which sits in an idyllic spot in an unspoilt, thickly wooded estuary, now cultivates and harvests more than five million oysters a year, making it one of the UK's largest oyster farms. The farm's Frenchman's Creek oysters are grown on the site of Cornish novelist Daphne Du Maurier's famed *Frenchman's Creek*. The conditions here – high freshwater input, good tidal flow and lots of vegetation in the water – help the oysters gain a high meat-to-shell ratio and a sweeter, nuttier taste much prized by oyster gourmets.

In February 2009 things really got interesting when a 300-year-old waterside pub right on the north bank of the Helford river came up for sale. The Wright Brothers snapped it up. The pub's kitchen is just a stone's throw from their oyster beds, so offered a perfect opportunity for a real 'farm-to-plate' gastro experience. It's a must-visit for seafood lovers, who can sit on the terrace and watch Ben or Mark, who work at the oysterage, bringing in the day's catch in a pretty little boat.

The pub has been renovated without losing any of its old nautical atmosphere. The former servery has been transformed into an oyster bar offering informal counter seating where you can enjoy the theatre of watching chefs shuck oysters and prepare shellfish. Or depending on what mood you're after, you can choose to eat in the main bar, with its darkened wood beams and open fire, in the cosy dining room or on the outside terrace where chefs grill fish, weather permitting, at the water's edge. And this being Cornwall, the pub caters for those wanting something sweet in the afternoon too; here the delicious cream teas include traditional Cornish 'splits' (soft sweet buns), freshly baked in the pub.

The Ferryboat Inn now has its own smoker for curing and smoking salmon and haddock. Ben is always experimenting and his new home-smoked creations often make their first appearance on the specials board. Filling the rest of the menu is easy: lobsters and crabs come straight from small boats with pots in the creeks; scallops, clams and winkles are hand-dived by local fishermen; while wet fish arrives with the likes of 'fisherman Dan'. Dan takes visitors on

fishing trips, then often stops off at the Ferryboat Inn to sell his group's catch of the day, usually boxes of jumping-fresh mackerel; you may well see other local fishermen there, who do the same with their bounties.

Ben bakes the daily bread and he sources many other ingredients from local Cornish producers. Some, like samphire and blackberries, he forages in the wild. He says: 'We're lucky to have such fantastic produce all around us and we want to really showcase the best of the area.'

Sharpham Estate

There's something wonderfully indulgent about arriving at a Georgian mansion by boat...then sitting down to an al-fresco meal of produce from its country estate. Yet it's easy to get to Sharpham by water – take ferries from Totnes' old waterfront or sail up the winding wooded valley from Dartmouth. Step ashore at Sharpham Reach into a food-lover's paradise.

Around this exquisite 18th-century stately home there's a 1,000-year-old dairy farm making some of the south-west's best-known cheeses, a vineyard producing some of the UK's highest-rated wines and an acclaimed café where scenic river views enhance your gastronomic experience. And, of course, there's a farm shop bulging at the seams with produce from the estate.

At the Vineyard Café, chef Rosie serves vegetables, salads, eggs, meat and cheeses from the surrounding organic farmland, complemented by fish from Dartmouth, all washed down with estate-grown wines and rounded off with her delicious hand-baked desserts and cakes.

Visitors can spy through windows on the cheesemaking process, which still uses traditional methods such as cutting, moulding and turning by hand. The vineyard tours tell more of a contemporary story of how cool-climate grapes growing on sheltered sloping river banks create some of England's finest wines.

Sharpham Estate (31)
Totnes, Devon TQ9 7UT
01803 732203
www.sharpham.com
Vineyard tours range from the self-guided version at £5 to the Sharpham Wine Experience tour at £49.50.
Open 10am–5pm Monday–Saturday March–Christmas Eve; open daily June–September.

The Vineyard Café
01803 732178
Open daily 10am–5pm Easter–September, but depends on weather.

Occombe's Best Ever Butchers

Those keen to follow the field-to-fork process should look no further than Occombe Farm. This working organic farm was established by an admirable local charity 'to reconnect people with food, farming and the countryside'.

The farm lies just a mile inland from busy Torbay Riviera beaches and is a Site of Special Scientific Interest with a network of wildlife cameras beaming live images to the visitor centre, well-marked nature trails and bird hides, plus an educational centre built from hay bales.

Occombe Farm (33)
Preston Down Road, Paignton, Devon TQ3 1RN
01803 520022
www.occombe.org.uk
Open 9am–5.30pm Monday–Saturday and 9.30am–4.30pm Sunday.

After wandering freely around pastures and barns, taking audio tours or watching farmers feeding Devon Ruby Red cattle, Dorset Down sheep and various pigs, ducks and chickens, head over to the onsite butchers. At this traditional butchery, watch butchers prepare beef, pork and lamb from the farm and ask them which cut is right for you. You can buy meat here or climb up the stairs to the café to sample what readers of *BBC Good Food* magazine voted the 'best ever' burgers.

If you're up for more observation then you can marvel at the goings-on in the onsite bakery through the viewing panel. Relax at the farm's café and enjoy lunch or coffee and a cake, knowing that everything is made from ingredients from the farm shop. The farm shop, as you'd expect, is packed with regional cheeses, home-made pasties, local fruit and veg and locally made drinks.

Pick of the Chippies

The combination of millions of holidaymakers wanting a quick snack and the daily availability of fresh fish from two separate coastlines means Devon has some of Britain's highest-rated fish-and-chip shops.

Hanbury's in Babbacombe – a licensed restaurant and seafood takeaway – has fine views over Torbay. David Hanbury's secret is a state-of-the-art, computerised, high-temperature, £75,000 Dutch gas range that cooks raw chips in six minutes flat. Hotter fat also means less-oily food and firmer fish. The range even has a special carbon filter to clean its own oil too. For something different try battered brill, smoked haddock, home-made fish chowder or poached cod fillets with parsley or cheese sauce. A nice touch is the daily papers to read while you wait – as all orders are cooked fresh.

Look out also for Braunton's two-storey, three-generation family-run fish-and-chip shop and café, Squires, which comes recommended by seafood guru Rick Stein. Squires is even licensed so you can enjoy a glass of wine with your battered cod.

Francine Baker's chippy has become a Plymouth institution by concentrating on perfecting the simple things: the only fish are plaice, cod and haddock, all cooked in pure vegetable oil. And Francine once made headlines…by creating the UK's biggest Spam fritter weighing three kilos and measuring almost half a metre wide.

Hanbury's
Princes Street, Babbacombe, Devon TQ1 3LW
Restaurant 01803 314616; takeaway
01803 329928
www.hanburys.net

Squires
Exeter Road, Braunton, Devon EX33 2JL
01271 815533

Francine's
North Prospect Road, Milehouse, Plymouth,
Devon PL2 3HY
01752 567577

The Purple Carrot Experience

Lewtrenchard Manor Hotel, a beautiful Jacobean country house hotel on the edge of Dartmoor, is determined to turn itself into a luxurious gastronomic destination. Not only have they spent £250,000 installing state-of-the-art kitchens, reviving a one-acre walled garden that produces 80 per cent of their fruit and veg and made the Head Chef into the General Manager…but they've created a unique high-tech food experience called The Purple Carrot.

If the highly rated hotel-restaurant is not quite foodie enough, diners can opt for The Purple Carrot experience. Here chef-patron Jason Hornbuckle welcomes you with champagne before introducing the rest of his team and giving a personal tour of the three-rosette kitchens. Then you'll be shown to a private table (made of local granite) in an adjoining room.

From here you can watch just what is happening in the kitchen on large wall-mounted flat-screen TVs. Four cameras zoom in on the chef's handiwork and action at the hobs. Jason wears a microphone to commentate as he prepares your special eight-course menu.

Between courses diners are welcome to pop into the kitchen to ask questions. 'It's like a chef's table in the kitchen but not as intimidating…or smelly,' says Jason.

The Purple Carrot
Lewtrenchard Manor, Lewdown,
Near Okehampton, Devon EX20 4PN
01566 783222
www.lewtrenchard.co.uk/purple_carrot.asp

Riverford Farm

**'I must be a bit of a nerd because I do get really excited by my vegetables,'
says Guy Watson, the man behind Riverford Farm, one of the country's
largest organic vegetable box delivery schemes. That sort of enthusiasm
rubs off, so you're sure to find a visit to Guy's farm a surprisingly
interesting and uplifting food experience.**

Amid the rolling Devon hills, visitors can tour the fields, learn secrets of good vegetable farming, watch cooking demonstrations, pick their own, cook their own – and most importantly – sit down in Riverford's Field Kitchen and eat the produce. The licensed restaurant (they serve organic wine and cider) is a modern wooden building with long communal tables. The atmosphere is relaxed and family-friendly, and the simple quality has impressed many diners – including Gordon Ramsay, who famously said: 'I knew it would be good but not *that* good'.

Chef Jane Baxter worked at The River Café in London and Dartmouth's Carved Angel before taking the helm at Riverford. Whether you choose the meat or vegetarian meals, Jane serves up big bowls of five or six different organic vegetables fresh from the fields. These offerings change with the season but Jane has plenty to choose from: Riverford grows around 100 varieties. And do save room for pudding; a renowned speciality is chocolate courgette cake. 'We like to use this recipe to persuade children of the virtues of vegetables,' says Jane.

Riverford is a totally family enterprise. Apart from its own fields, the restaurant's main suppliers are Guy's brother Oliver's dairy farm next door (milk, clotted cream and yogurt) and his other brother Ben's four local farm deli and butchers shops (at Riverford, Sidmouth, Totnes and Kitley, near Plymouth).

Jane also runs cookery courses in the Field Kitchen that include a short tour of the farm, demonstrations, printed recipes to take away and a full lunch. Children's 'pick and cook' days are proving very popular during school holidays, too. The kids help with planting and picking in the fields then go back to the Field Kitchen to cook their 'crop' themselves. The farm also hosts nature walks, trailer rides, children's suppers and autumnal pumpkin days.

Stringent planning laws in South Devon's beautiful but heavily protected rolling countryside mean that Field Kitchen diners must book a table and take a tour of the farm. The guided tours impart more of Guy Watson's passion for vegetables. You are driven around the 1,000 acres in a trailer pulled by a tractor to see what's going on at that particular time of the year; if you're not keen on a bumpy ride you can walk the tour using an audio guide.

The tours can mean sheltering in the polytunnels in winter, watching spring crops being planted, investigating strawberry fields in June and salad crops in July or joining the pumpkin harvest in October. You'll also see their home-made canopied

Riverford Farm 28
Wash Barn, Buckfastleigh, Devon TQ11 0JU
0845 600 2311
www.riverford.co.uk
Open weekends, some weekdays and every day in school holidays February–December. Farm tours start at 11am; self-guided tours are free and guided tours cost £5 adults and £4 children (3–12).

Monthly cookery demonstrations in the Field Kitchen cost £60 including coffee on arrival and a 2-course lunch afterwards.

Field Kitchen
01803 762074
Sat at communal tables there's a 2-course lunch for £15.95 (children £7.95) and a 2-course dinner for £18.50 (children £9.75). Booking essential.

Riverford Farm Shop 29
Staverton, Totnes, Devon TQ9 6AF
01803 762523
www.riverfordfarmshop.co.uk
Open 9am–6pm Monday–Saturday (late opening Wednesday at 10am) and 10am–4pm Sunday.

Also at:
Riverford at Kitley
Yealmpton, Plymouth, Devon PL8 2LT
01752 880925

Riverford goes to Town
38 High Street, Totnes, Devon TQ9 5RY
01803 863959

'rigs' that roll around the fields to shelter the pickers and crops in rough weather and you'll realise how labour-intensive the organic farm operation is. Riverford fields are often crowded with planters or pickers.

Visitors will come away with a deeper understanding of the Riverford farming process, for example, how Oliver's dairy herd next door help out by supplying nutritious manure and eating up any surplus veg. The brothers rotate their pastures so the cows graze on fallow fields to allow the soil to recover.

For a couple of hours you'll get up close and personal with modern organic farming – picking, poking, sniffing and tasting samples as you go. And most visitors end up with some muddy samples to take home. You may never look at a humble carrot in the same way ever again.

Michael Caines

It could be the best food surprise of your life. You take a table on the cobbles in Exeter's historic Cathedral Yard and ask for a quick snack...but what arrives is officially 'the world's greatest sandwich'. The 'Rustic Ruby' is a mouth-watering, colourful-looking combination of some of the south-west's best ingredients. The baguette is spread with garlic and parsley butter and filled with Red Ruby beef from hand-reared cows at Piper's Farm 10 miles away, with a celeriac *remoulade*, mixed leaves and crispy shallots from Rowswell Farm in Barrington, Somerset.

It's the creation of one of Devon chef Michael Caines' young protégés – Seth Ward – who represented Britain in the Sandwich World Cup in the gourmet capital of Paris and won the Cup. The panel of international food judges preferred it to all the flamboyant creations from highly rated chefs, including entries from France, Switzerland and Belgium. This world-class sandwich is available only at the Well House Tavern and the MC Café Bar at the ABode Hotel in Exeter.

Of course, supervising chef Michael Caines approved Seth's competition entry and was delighted when he won. 'I'm very proud of Seth. Great food needs to be inclusive not exclusive. It is important to offer quality at every level. The key to Seth's creation is local quality, even down to using local Somerset shallots and sea salt from Cornwall.'

At the other end of the dining scale is Michael's restaurant in the luxury country house hotel Gidleigh Park near Chagford on the edge of Dartmoor. You may not be able to order Seth's sandwich there but what you do get is two-Michelin-starred, four-rosette food. It's the south-west's highest-rated restaurant. Expect fabulous food and plenty of the freshest, finest local produce.

You'll find similar standards, if not accolades, at Michael's restaurant at the Bath Priory Hotel, which currently has one Michelin star. Michael's restaurant at ABode Exeter is another more affordable way to sample his food.

Michael, who was born and brought up in Devon, is famous for overcoming the handicap of losing a hand in a motorbike accident, which by a weird trick of fate also befell Seth. Michael was awarded an MBE for his tireless charity work. He endears himself to locals by often speaking out, not to promote himself or his restaurants, but to praise his home county. 'If Devon was in France or Italy it would be famous as a great food region,' he says. 'In Devon there's always a food experience to match the location. It may be a Devon ice cream on a sunny beach, a ploughman's with some interesting local cheese or a glass of Sharpham's Devon wine down in the South Hams. And all visitors should try a proper cream tea with clotted cream and home-made scones.'

Michael Caines 45
ABode Exeter, Cathedral Yard,
Exeter, Devon EX1 1HD
01392 223638
www.abodehotels.co.uk/exeter

Gidleigh Park 23
Chagford, Devon TQ13 8HH
01647 432367
www.michaelcaines.com

Also at:
The Bath Priory Hotel, Restaurant & Spa
Weston Road, Bath BA1 2XT
01225 331922
www.thebathpriory.co.uk

Devonshire Cream Teas

Whether you sit on the plastic chairs among the pot plants in Heather Knee's walled garden off the village High Street or inside among her collection of novelty teapots, there's little to suggest that you are about to experience the finest of regional delicacies.

A traditional Devonshire cream tea is a British classic rooted way back in history. Tradition has it that a warm scone is served whole, then broken into halves by the eater who covers the exposed surfaces with clotted cream and jam. The apparent simplicity of the dish disguises the expertise of its creation.

Heather Knee, of the Georgian Tea Room in Topsham, learned how to make clotted cream from her mother on their farmhouse Aga. 'I just heat it, then take the crust off,' she shrugs in her broad Devon accent, as if it was something everyone does. In fact, it takes many hours of gently 'scalding' the creamiest milk – that's why it originated in Devon's rich dairy pastures. The mixture is then left in shallow dishes for the cream to rise in its characteristic way and form a thick yellow crust. Then Heather carefully skims the clotted cream off the top.

Clotted cream has a slight caramel richness and a thick texture, and should stay on a spoon or knife like a chunk of butter. Although it is 60 per cent fat, it is an excellent source of minerals and vitamins A, B12 and D. Local legend suggests that the first fluffy dollops were dished out by the Benedictine monks of Tavistock to thank villagers for repairing their abbey.

Today you'll find clotted cream sold everywhere across the south-west; in fact, little pots of the stuff are transported all over the world. Cream teas are commonplace too, although it can sometimes be difficult to find the finest examples among the batch of substandard frozen scones and supermarket jam types dotted about. But fret no more. Heather's Georgian Tea Room offers what's considered to be one of the best cream teas by locals. She's won *Devon Life* magazine's 'Best Tearoom' title for seven years.

In her beautiful B&B in the riverside village of Topsham, Heather's up at 5.30am each morning to bake scones; they are best if eaten on the same day. Her 'secret family recipe' includes eggs from Cobley Farm near Crediton and unsalted local butter. She rewarms the scones in the oven later just before serving.

On the jam front, there are at least eight to choose from – including classic conserves of strawberry and raspberry but also greengage and damson jams – all, of course, made by Heather's fair hands from local fruit. Experts say you can tell home-made jam because it is runny, but Heather's is stiff enough to stand a spoon up in thanks to the addition of pectin. 'Strawberry jam is too runny without it and you can't get enough on the scone,' she explains.

Georgian Tea Room
Broadway House, 35 High Street,
Topsham, Devon EX3 0ED
01392 873465
www.broadwayhouse.com
Open 8am–5pm Tuesday–Saturday.

Other great venues for a proper Devonshire cream tea include these *crème de la cream* venues:

Southern Cross Tea Rooms
Newton Poppleford, Near Sidmouth,
Devon EX10 0DU
01395 568439
www.southerncrossdevon.co.uk
Open daily 11am–5pm except November–February when closed Monday and Tuesday.

Docton Mill Tea Room
Lymebridge, Hartland, Devon EX39 6EA
01237 441369
www.doctonmill.co.uk
Open daily 10am–5pm March–October.

Dartmoor Tearooms
3 Cross Street, Moretonhampstead,
Devon TQ13 8NL
01647 441116
www.dartmoortearooms.co.uk
Open 10.30am–5pm Wednesday–Saturday,
11am–5pm Sunday March–October.
Also open on bank holidays.

Her full cream tea involves two scones as tall as they are round, served on floral china plates, with cream, jam and a pot of tea or mug of coffee with free top-ups. 'No one has ever eaten three of these scones,' she says proudly. Indeed, they are more like rich, thick, soft biscuits with a crunchy crust. One is enough for all but the very hungriest of visitors.

Incidentally, down in the south-west, scones are called 'scoanes' rather than the more northern pronunciation 'scons'. And for perfect regional etiquette, note that in Devon the cream goes on first, taking the place of butter. Whereas in Cornwall it's normal to put the jam on first as Cornish clotted cream is traditionally runnier and wouldn't form a thick platform for all that luscious jam.

Hound of the Basket Meals

Great British food experiences aren't all about fine dining in luxury venues, and there's nothing fine or luxurious about Hound of the Basket Meals. Instead it shows how careful presentation and use of good local ingredients can elevate even the humblest of snacks to star status.

The bleak spot of Hound Tor on Dartmoor inspired Conan Doyle to write *The Hound of the Baskervilles* 100 years ago. Nowadays you'll find Jayne Hutching's van in the parking space beneath the Tor throughout the year, whatever the weather.

Pick from 17 types of tea served in Jayne's collection of 50 different floral china mugs. The hefty chunks of moist fruitcake are made by local housewife Anne Smith (to her great grandmother's recipe), crab in sandwiches comes from Brixham and local ice cream arrives topped with dollops of Chagford clotted cream.

Jayne is rightly proud of her meaty sausages and burgers, which are either home-made from local beef or made to an old family recipe by George Smith's butchers in Ashburton. All are served in proper bread rolls from Thomas' traditional bakery in Bovey Tracey.

The Times once called this 'Britain's finest appointed tea van'. The burgers have cult status among Dartmoor aficionados and some locals drive miles just to eat here.

Hound of the Basket Meals 25
Hound Tor, Dartmoor, Devon

WG Smith & Sons 27
42 East Street, Ashburton, Devon TQ13 7AX
01364 652250

Thomas Of Bovey 26
7 Station Road, Bovey Tracey,
Newton Abbot, Devon TQ13 9AL
01626 834463

Crediton Farmers' Market

It's one of Britain's most local farmers' markets since most stallholders live less than 10 miles away. And it's also one of the best-sited markets – Crediton's smart new Town Square surrounded by old shops and houses was purpose-built to house it. Little wonder then that this monthly market, in the heart of Mid Devon's rolling hills of red-soil, was recently voted best farmers' market by the readers of *Devon Life* magazine…for the third year running.

Browse 35 stalls to find food miles that put supermarkets to shame. Goat's cheese travels just three miles from Norsworthy Farm, organic seasonal vegetables were picked four miles from the market at Linscombe Farm and naturally reared, traditional Red Ruby beef grazed just five miles away at North Down Farm.

In such a sleepy rural town the market is also a major community event with a town council 'surgery' stall and performances by local school bands, choirs and clubs. Back at the stalls, you'll see the wares offered by the many inventive farmers who have diversified successfully. Look for port terrine from North Down Farm, gravadlax from Tracey Mill Trout Farm, traditional ginger beer from Sandford Orchards and even hand-made herbal teas from Christow.

Just don't ask for a free carrier bag – stallholders led the campaign to make Crediton a plastic-bag-free zone in November 2008.

Crediton Farmers' Market 38
Town Square, Market Street, Crediton, Devon
The first Saturday morning each month.

Also recommended are farmers' markets in:
Kingsbridge (first Saturday, Town Square) 30
Tavistock (second and fourth Saturdays,
Bedford Square) 20
Exeter (every Thursday South Street/Fore
Street junction) 40
Exmouth (second Wednesday, The Strand) 37
Newton Abbot (every Tuesday,
Courtenay Street) 35

Yearlstone Vineyard

Devon is a hot spot of small wine producers. The county now has about 30 vineyards, many planted in the last few years. The first vineyard to exploit Devon's mild, well-watered conditions was Yearlstone, between Exeter and Tiverton. The distinctive red sandstone here is among the most sought-after by vine growers anywhere in the world.

For the rest of us it's an inspiring spot to visit too. Yearlstone stands on a steep natural amphitheatre above the cricket pitch of the picturesque village of Bickleigh, looking south over the River Exe and rolling hills of Mid Devon.

There are eight acres under vine here with a modern winery producing a small range of white, red and rosé plus a sparkling brut. At the time of writing Yearlstone's wines are ranked Britain's fourth best and it's rated in 2008 as the 'fastest improving vineyard'. After a guided or self-guided tour, visitors can soak up the view from Charlotte's Kitchen, a licensed terrace café, with a glass of Sparkling Vintage Brut made with the classic *méthode champenoise*, an award-winning rosé or the barrel-aged dry white (number 6).

Other Devon vineyards worth a visit include Sharpham, which sells more than 100,000 bottles a year (see page 28), Kenton, where a farm has been converted to a vineyard and Old Walls where Romans made wine 2,000 years ago.

Yearlstone Vineyard (46)
Bickleigh, Devon EX16 8RL
01884 855726
www.yearlstone.co.uk
Open 11am–4pm Friday–Sunday.

Sharpham Vineyard (32)
www.sharpham.com

Kenton Vineyard (41)
www.kentonvineyard.co.uk

Old Walls Vineyard (36)
www.oldwallsvineyard.co.uk

Otterton Mill

There's been a waterwheel grinding flour for a thousand years at this scenic spot by the River Otter. The water-powered mill still produces stoneground flour at the heart of this complex of restored red sandstone buildings. It's free to watch the milling and the millers are happy to explain the process.

Follow your nose to the onsite bakery and its shelves of bread, scones, biscuits and cakes – all made from the mill's wholemeal flour. Head baker Roy runs traditional baking courses here, too.

Across the courtyard, the Devon Food Shop sells only local food and drink, including Luscombe ciders from Buckfastleigh, O'Hanlon's Beers from Clyst St Lawrence, organic Otter valley vegetables, the mill's own cookbook and even organic dog biscuits made from Otterton flour.

Ingredients at the licensed restaurant, café and takeaway are super-local and you may well see unusual wild 'game' dishes, such as grey squirrel, as well as Devon cheese tasting events or Harvest Festivals complete with hymns and samples. In the evening the mill site doubles up as a top-class folk music venue.

Follow a river-bank path to the World Heritage Coast at Budleigh Salterton to spot trout, otters and kingfishers. Squirrels, though, tend to keep a low profile.

Otterton Mill (42)
Otterton, Near Budleigh Salterton,
Devon EX9 7HG
01395 568521
www.ottertonmill.com

Darts Farm

Is this the biggest farm shop in the world? Probably. It's difficult to describe Darts Farm in any other way. A national newspaper likened it to 'finding Selfridges food hall dumped in the middle of a field'. What started as a pick-your-own operation run from a wooden shed has grown into a complex of inspiring food experiences standing among 500 acres of family farmland in the picturesque Clyst Valley in East Devon.

Darts Farm 39
Clyst St George, Topsham, Exeter,
Devon EX3 0QH
01392 878200
www.dartsfarm.co.uk

The heart of the business is very much fresh fruit and vegetables straight from surrounding fields (more than 50 different varieties) but brothers Michael, James and Paul Dart have gradually converted and extended old animal barns to create a venue for lovers of all types of top-quality local produce.

Some visitors head straight for the extraordinary fish shop, café and takeaway run in a wooden shed by charismatic scallop-diver and chef Dave Kerley. Line-caught fish arrive straight from day boats at Exmouth and Brixham. Pick what you want from the wet fish counter (everything from John Dory to mackerel). They'll sell it to you, prepare it, tell you how to cook it, fry it battered with chips to take away...or even grill it to eat with some salad and bread at a simple table alongside the shed. The choice is yours.

In the next converted barn are a couple of old Devon cider makers, producing award-winning Green Valley Cyder with a wooden board-and-cloth press using apples from orchards at Whimple and Newton Poppleford. Ask nicely and you'll get a free taste. They also sell a huge selection of local ciders and at least 100 beers from the south-west.

You'll find Gerald Davies, three-times winner of the *Devon Life* Butcher of the Year Award, in what was once a cowshed. His family company has its own farm, abattoir and smokery in North Devon and it sells only locally reared, naturally fed, well-hung meat as well as making all its own sausages and bacon.

Then there's a deli and food hall that stock more than 10,000 different top-quality products – all personally tested and approved by Michael Dart. You'll find marmalade made by 86-year-old Doris in Clyst St George, wine from the three vineyards within five miles and pickled onions from Ede's of St Thomas in Exeter. 'We can't order what we need,' says Michael. 'He only delivers what he's made that week and tells us we can't have any more.' Every product seems to have a story. Midfields Granola, for example, is made in an Aga by a woman in Mortenhampstead, a cook from Tiverton drops off hand-made chocolates in the back of his car and a clutch of local families supply their traditional Devon fudges.

The site is still growing, there are now 300 parking spaces, a spa upstairs and upmarket lifestyle shops, such as Cotswold Outdoor, in surrounding barns. Visitors can sample much of the produce in Darts' restaurant, coffee bar and deli café.

"It's like finding Selfridges food hall dumped in the middle of a field."

And for those wanting more there's the Darts Farm Food Club, offering regular 'catch and cook' fishing days, cooking demonstrations, trips to local suppliers such as Otter Brewery, meat masterclasses and superb dinners where local suppliers introduce each of the ingredients.

But you don't have to be a member to enjoy all that Darts Farm offers: anyone can tuck in at hog roasts, kids can run till dizzy in the children's field with activities and rare-breed animals, and there's almost always something in the pick-your-own fields. And if you fancy something more along the lines of peace and quiet, there are walks around the fields on paths with outstanding views across the valley, Darts' coarse-fishing lakes and the birdwatching hides.

River Cottage Local Produce Store & Canteen

Chef and author Hugh Fearnley-Whittingstall quietly moved his entire River Cottage operation from Dorset to Devon a few years ago. He is now based at the 60-acre Park Farm near Musbury, Axminster. More accessible for visitors though, is the old pub he's converted into River Cottage Local Produce Store and Canteen on Axminster's Trinity Square. This public showcase for Hugh's way of growing, sourcing, preparing and cooking food won't disappoint.

You may not see Hugh himself but the shop is open seven days a week and is full of top produce from the south-west. As Hugh says: 'We have set up this store as a real alternative to the supermarket. We stock a wide selection of everyday food items such as milk, eggs, meat and poultry and virtually all of our produce is sourced locally'. Shelves are bulging with 60 types of British cheese, local bread and, of course, free-range chickens…and there is, predictably, the full range of River Cottage paraphernalia.

Alongside the shop and deli, the Canteen section is an all-day restaurant. Décor is trendily basic but the restaurant serves excellent locally sourced, seasonal food at reasonable prices. Menus change daily depending on 'what comes in from farmers and fishermen,' says Hugh. Dishes could be some masterpiece he has cooked in front of millions on TV, such as mashed courgette on toast or roast organic meats, or it could be a selection of fresh ingredients simply prepared in the kitchen that day.

There'll be some delicious treat on offer whatever time you arrive. Breakfast usually includes hot Town Mill Bakery rolls with Sydling Brook Farm bacon cured to Hugh's recipe, while lunch might feature fresh line-caught sea bass from Lyme Bay, pearled spelt risotto and locally foraged wild ingredients. An afternoon cream tea comes with local organic butter, clotted cream and jams. And if you come late in the day, dinner could be roast organic free-range chicken with wild garlic mash.

Suppliers like Tom's Pies and Filbert's Bees are at the shop regularly talking about their produce. And the place is generally a hub of activity with tastings, book signings and live music evenings.

There are even more events at Park Farm – River Cottage HQ – a few miles away. Hugh and his team of food specialists have established what is almost a theme park for foodies. There is a long list of day courses available in food skills like curing and smoking, cidermaking and mushroom foraging, regular Sunday lunches in the threshing barn preceded by a farm tour, special themed visitor days, seasonal produce fairs, plus evening dinners, talks and parties. You'll need to book in advance for any event and you never know you may even meet Mr FW himself.

River Cottage Local Produce Store and Canteen 47
Trinity Square, Axminster, Devon EX13 5AN
01297 631715
www.rivercottage.net
Shop open 8.30am–5pm Monday–Saturday and 10.30am–4.30pm Sunday.
Canteen open 9am–5pm Monday–Saturday, 6.30–9.30pm Tuesday–Saturday and 10.30am–3pm Sunday.

Somerset Cider

Ancient doors on an old stone barn creak open to reveal piles of dusty, old, wooden farm tools and horse harnesses. Inside are the family's traditional wooden presses – still used every autumn to make cider from apples grown in the orchards outside. It's like a Hollywood film-maker's version of a Somerset cider farm...except that it's all real.

The Perry family have been growing apples and pressing them into cider here for more than 500 years. The 16th-century thatched barn sits in a picturesque village deep in rural Somerset, but once a year the quaint and quiet scene transforms into the busy heart of this cider-making operation. First, apples are sorted by variety (30 different types are grown), quality and ripeness, then washed and crushed to pulp. The pulp is wrapped in cloth and laid between wooden racks, creating what cider makers call 'a cheese' about 12 layers high. Said 'cheese' is wheeled under a hydraulic press to squeeze out the juice. Perry's presses extract over 450 litres from a tonne of apples and can press 10 tonnes every day. Visitors can peep into the cellar where barrels are left for four to six weeks to ferment naturally until the cider reaches around 6% ABV.

It's at this picture-postcard cottage industry that the Perrys create some of Britain's most acclaimed ciders. Twice they have won the Supreme Champion Cider Award at the Royal Bath & West Show, where more than 200 of the world's top ciders battle for the judges' favour. 'We believe our success stems from preserving the art of "real cider" making – traditionally crafted, free from artificial colours, flavours, sweeteners and pressed from real Somerset apples,' they say.

Wander freely round Perry's little museum of videos and photos, the cider mills and farm shop to catch a glimpse of cider's rural roots. Most importantly, make sure you get a free taste of each of the ciders, ranging from traditional still ciders from the barrel to sparkling vintage and single-apple variety bottled ciders. Unusually, the farm's tea room also serves cider.

Across the south-west you'll find plenty of cider makers to visit. But in Somerset the traditions are strongest, from tiny family orchards making rough farmhouse 'scrumpy' to commercial farms producing thousands of bottles for global distribution. The mild climate, rich soils and geography of the region seem to create top-quality apples, many unique to Somerset.

A few miles east of Perry's Cider Farm, visitors can tour Pass Vale, where local character Julian Temperley makes traditional farmhouse cider, cider brandy and bottle-fermented sparkling ciders using the *méthode champenoise*. Julian claims this technique was being used in Somerset more than 400 years ago...long before the French claim to have invented it.

Perry's Cider Farm 49
Dowlish Wake, Ilminster, Somerset TA19 0NY
01460 55195
www.perryscider.co.uk

Burrow Hill Cider 50
Pass Vale Farm, Kingsbury Episcopi,
Martock, Somerset TA12 6BU
01460 240782
www.ciderbrandy.co.uk

Mark Hix

Local lad Mark Hix has done rather well since leaving Weymouth Catering College. After a glittering career at some of London's top restaurants, Mark now owns the 'Oyster and Chop House' in Smithfield Market, is Director of Food at Brown's Hotel in London and is an acclaimed food writer and TV chef.

Yet the best place to see Mark in action is back in his native Dorset. His seafood restaurant overlooks the harbour in Lyme Regis. It's an inspirational spot to enjoy lobster and chips or a dozen oysters. And if you're prepared to sacrifice sea views for watching chefs at work while you eat there's a chef's table down in the kitchen.

Hix Oyster and Fish House 48
Cobb Road, Lyme Regis, Dorset DT7 3JP
01297 446910
www.hixoysterandfishhouse.co.uk

Mark also holds monthly demonstrations in this kitchen, preparing, cooking and serving four-course seasonal lunches. At busy times these 'kitchen table' events are held in Mark's home in nearby Charmouth; he also invites other chefs for regular masterclasses in the restaurant.

The food itself is disarmingly simple, relying on good fresh ingredients more than exotic techniques. How fresh? Well, Mark may bring salad leaves to work from his garden and the menu could even contain fish caught by him the day before.

Poole's Catch of the Day

One of the world's biggest harbours, with beaches and watersports that attract thousands of visitors, Poole Harbour is also a great spot for food lovers – thanks to abundant seafood and day fishermen.

Among Poole's boatyards you'll find where much of this nautical harvest ends up: Frank Greenslades. This humble shop is one of Rick Stein's favourite fishmongers, where wholesalers, chefs and the public can buy the fishermen's catches. Expect to find everything from sea bass and squid to oysters and lobster.

Frank Greenslades 64
16 New Quay Road, Poole, Dorset BH15 4AF
01202 672199

Wander across the old swing bridge and you'll find yourself in Poole's old town. Fishermen sometimes moor at the harbourside here to sell to passers-by; while other boats offer fishing trips. The oldest quayside pub is the Poole Arms, distinctively faced with green 'Poole pottery' tiles. It calls itself a 'specialist fish pub' and features an ever-changing menu of home-made fish soups and pies plus a blackboard of 'catches of the day'.

The Poole Arms 65
The Quay, Poole, Dorset BH15 1HJ
01202 673450

A few metres inland is the Storm seafood restaurant run by Pete 'The Prawn' Miles – a fisherman by day and chef by night. Pete often takes visitors out fishing and cooks them fresh prawns on his boat moored by Brownsea Island.

Storm 66
16 High Street, Poole, Dorset BH15 1BP
01202 674970
www.stormfish.co.uk

Pamphill Dairy Farm Shop

Thirty years ago Joyce Richards began selling eggs from her kitchen window at Chilbridge farmhouse on National Trust land near the pretty village of Pamphill. As trade grew, sales expanded into nearby 18th-century milking parlours and soon surrounding fields were planted up.

Now the Richards family presides over a thriving foodie collection. There's 'wholesome farmhouse fayre' such as home-made soups and freshly baked scones with clotted cream in the restaurant. The farm shop stocks local produce, including the Richards' own veg and Barford Farm's wondrous hand-made ice cream. The onsite butchery sells the farm's home-matured Aberdeen Angus beef; it's also the main outlet for the Devon Ruby Red beef from the Kingston Lacy estate, plus local game and home-made sausages and pies. You'll also come across a selection of other traditional rural trades – an animal feed store, florist, furniture maker, craft shops and a saddlery.

Further north, in the Wiltshire hills east of Bath, Lady Venetia Fuller also converted old dairy buildings on her family's organic estate. Neston Park Farm Shop now has an in-house artisan bakery, café and deli. Its butcher sells the estate's organic 'Black and Tan' beef and there are food courses, tastings, talks, outside barbecues and nature trails (with picnics available in the shop).

Pamphill Dairy 63
Chilbridge Farm, Wimborne,
Dorset BH21 4DY
Shop 01202 880618;
restaurant 01202 857131
www.pamphilldairy.com

Neston Park Farm Shop 56
Bath Rd, Atworth, Wiltshire SN12 8HP
01225 700881
www.nestonparkfarmshop.com

Long Crichel Bakery

Buying a 200-year-old brick stable deep in rural Dorset prompted a major life change for two architects. They pondered what to do with the building until 'eventually we hit upon the idea of a bakery,' despite having no prior knowledge of bread-making. It sounded like a recipe for disaster.

But Jamie and Rose Campbell taught themselves the skills of artisan baking and a decade later Long Crichel Bakery has become one of the south-west's finest. It produces an eclectic range of traditional hand-made organic bread and cakes in a huge wood-fuelled oven. At the last count there were 12 types of bread (including raisin-and-walnut and malted five-seed) and more than a dozen cakes, ranging from buttery almond croissants to sticky ginger cake.

Visit the bakery just to smell the wood-fired aroma, take a guided tour or browse the vast array of the Campbells' own produce, including home-made muesli, jam, chutney and herbal teas, as well as the vegetables, fruit, herbs and flowers from their garden. Behind its high cob walls they have cultivated this garden to be something of an all-year food factory.

And even if you can't find the bakery in the winding Dorset lanes, you can still try their patisseries in their Elizabethan tea room and shop opposite the minster in the nearby market town of Wimborne.

Long Crichel Bakery 61
Long Crichel, Wimborne, Dorset BH21 5JU
01258 830852
www.longcrichelbakery.co.uk

Long Crichel Shop and Tea Rooms 62
7 Cook Row, Wimborne, Dorset BH21 1LB
01202 887765

Stourhead Farm Shop

Visitors from all over the world know about Stourhead's grand Palladian mansion and stunning 18th-century landscaped gardens. What most of them don't know, however, is that these are surrounded by a huge estate. The estate is owned jointly by the National Trust and by the original occupants of this stately home, the Hoare family. Stourhead combines prehistoric hill-forts and burial mounds with ancient hamlets and working farms. In this prime south Wiltshire countryside, there are thousands of acres of lush sunny pasture on well-watered slopes. Such conditions allow the estate farms to use traditional expertise to raise and grow quality produce.

In 2005 one of the tenant farmers had the idea of selling produce directly to the National Trust visitors of the house and gardens. And so Stourhead Farm Shop was 'born' and opened in a prettily converted stone cowshed next to the visitors' car park. Since then, it has developed into a well-respected outlet for all the estate's farmers and vegetable gardeners and for the best other local producers.

The man behind the 'birth' of the farm shop is tenant farmer Stephen Harris, who has a beef farm on the estate with its own butchery. The shop sells his well-hung beef, his home-cured bacon and hams, and 10 types of home-made sausage including the popular 'Stourhead Sizzler' – a mix of pork and venison from the wild roe deer in the estate woods flavoured with port and juniper berries. Stephen's Stourhead pastrami is cured in a spicy seasoning for up to five days before being cooked by a local chef and returned to the farm for slicing.

The shop's ethos is to 'always take food miles into consideration and buy as locally as we can'. You'll find fresh game from the estate when it's in season along with estate-made meat pies and free-range eggs, bread, jams and pickles. There's a colourful and ever-changing supply of seasonal fruit and vegetables from Stourton House Flower Garden next door, which is well worth a visit for its rambling garden shop and fabulous cream teas.

The Stourhead estate was so named because it contains the source of the River Stour, which is marked by an impressive monument to the north of the gardens. With so much water rising here, the estate now bottles its own mineral water. And, of course, those enterprising farmers ensure that this is on sale in the farm shop.

The Stourhead Farmers' Market is held, somewhat irregularly, in the main car park and the courtyard by the National Trust shop; if you are lucky enough to happen upon it you'll be rewarded with visiting producers from Dorset, Wiltshire and Somerset. Also, in a modern stone building alongside the visitor centre, is the National Trust's restaurant (you don't have to pay for entry to eat here). The menu is packed with all things local, including organic meat from the estate and vegetables from Stourhead House's own walled garden – look out for the beetroot, lettuce, potato, leek, squash and herbs.

Stourhead Farm Shop 57
High Street, Stourton, Warminster,
Wiltshire BA12 6QF
01747 841164
www.stourhead-farm-shop.co.uk

Stourhead House 58
Stourton, Warminster, Wiltshire BA12 6QD
01747 841152
www.nationaltrust.org.uk/main/w-stourhead

Stourton House Flower Garden 59
Stourton House, Stourton,
Warminster, Wiltshire BA12 6QF
01747 840417
www.theheartofagarden.com/stourtonhouse.htm

The Spread Eagle 60
Church Lawn, Stourton, Warminster,
Wiltshire BA12 6QE
01747 840587
www.spreadeagleinn.com

And, if your appetite can stand more feeding, then further down the hill, by the church and entrance to the garden, you'll find fine food served at the Spread Eagle pub, which is leased from the National Trust. The unspoilt Georgian interior furnished with National Trust antiques makes it a suitably grand spot to explore a menu that includes a traditional ploughman's with local bread, Dorset Blue cheese or Keene's mature Cheddar and home-made chutney as well as plenty of rural specialities like traditional country pies, slow-cooked stews and Wiltshire ham.

Cheddar from Cheddar

The Somerset village of Cheddar seems an unlikely birthplace for the world's most popular cheese. It stands to the south of the Mendip Hills at the mouth of Britain's biggest gorge and next to the spectacular Cheddar Caves. Summer visitors may think the sleepy rural community has been swamped by tourism – but beyond the busy weekend car parks, food and drink producers still thrive here.

Cheddar Gorge Cheese Company 52
The Cliffs, Cheddar Gorge,
Somerset BS27 3QA
01934 742810
www.cheddargorgecheeseco.co.uk

Pride of place goes to John Spencer's Cheddar Gorge Cheese Company. John has spent the last six years reviving traditional cheesemaking in the village. Ignore the caves and gorge for a moment and pop into the dairy to watch John, wife Katherine and their three cheesemakers at work. The viewing gallery provides a lesson in how village farmers invented a process 1,000 years ago that went on to conquer the world. Farmers used excess milk to make cheese and discovered pressing excess moisture from fresh curd made cheese last longer. Cheddar's cheesemakers refined this by cutting curd into strips, stacking and turning them by hand so the last remnants of whey drained away. Today, all over the world, this style of cheese production is known as 'cheddaring'.

At the dairy, onlookers can watch cheesemakers still 'cheddaring' by hand in a long open vat. They use only unpasteurised milk, from a single herd grazing on the lush pastures around the village. In some ways this is the only authentic Cheddar cheese – it's the only one made and matured within the parish. And this isn't just geographical point-scoring because John's produce is already winning global acclaim. His cheese won 'Best Cheddar' at the World Cheese Awards in 2008. Says John: 'As a small artisan maker competing against producers from all over the world we are all thrilled. It does seem fitting that the best Cheddar has returned to its birthplace'.

Historians know cheese has been produced in Cheddar since at least 1170. They have found a written order from King Henry II from that year to purchase a massive 10,420lb of cheese from the village at a farthing per pound. Many years later, in 1901, Scott took 3,500lb of Cheddar on his famous South Pole expedition.

You don't have to buy quite those quantities at the shop but it's definitely worth trying a chunk of unpasteurised Cheddar. This has a depth of flavour absent from the rindless blocks in supermarkets that have been made quickly by a mechanised process. Mass producers don't have time for the traditional three-day process, from the milk filling the vat until the cheese is put into store.

The lush pastures, careful processes and traditional recipes help create John's world-beating cheese, but there's one more secret ingredient to the Cheddar cheese story…the caves. Strong Cheddar needs to mature and form a rind in its cheesecloth dressing at constant temperatures for up to 18 months. Caves provide an ideal environment for this. John persuaded Lord Bath of Longleat,

"It does seem fitting that the world's best Cheddar has returned to its birthplace."

owner of Cheddar's famous show caves, to let him store the cheese underground, just as it was kept hundreds of years ago. Now the stacks of John's cheese can be seen – and smelled – maturing there by cave visitors.

Amazingly, Cheddar village produces another great food: the strawberry. So many were produced on the sunny slopes around the village that a railway called 'The Strawberry Line' opened in 1869 to provide a fast link with markets in Birmingham and London on trains called the 'Strawberry Specials'.

Big tasty strawberries are still grown here. On any road to and from Cheddar in the summer you'll spot roadside stalls selling punnets of fresh strawberries and fields where you can pick your own.

Somerset Smoked Eel

The Pattisson family smokery has been a source of top-quality smoked eel and salmon for almost 30 years. And once Jesse and Charlie opened a little restaurant in the barn next door serving food straight from the smokers it became an instant hit with the foodies of Somerset.

Most ingredients in the smokery, shop and restaurant are ultra-local – meat comes from farms around the Somerset Levels – but the eels are sourced from chalk rivers across southern England; apparently Somerset eels taste too 'muddy'.

The Pattissons now sell more than 40 smoked foods in the little shop on the farm – including smoked chicken, duck, lamb and trout, plus more exotic creations such as smoked black pudding, olives, herrings and cheese. Yet it's all small-scale, low-tech and non-mechanised.

You can eat here too, in the barn or outside overlooking the Somerset Levels. Dishes are simple: smoked meat or fish with local salad and potatoes, and home-made soups, puddings and cakes. It's a top spot for a plate of smoked eel on warm rye bread, washed down with a glass of Burrow Hill cider (see page 42), and all the while with a hint of wood smoke in the air.

Brown and Forrest 51
Bowdens Farm Smokery,
Hambridge, Somerset TA10 0BP
01458 250875
www.smokedeel.co.uk

Bath Buns

The attractions of Bath's Roman remains and Georgian architecture are famous around the world. Less well-known, however, are the historic Bath buns that have been refuelling visitors for hundreds of years.

Start with the Sally Lunn bun, which is served in the medieval bakery where she invented the recipe. Sally was a French refugee – hence the rich, airy brioche-style bun, served with a choice of toppings from clotted cream and jam to cinnamon butter and lemon curd. The bun is still hand-made to a secret recipe that is held with the deeds of this pretty half-timbered tea shop.

A mere 100 metres away you can try a different local speciality – the smaller, more scone-like Bath bun with crumbled sugar lump in its middle. Sample one in the restaurant in the Georgian Pump Room, along with, if you can stomach it, a glass of the famous spa water (it actually tastes disgusting). Famous Bath physician Dr Oliver is believed to have invented this sweet bun but found his patients loved them too much. Their waistlines expanded at such an alarming rate, he replaced the bun with his next invention – the savoury dry Bath Oliver biscuit.

Sally Lunn's House 54
4 North Parade Passage, Bath
BA1 1NX
01225 461634
www.sallylunns.co.uk

The Pump Room 55
The Roman Baths, Stall Street, Bath
BA1 1LZ
01225 444477
www.romanbaths.co.uk

Roger Jones

Michelin-starred chef Roger Jones blindfolds his diners and then takes them on secretive trips to his secret spot in the woods where he takes the blindfold off and helps them gather English truffles. With blindfolds back on, Roger brings the visitors back so that they can enjoy this precious fungi in his village gastro-pub – the Harrow at Little Bedwyn.

Roger Jones 67
The Harrow at Little Bedwyn,
Near Marlborough, Wiltshire SN8 3JP
01672 870871
www.theharrowatlittlebedwyn.co.uk

The blindfolded trip isn't obligatory and you may prefer just to relax in one of the highest-rated pub restaurants in England while Roger and his family do the snuffling on your behalf. In autumn they gather 20kg of truffles a week. 'There is nowhere else in Britain with that amount,' Roger says.

Truffles obviously feature prominently on the menu. Highlights include dishes such as line-caught turbot with truffle oil, truffle risotto or pork faggots with apple and truffle. But there are plenty of other fine ingredients, too, with a preference for free-range, organic, traceable and hand-reared produce.

What's more, there's one of Britain's finest wine lists. Its 60 pages feature 1,000 bins, and many rare wines are available by the glass, including Penfolds Grange, Vintage Krug and Dom Perignon Onetheque. Roger takes wine so seriously that he stocks 18 different glass shapes to complement the different grape varieties.

The Royal Oak, Bishopstone

Follow a single-track lane deep into the Wiltshire Downs to find the Royal Oak pub. It's famous locally for its good food...but this is more than just another country gastro-pub.

The Royal Oak 68
Cues Lane, Bishopstone, Wiltshire SN6 8PP
01793 790481
www.royaloakbishopstone.co.uk
www.helenbrowningorganics.co.uk

The Royal Oak is owned by organic farmer Helen Browning, whose 1,337-acre Eastbrook Farm surrounds it. Helen has turned the pub into both a showcase for her farm's produce and a one-stop food adventure. For starters, the pub menu includes fresh fruit, veg and meat from the surrounding fields. The kitchen sources food grown by a team of village volunteers in their own gardens, as well as food from its own allotment. In a unique swap shop, Helen supplies the seeds and their resulting produce is traded for free food and drinks at the bar. There's also a farm shop at the pub, selling produce from Helen's and other local farms.

If you fancy you can take a farm tour, sometimes on the back of a tractor and trailer, or use a free map to wander across the fields with a picnic hamper from the pub. The pub's chef Liz Franklin, a regular on TV's *Ready Steady Cook*, has plenty of experience and favours foraged ingredients from local hedgerows, such as crab apples, blackberries and nettles, in her seasonal menus.

An Eco-gourmet Mecca

Diners enjoy sophisticated food at Bordeaux Quay's restaurant overlooking the heart of Bristol's trendy waterfront. Amid the converted warehouses, harbourside piazzas and lively bars they could be excused for thinking it is just another smart urban eatery. But Bordeaux Quay is very much more than just a restaurant – some food writers have even called it 'the future of food'.

Bordeaux Quay 53
V-Shed, Canons Way, Bristol BS1 5UH
0117 906 5550
www.bordeaux-quay.co.uk

Bordeaux Quay is Britain's first eco-restaurant complex. It's dedicated to doing things in the right way and teaching others to do the same. But what does being committed to sustainable food practices, responsible energy use, zero waste and community food education actually mean to customers? Visitors might spot the free bottled and filtered tap-water (still or sparkling) with their meals or admire the sturdy brown-paper bags in place of plastic carriers in the shop, but the full message of Bordeaux Quay might get lost in the recycled rain-water toilets and comprehensive composting system if it wasn't for the excellent quality of the food here. Happily, the site features an acclaimed fine restaurant combining classic European cooking with the best local and seasonal ingredients from the south-west. Expect dishes such as salad of langoustines, squid and clams with green chilli and lemon or duck-liver parfait with quince jelly.

The enormous old warehouse, named after the wine from Bordeaux that used to be unloaded here by the barrel, also includes a stylish brasserie, innovative wine bar, organic artisan bakery, deli and takeaway, and a big, busy cookery school. You'll find top-quality food and drink throughout the building – from award-winning potato bread baked onsite to the bar's menu of more than 70 cocktails and 250 spirits.

'BQ', as locals call it, is the brainchild of Barny Haughton, a former French teacher who opened a pioneering organic restaurant in Bristol more than 20 years ago. Back then it was so unfashionable to be organic he didn't dare publicise the fact. He has since trained more than 40 chefs who have gone on to spread his message of local, seasonal, organic slow food.

After years of planning, the quietly spoken chef opened this pioneering business in a huge converted warehouse. 'Bordeaux Quay is much more than a place to eat, it links eating, cooking and learning,' he says. 'We believe that nothing we do has a more direct impact on us and the environment than the way we choose to grow, shop for and eat food.' Among other things, this philosophy means most ingredients are sourced from within 50 miles, are organic where possible and menus change daily to reflect what is fresh and seasonal. 'If it grows in the west country I won't buy it from anywhere else,' says Barny, who has compiled a book for the Cookery School entitled *For Every Season*.

BQ's message is also promoted by a packed diary of events. There are all the wine tastings, themed nights, celebrity chef appearances and gastro-demonstrations you'd expect at a top foodie restaurant; a masterclass here may

> "...nothing we do has a more direct impact on us and the environment than the way we choose to grow, shop for and eat food."

show you how, among other things, to make a twice-baked cheese soufflé. But there is also a unique range of workshops and courses aimed at involving the sort of people who don't normally go to gourmet food events. The Cookery School is run as a not-for-profit venture – all revenue is returned to a community fund, which finances more food educational work with schools and community groups. This means that there are highly accessible courses including 'how to shop for food' and 'cooking on a budget'. There's even a series of lessons to introduce children to the basics of cooking…and in many ways that really is the future of food.

South-east England

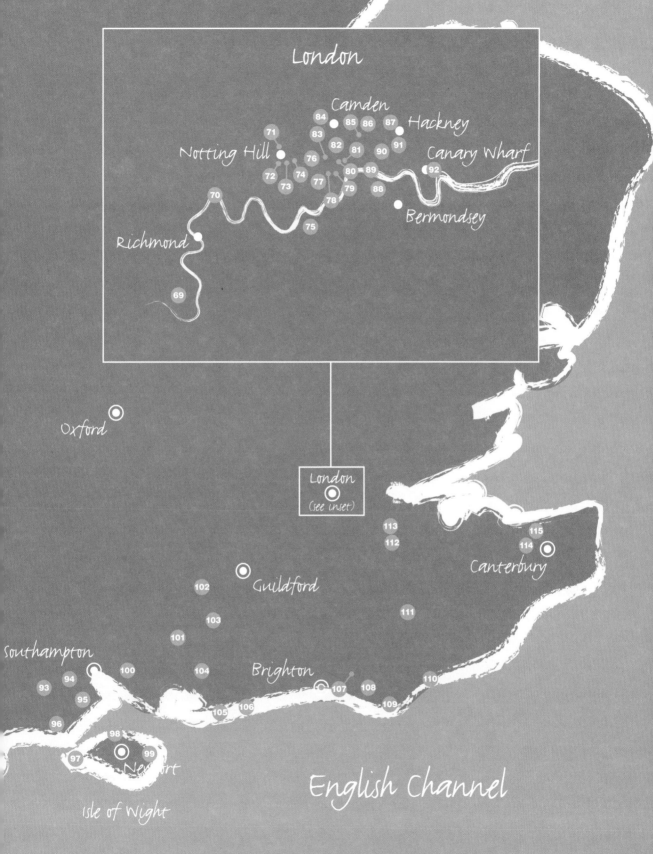

London

Camden
84 85 86 87 Hackney
71 83
Notting Hill 82 81 Canary Wharf
76 90 91
72 74 80 89 92
73 77 79 88
70 78
75 Bermondsey
Richmond

69

Oxford

London
(see inset)

113
112
115
114 Canterbury

102
Guildford

103
111
101

Southampton
100
93 94 104 Brighton
95 110
107 108
96 105 106 109
98
97 99
Newport

Isle of Wight

English Channel

Hampton Court Royal Kitchens

Hampton Court Palace, famously, was the favourite home of Tudor lothario King Henry VIII. Another claim to fame is that this magnificent palace also houses Europe's largest surviving Renaissance kitchens. These straddle over a third of the palace's ground floor in an intricate network of courtyards, cloisters, larders (Wet, Flesh and Dry), preparation areas and kitchens.

Supplying freshly cooked food for the 600 or so members of the Court (and the king himself, if you think of his size) was a major operation, involving formidable logistics. Over 200 servants worked in the kitchens, on tasks ranging from slaughtering and plucking poultry to creating elaborate confectionery.

Visiting today it's possible to follow the food trail, making your way from the courtyard where stores were unloaded – via the huge, high-ceilinged Great Kitchen, with its enormous roasting fireplaces – to the sumptuous Great Hall, where most of the courtiers ate.

In a fascinating research project, the palace employs a knowledgeable team of food historians, in full period dress, to cook recreations of meals that would have been served to Henry, in the very same kitchens. This team offers periodic Tudor cookery demonstrations – complete with meat roasting on spits before the blazing fires – a vivid insight into kitchen life all those centuries ago.

Hampton Court Palace 69
East Molesey, Surrey KT8 9AU
0844 482 7777
www.hrp.org.uk/HamptonCourtPalace
Open daily 10am–4.30pm end October–end March; 10am–6pm end March–end October. Your admission ticket (£14 for adults; £7 for under-16s) gives free access to live cookery demonstrations (once or twice a month, please check website for details).

The Original Maids of Honour

There's a chance to sample food history at this pretty, old-fashioned bakery-cum-tea room, literally on the doorstep of Kew Gardens. The Newens family has long been making their traditional Maids of Honour – small, sweet curd-cheese tartlets with their own venerable history.

By the early 18th century Richmond was noted for these tiny treats: there was even a Maids of Honour shop that specialised in their production. It was also in Richmond that Robert Newens served an apprenticeship before setting up his own premises for selling these tarts; the Kew Road branch came later in 1868.

Today, John Newens carries on the family tradition of baking Maids of Honour on the premises; and not surprisingly, the recipe is a closely guarded secret. The tea rooms are pleasantly sedate, offering a glimpse into an England where everything stopped at four o'clock for a cup of tea.

Newens 70
288 Kew Road, Kew, Surrey TW9 3DU
020 8940 2752
www.theoriginalmaidsofhonour.co.uk

The clientele ranges from elderly ladies, many of whom have been coming here for years, to Japanese or American tourists, enjoying the quintessentially English afternoon tea ritual. Newens' baking expertise makes eating here a delight. For the full experience arrive hungry enough for a slice of one of their justly famous pies – steak, chicken, chicken and ham or salmon – then round off with one of their mouth-watering Maids of Honour.

Tavola

Tavola 🔢72
155 Westbourne Grove, London W11 2RS
020 7229 0571

An appetising gem of a food shop, Tavola in Westbourne Grove is run with an eye for quality by husband-and-wife team Alastair and Sharon Little. A noted chef and early champion of authentic Italian food in London, Alastair cooks up a storm for the demanding local foodistas.

The interior of this small, attractive shop is dominated by a central table upon which a daily changing selection of Alastair's freshly prepared *traiteur* dishes appear: seriously tasty Sicilian *caponata* (a cooked aubergine salad), a slow-roast tomato salad, fresh crab cakes and broad bean salad with garlic, parsley and chilli. Alastair was advocating seasonality long before it was de rigueur and the food here reflects the seasons, moving from summer soups such as *pappa al pomodoro* (bread and tomato) or gazpacho to hearty autumn minestrone or red Thai-spiced squash.

Tavola has an exemplary, carefully selected range of foodstuffs, from attractive fresh fruit and vegetables in crates by the door to excellent olive oils and vinegars, piled high on shelves. The name 'tavola' ('table') also reflects the appealing range of tableware, from fine linen napkins to colourful glassware and rustic ceramics on sale – all sourced and chosen by Sharon Little, who manages the shop with consummate charm and panache.

Books for Cooks

Books For Cooks 🔢71
4 Blenheim Crescent, London W11 1NN
020 7221 1992
www.booksforcooks.com

Tucked away in a Portobello side-street, but marked by a cheery red awning, this small, unassuming-looking, independent bookshop has achieved legendary status among foodies. Step inside and you'll discover why. There are neatly arranged shelves and display tables full to the brim with a comprehensive stock of about 8,000 cookery and food-related books – from the latest cookbooks from celebrity chefs and food writers to obscure publications from little-known publishers.

For those who like to drool over beautiful pictures of food, there is gastro-porn aplenty; equally, the scholarly will discover tomes of detailed, specialist food history. Want to know how to make a pizza oven in your garden, learn more about Afghani cuisine or the chemistry of cookery? Then, this is *the* place to come; the knowledgeable staff are positively happy to help.

A handful of tables and chairs in the back offer customers a chance to sit and sample appetising cooking from the tiny Books for Cooks test kitchen, with recipes ranging from in-house classics to trial ones from not-yet-published titles.

Cookery workshops on subjects from Sri Lankan food to knife skills take place in the demonstration kitchen upstairs, many taught by former Books for Cooks staff (such as Celia Brooks Brown) who have gone on to successful careers in food writing.

Northcote Road

There's a noticeable buzz around Northcote Road on a Saturday. Locals stop and chat, stallholders shout and joke, shops bustle with browsers, bars and cafés spill out on to the street. It's a great place to hang out, as many locals do at Battersea's most original shopping strip. Unusual, independent retailers and a small but special Saturday street market exist side-by-side with more predictable retailers – working proof that British high streets can not only survive, but flourish in the face of competition from supermarkets when quality and diversity of food is the attraction.

Despite high-street butchers being an endangered species these days, Northcote Road offers two outstanding examples, one for each side of the road. On the north side is Hennessy's offering free-range or organic meat and poultry. Across the road, Dove's, run with pride by the genial Bob Dove, is a picturesque old shop, founded by Henry George Dove in 1889. With an emphasis on traceability, Dove's is noted particularly for its beef, hung for 14–21 days to develop its flavour, and its home-made pies, a real take-home treat.

For sheer obsessive uniqueness, The Hive Honey Shop is hard to beat. This small, cosy, honey-scented shop run by third-generation beekeeper James Hamill is packed with bee- and honey-related products, from impressive frames of honeycomb to specialist beekeeping kit. Pride of place goes to an extensive, ever-changing seasonal array of over 80 raw honeys ranging from dark, rich bell-heather honey from Dorset to a buttery acacia honey from Prague. A selection of tasting jars offers you the chance to sample and decide for yourself which honey hits the spot. A high, glass-sided beehive inside the shop offers an insight into the life of the honey bee and is a perennial source of fascination to visiting kids.

Lovers of fine wine are catered for by notable independent wine merchants Philglas & Swiggot, founded in 1991. Knowledgeable staff in this discreetly smart shop offer guidance to the range of around 800 wines, catering for both wine buffs and novices. Down the road, veteran Italian deli Salumeria Napoli strikes a pleasantly old-fashioned note: a friendly, down-to-earth business offering excellent, authentic home-made sauces, pasta and charcuterie. And it's impossible to not find yourself drifting into Gail's, an upmarket, artisanal bakery-cum-café with a mouth-watering array of breads, cakes and pastries.

Adding to the street's character is Northcote Road Market, with stalls offering everything from colourful bunches of flowers to fruit and veg. Particularly eye-catching is Breadstall, with a tempting display of breads sourced from seven different bakeries, freshly baked sausage rolls and hand-made *pizza al taglio*. Saturday sees the largest number of market stalls on the road, including the locally famous Northcote Fisheries, which pulls in a queue for its fresh fish, and the cake stall Eat Me, with richly colourful muffins and cupcakes.

Northcote Road
London SW11

Hennessy's
80 Northcote Road, London SW11 6QN
020 7228 7996
www.hennessybutchers.co.uk

A Dove & Son
71 Northcote Road, London SW11 6PJ
020 7223 5191
www.doveandson.co.uk

The Hive Honey Shop
93 Northcote Road, London SW11 6PL
020 7924 6233
www.thehivehoneyshop.co.uk

Philglas & Swiggot
21 Northcote Road, London SW11 1NG
020 7924 4494
www.philglas-swiggot.com

Salumeria Napoli
69 Northcote Road, London SW11 1NP
020 7228 2445

Gail's Bakery
64 Northcote Road, London SW11 6QL
020 7924 6330
www.gailsbread.co.uk

Lola Rojo
78 Northcote Road, London SW11 6QL
020 7350 2262
www.lolarojo.net

Recipease
48–50 St Johns Road, London SW11 1PR
0845 279 7272
www.jamieoliver.com/recipease

There's no shortage of restaurants, bars and cafés to choose from along the road. A particular highlight is Lola Rojo, an acclaimed tapas bar that buzzes with happy diners, tucked cosily inside or perched outside, nibbling on stylish contemporary tapas, such as the knock-out confit of suckling pig with vanilla apple purée and crispy vegetables. No wonder it's been named best Spanish restaurant in London.

The Northcote Road foodie hub ends dramatically at Battersea Rise, where deep-fried fast food and chain store schintz takes over. But even here, it's encouraging to see that Jamie Oliver has opened his concept food shop and cookery school Recipease. Surely it's only a matter of time before Heston Blumenthal takes over the local McDonalds?

Chocs in the City

When was the last time you bought yourself some hand-made chocolates? Food hall chocolate counters no longer hold the monopoly on such treats. These days London's chocolate scene is bursting with talented chocolatiers who are setting up their own shrines to cocoa.

An early advocate of quality chocolate in the capital was Chantal Coady, who opened her first delectable chocolate shop Rococo in the King's Road in 1983. Today she has three branches, including her elegant flagship shop in Belgravia. Here you can do more than browse and buy Rococo's trademark chocolates – from flavoured bars such as milk chocolate with sea salt (with its lingering caramel-like taste) to violet wafers – there's a glass 'window' in the floor through which you can gaze at the goings-on downstairs. Rococo's talented head chocolatier Laurent Couchaux works in his basement laboratory, meticulously creating dainty delights before passing them through the fabulous chocolate-enrobing machine.

Take a break from all that gawping and enjoy a cup of luxuriously rich hot chocolate inside the shop or outside under the shade of a tree in the small, charming Moroccan-inspired courtyard garden, attractively decorated with blue tiles and painted doors that are surrounded by herbs, used as flavourings for the chocolates. If Monsieur Couchaux's work has you reaching for your apron, then you too can learn the art of chocolate-making at Rococo's School of Chocolate.

Elsewhere, founded in 1999, Artisan du Chocolat rapidly made a name for itself with sophisticated hand-made chocolates of innovative flavours such as banana and thyme, tonka bean and trademark tobacco; the team have also worked with top chefs including Gordon Ramsay and Heston Blumenthal. At their contemporary West London shop you can admire the beautiful packaged boxes on display while sampling such creations as sea salt liquid caramels, 'O's (thin chocolate discs with assorted fillings of fruit coulis, pralines and liquid caramel) and South Sea Pearls. Its gleaming white space, dominated by a giant canopy-like light decorated with a wrap-around image of a cocoa plantation, offers chocolate-lovers somewhere to share 'chocolate tapas' or enjoy sophisticated choctails, such as Cacao Martini.

Just down the road from Artisan du Chocolat sits the chic minimalist chocolate boutique of Melt. Watch with awe and fascination in the chocolate kitchen as the head chocolatier, Chika Watanabe, crafts indulgent delights such as olive caramel bonbons (a salty-sweet combination of olive tapenade with caramel all encased within chocolate) or playful Love bars (with a secret pocket for your own message).

Chocolatier Paul A Young has quickly achieved a cult following for his artisanal chocolates, made by his fair hands in the basement of his smart, eponymous Islington shop. Signature chocolates include his Marmite truffles – which you'll either love or hate – and sea-salted caramel and raspberry ganache. Paul

Rococo
5 Motcomb Street, London SW1X 8JU
020 7245 0993
www.rococochocolates.com

Artisan du Chocolat
81 Westbourne Grove, London W2 4UL
0845 270 6996
www.artisanduchocolat.com

Melt
59 Ledbury Road, London W11 2AA
020 7727 5030
www.meltchocolates.com

Paul A Young
33 Camden Passage, London N1 8EA
020 7424 5750
www.paulayoung.co.uk

Cocomaya
12 Connaught Street, London W2 2AF
020 7706 2770
www.cocomaya.co.uk

William Curley
10 Paved Court, Richmond, Surrey TW9 1LZ
020 8332 3002
www.williamcurley.co.uk

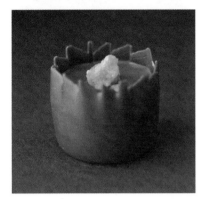

changes his range with the seasons: summer creations might be Pimm's cocktail (strawberry, mint and cucumber) whereas winter greets Christmas pudding truffles.

In contrast to the elegant minimalism favoured by many chocolatiers, Cocomaya is gloriously over the top. And the chocolates take centre stage, laid out in profusion on beautiful, colourful plates on a long central table. In his onsite kitchen, chocolatier Jonathan Deddis creates chocolates as vivacious as their setting and tasting as good as they look. Expect to find refreshing passion fruit or lemon flavours as well as rich chocolate truffles and seriously good chocolate-coated nuts.

A peaceful side-street in leafy Richmond is a somewhat surprising home to the creative talents of husband-and-wife team William and Suzue Curley, acclaimed for their exquisite chocolates and patisserie, at their shop William Curley. Suzue's Japanese roots manifest themselves in chocolates flavoured with ingredients such as yuzu (a rare Japanese citrus fruit) or Japanese black vinegar. Their beautifully crafted confections are wonderfully edible miniature works of art.

Berry Brothers & Rudd

As wine shops go, you'll struggle to find one with as much vintage refinement as Berry Brothers & Rudd. Founded by a widow in 1698, just a goblet's throw from St James' Palace, it began as a humble grocer's shop called The Coffee Mill – the old sign still hangs outside to this day – before branching into the wine business.

The wooden shopfront maintains a suitable air of grandeur and antiquity for a business that has been supplying the British Royal Family with its tipples since 1760. Attentive, immaculately dressed staff tread the sloping wooden floorboards offering knowledgeable advice about the extensive range of fine wines, but there aren't any bottles to view in the main shop. Most of the formidably large stock remains in a temperature-controlled warehouse.

The huge old coffee scales are on display, however, and weren't just used for measuring quantities of roasted beans; from 1765 they weighed their customers – such illuminati as Lord Byron, William Pitt the Younger and the Aga Khan.

Down below are the famous Berry Brothers' warren-like cellars, named after Napoleon III who dropped by during his exile. Nowadays these form the backdrop for palate-whetting events such as wine tastings and grand dinners.

Berry Brothers & Rudd 79
3 St James's Street, London SW1A 1EG
0800 280 2440
www.bbr.com

Algerian Coffee Stores

Behind a lovely cheery red, old-fashioned shop front, in among Soho's bars, cafés, restaurants and sex shops, sits this venerable coffee shop, founded in 1887 by Algerian businessman Mr Hassan. Run for decades now by the Crocetta family, the shop sells not only an impressive range of own-roasted coffees (their best-selling Formula Rossa is so smooth), but also a wide selection of teas and infusions – from Russian Caravan to Yerba Mate.

Step inside the shop and you are greeted by both the intoxicating smell of freshly roasted coffee and by the fragrant aromas of the cardamom and cloves used to flavour it. Enthusiasts might think they've died and gone to heaven, such is the array of teas and coffees on the shelves behind the counter. What's more, the shop also stocks coffee- and tea-making equipment – from gleaming stove-top espresso makers and grinders to tea-infuser mugs and caddies. Down-to-earth and friendly, the staff are happy to advise and guide you on their extensive stock.

Customers can also sample one of the store's reasonably priced takeaway cappuccinos or espressos; the painted wooden sign in the doorway says it all: 'No seating. No inflated prices. Just a pure caffeine shot'.

Algerian Coffee Stores 80
52 Old Compton Street, London W1D 4PB
020 7437 2480
www.algcoffee.co.uk

Fortnum & Mason

Fortnum & Mason (82)
181 Piccadilly, London W1A 1ER
020 7734 8040
www.fortnumandmason.com

This grand old man of London's food retailing scene is still going strong today. Founded in 1707, the business was set up by William Fortnum, an enterprising footman at the court of Queen Anne, who teamed up with his landlord Hugh Mason to offer groceries to royalty and the aristocracy. Today, following a major revamp in time for its tercentenary celebrations in 2007, Fortnum's offers a distinctly luxurious food shopping experience.

Frock-coated staff open the door for you, while inside the store's glittering chandeliers sparkle from on high and the trademark red carpets cushion every footstep for browsing customers. Wander back and forth between such departments as Tea and Coffee, Chocolate and Hampers, choosing from exquisitely packaged goodies and sampling whatever delights are on offer.

Fortnum's embraces gastro-patriotism with gusto, stocking British treats from Highgrove beefburgers to Shropshire Blue cheese along with its own honey, made in four smart hives on the building's rooftop. You can buy a bottle from the impressive wine department, with its selection of champagnes and rare wines, and drink it in style at Fortnum's 1707 wine bar for a small fee. Would-be diners are also well catered for: from the brasserie-style Fountain Restaurant, noted for its Welsh rarebit, to the sedate St James' restaurant offering lunch and a truly indulgent afternoon tea.

The Oldest Pie and Mash Shop

M Manze (88)
87 Tower Bridge Road, London SE1 4TW
020 7407 2985
www.manze.co.uk

Jellied eels. Pie and mash. These traditional and iconic Cockney dishes – once staples of London's East End-dwelling working class – are increasingly hard to find in the capital. But London's oldest pie and mash shop, Manze's, is still going strong.

The shop was established in 1891 by Robert Cooke, then bought by Michele Manze in 1902; today it is still run by the Manze family on its original premises, just down the road from the River Thames from where, historically, the eels were caught. As you might expect from such an institution, the Manze family take great pride in maintaining a tradition, still using the same recipes for their pies and their 'liquor' (parsley sauce) that Michele Manze used back in the day.

The interior is at once straightforward and splendidly evocative: narrow wooden benches at white marble-topped tables with the trademark green-and-white tiled walls and mirrors. Staff are friendly and down to earth. Regular customers, from builders to old age pensioners, make their way here to grab a seat and tuck into the gargantuan portions of Manze's home-made meat pies freshly baked each day, served with helpings of mashed potato and startlingly green liquor or platefuls of stewed or jellied eels.

Postcard Teas

Britain has long been known as a nation of tea-drinkers, from delicate ladies sipping from dainty china cups to helmet-clad builders dunking digestives into steaming mugs. Yet nowadays all too often a cup of tea is a perfunctory affair, made by simply plonking a teabag into hot water. Not so at Postcard Teas, Tim d'Offay's exquisite tea shop, a civilised, peaceful oasis located just a couple of minutes' away from the hurly-burly of Oxford Street. On offer here is a select range of black, green, oolong, white and flavoured teas that Tim sources and imports direct from master tea makers and small-scale family producers, all stylishly packaged in strikingly decorated tins he designs himself. Each tea is also available in an attractive package, which can be posted to friends abroad – a tea 'postcard' from Postcard Teas.

The collection reflects Tim's genuine and deep-felt love for the leafy stuff, which has seen him spend over 10 years travelling regularly to China, India, Japan, Korea, Sri Lanka and Taiwan to meet and work with the world's finest artisanal tea makers. His list of teas and the places they come from is a wonderfully evocative one: Sparrow's Tongue tea, made in Korea by Mr Ha, Moonlight White tea from the Doke Estate in Bihar (near Buddha's birthplace), Yimu Oolong made by Master Hsieh in Nantou County, Taiwan. Of particular interest to tea cogniscenti is the range of rare teas, hand-made in tiny quantities each year, such as Emperor Jiaqing Tribute Phoenix, an old tea tree oolong made by Master Wang, or Jin Damo 800-year-old tree Pu-erh, made by Master Liu. Tim's own photographs of his tea travels are on display, showing the beautiful places in which the beverage you're drinking has been grown and the people who work there.

Customers here range from tea enthusiasts, on a quest for an exceptional Darjeeling or an aged Pu-erh, to intrigued passers-by who have stopped to admire the window display and popped in to find out more. Potential tea buyers visiting Postcard Teas are offered the chance to sample any tea they're interested in, taking a seat at the long, communal table in the main room. Tim himself or a member of his unfailingly courteous staff will come and take an order, offering advice or recommendations. The tea is carefully brewed and served in beautiful, individual china cups to be inhaled, sipped and savoured; this is a leisurely process, not for people in a rush. For those wishing to learn more, tutored tastings with Tim are also offered.

Adding to the special nature of this place is the display of artefacts and craft objects, some, but not all, tea-related. Pride of place goes to a gleaming array of hand-made, tin, brass and copper Japanese tea caddies, made by Kaikado of Kyoto, a family-run business that has been meticulously making these metal caddies since 1875. Other desirable objects range from hand-painted colourful Chinese teapots, decorated with blossoms, to dainty Japanese boxes of pure gold leaf, to be sprinkled over tea or food. Downstairs, a small gallery offers a changing exhibition of craft, from lacquerwork to fine ceramics.

Postcard Teas 83
9 Dering Street, London W1S 1AG
020 7629 3654
www.postcardteas.com

Teasmiths 90
6 Lamb Street, London E1 6EA
020 7247 1333
www.teasmith.co.uk

Teasmiths in Spitalfields Market is another London tea grotto offering a chance to learn more about this refined world, with a self-styled 'tea bar' stocking an extensive range of premium leaf products. Here, customers can taste the tea of their choice in three infusions, assessing the changes in flavour. A partnership with noted chocolatier and patissier William Curley (see page 63) means that tea-drinkers here can also sample treats such as green-tea-flavoured cakes and chocolates. Tastings and masterclasses are also on offer.

Neal's Yard Dairy

A visit to the Borough Market branch of Neal's Yard Dairy – a high-ceilinged, spacious establishment – demonstrates just how vibrant the farmhouse cheese scene is. A splendid array of farmhouse cheeses, from huge cloth-bound Cheddars on shelves to tiny goat's cheeses in the counters with all sorts in between, is on show. Cheeses are grouped together by type – hard, soft, washed rind, blue, goat's, sheep's and cow's – helping you to locate the cheese you want. The range of textures and tastes on offer here is most extraordinary, from the delicate flavour and soft texture of a fresh goat's cheese such as Perroche to the rich caramel flavours of Coolea from County Cork, Ireland.

Founded in 1979, Neal's Yard Dairy is well known to lovers of British and Irish farmhouse cheeses. Under the watchful eye of Randolph Hodgson, Neal's Yard Dairy is far more than an excellent cheesemongers, it has played a vital role in championing farmhouse cheeses and promoting them both at home and abroad.

The resurgence in artisanal cheesemaking (and of an appreciative market for said cheeses) has seen cheesemakers reviving historic farmhouse cheeses that were in decline or no longer being made traditionally, such as Gorwydd Farm making an artisanal Caerphilly in Wales (see page 233) or the Clarkes creating Sparkenhoe Red Leicester in Leicestershire.

Excitingly, however, many cheesemakers today are returning to traditional methods and using them to create totally new cheeses, such as Charles Martell's pungent Stinking Bishop or Robin Congdon's Beenleigh Blue. Randolph Hodgson himself has teamed up with acclaimed cheesemaker Joe Schneider to create Stichelton, a blue cheese made in Nottinghamshire using raw milk (see page 162), unlike Stilton which nowadays must be made using pasteurised milk.

All these cheeses, and many more besides, are on sale at Neal's Yard Dairy, offering what is to some a bewildering amount of choice. Fortunately, tasting lies at the heart of Neal's Yard Dairy's ethos, so you can cruise your way on a journey of cheesy loveliness. Friendly, helpful staff greet you and immediately ask what you'd like to try, cutting off pieces of cheese for you to taste and talking through your thoughts, offering suggestions, guidance and recommendations. A request to try a Cheddar turns into an opportunity to sample the three artisanal Somerset Cheddars in stock, side-by-side, so you can work out for yourself which you prefer. A visiting British or Irish cheesemaker is often to be found standing outside the door handing out samples of their cheeses, happy to explain how it is made.

Behind the scenes the staff at Neal's Yard Dairy work very closely with the cheesemakers to ensure that the cheeses are sold in peak condition. A number of cheeses are bought in as young cheeses to be aged by Neal's Yard Dairy in their maturing rooms in Bermondsey under the railway arches.

Neal's Yard Dairy 81
6 Park Street, London SE1 9AB
020 7367 0799
www.nealsyarddairy.co.uk

Also at:
17 Shorts Gardens,
London WC2H 9AT
020 7240 5700

"Tasting lies at the heart of their ethos, so cruise your way on a journey of cheesy loveliness."

The emphasis on tasting a cheese before you buy it reflects the way that hand-made cheeses – as opposed to a uniform mass-produced product – change from batch to batch. You can return to the shop a week later, ask for a cheese that you enjoyed before, be offered a taste and realise – with surprise – that it tastes different this time. Variations in the milk (depending on what the cows, sheep or goats are eating), the weather, the season and the starter culture being used by the cheesemaker all influence a cheese's taste.

Fromage-o-philes beware, you can indulge your obsession further at the wonderful informal-but-informative tutored tastings at Neal's Yard Dairy.

Borough Market

While trains rumble overhead a magical transformation has taken place over the past decade in what was a historic wholesale market under the railway arches by London Bridge. Borough Market has become one of the capital's most celebrated foodie attractions, housing over 150 stalls selling everything from everyday fruit and veg, bread, meat, fish and cheese to such specialist foods as biodynamic salad leaves and Portuguese honey. And the 'Borough Market effect' has spilled into the streets around and about, too, so that a visit here is about so much more than just the shopping. Enjoy the noise and spectacle of the market while you sip a latte, grab a chorizo and rocket roll or sit down for modern British fare; you could easily spend breakfast, lunch and dinner here, with plenty of snacks in between.

The historic market site is a handsome construction, housed under a high glass roof supported by green metal pillars, with the market extending beyond it into areas under the railway arches. Finding your way round is part of the fun here, as you spot tucked-away stalls that you missed on the last wander round.

Visiting Borough Market is an atmospheric and appetising experience, with food candy aplenty – from striking displays of meat, fish, seafood and game to attractive arrangements of seasonal fruit and vegetables. Thursday is the Market's quietest day, with the fewest stalls open, while Friday is a favourite day for serious food shoppers who wish to avoid the thronging crowd on Saturday, the market's busiest day in terms of both traders and footfall.

Unlike the local focus of most farmers' markets, Borough Market is a cosmopolitan affair with shoppers able to sample good things to eat from around the world. Spanish food, for example, is represented by Brindisa, noted for its melt-in-your-mouth cured hams and Flavours of Spain's stall, which specialises in unique foods from Galicia, such as monkfish liver with sea urchin or prime smoked mackerel in olive oil. Ital-o-philes are spoilt for choice when it comes to olive oils, cheeses and cured meats. Giuseppe Mele beats the drum for his native Southern Italian cuisine with De Calabria's rich green olive oil, unpasteurised mixed blossom honey and nduja, a spicy salami. From further afield come Mexican dried chillies and fresh tomatillos on Cool Chile's stall or Argentinian foods from Porteña.

Sitting alongside the international array is some of the best cuisine Britain has to offer. You'll find great meat and game (one of the market's strong points), with a number of farmers selling their own meat, such as Ginger Pig, Sillfield Farm, Wild Beef and Gamston Wood, which sells own-produced ostrich meat. In fact, keep a keen eye out for the myriad offerings of delicious British foods throughout the market, including Shellseekers diver-caught scallops from Dorset, Mrs King's Pork Pies (which have a devoted following) and England Preserves' great jams and chutneys.

Borough Market 89
Southwark Street, London SE1 1TL
www.boroughmarket.org.uk
Open 11am–5pm Thursday, 12–6pm Friday
and 8am–5pm Saturday.

Brindisa Shop
Stoney Street, London SE1 9AF
020 7407 1036
www.brindisashops.com

Flavours of Spain
0870 330 2879
www.flavoursofspain.co.uk

Cool Chile Co
0870 902 1145
www.coolchile.co.uk

Porteña
020 7740 2196
www.portena.co.uk

The Ginger Pig
020 7403 4721
www.thegingerpig.co.uk

Sillfield Farm
01539 567609
www.sillfield.co.uk

Wild Beef
01647 433433

Gamston Wood Farm
01777 838858
www.gamstonwoodfarm.com

Shellseekers
07787 516258

Mrs King's Pork Pies
01159 894101

England Preserves
020 8692 0806

> **"Sitting alongside the international array of foods is some of the best food Britain has to offer."**

Boerenkaas Dutch Farmhouse Cheese
07783 542310
www.dutchfarmhousecheese.co.uk

Mons Ltd
020 7064 6912

KaseSwiss
07783 542310
www.kaseswiss.com

Kappacasein
www.kappacasein.com

Monmouth Coffee Company
2 Park Street, London SE1 9AB
020 7232 3010
www.monmouthcoffee.co.uk

Konditor & Cook
10 Stoney Street, London SE1 9AD
020 7407 5100
www.konditorandcook.com

German Deli
3 Park Street, London SE1 9AB
020 7378 0000
www.germandeli.co.uk

Brindisa Tapas
18–20 Southwark St, London SE1 1TJ
020 7357 8880
www.tapasbrindisa.com

Wright Brothers
11 Stoney Street, London SE1 9AD
020 7403 9554
www.wrightbros.eu.com

Roast
The Floral Hall, Stoney Street,
London SE1 1TL
020 7015 1863
www.roast-restaurant.com

Cheese-lovers beware, Borough Market's selection of lactic delights is vast and irresistible (see also Neal's Yard Dairy, page 68). You'll find that some stalls offer one excellent cheese – great Comte, superb Parmesan, traditional Cheshire or artisanal Caerphilly – while others display a range of cheeses from one nationality. Mons, for example, specialises in raw milk, French cheeses, such as a voluptuous washed rind Langres, an intriguing soft Tomme Crayeuse and Tarentis goat's cheese. Boerenkaas offers a rare chance to try farmhouse Dutch cheeses, such as 3½-year-old aged Gouda or Olde Remeker. KaseSwiss' mouth-watering range of fine Swiss cheeses includes a spectacular aged Emmentaler and a Gruyère Vieux.

You may want to skip breakfast before a planned visit (or at least come peckish) as many of the stalls offer takeaway food and part of the fun is choosing what you want to snack on next. Brindisa's grilled chorizo sandwiches have achieved cult status as the long, patient lunchtime queue outside the shop testifies. Fromage-o-philes should hunt out the Kappacasein's raclette stall, where buttery Ogleshield cheese is transformed into the classic Swiss dish of shaved melted cheese over new potatoes with cornichons and pickled onions. Plus, there's oysters from Colchester, falafel, chicken wraps, venison burgers…the list could go on.

But there's more than stalls to visit: foodie shops abound. Monmouth Coffee Company occupies a prime spot at the edge of the market. As you'd expect, its speciality is coffee, ethically sourced from farms, estates and cooperatives and freshly and expertly roasted in-house at its Maltby Street roastery. Customers flock here for coffee beans or to sit outside for a lingering coffee with some simple but good bread and jam. Next door, Konditor & Cook offer delicious and delectable baked goods, from eye-catching cakes to moreish biscuits. Just around the corner, the cosy German Deli offers Londoners a rare chance to purchase authentic German ingredients, from cooking and slicing sausages to potato dumplings.

Would-be diners looking to sit down and enjoy a meal have plenty to choose from. On the corner of the market, Brindisa Tapas – a relaxed tapas bar venture from the noted Spanish food importers – is perpetually busy with happy folk tucking into tasty portions of, for example, deep-fried Monte Enebro goat's cheese with orange flower honey. Their popular Friday and Saturday breakfast menu includes grilled chorizo, fried egg and fried potatoes or scrambled eggs with peppers. Seafood fans should head to the Wright Brothers' Oyster and Porter House on Stoney Street (see also page 26). Here you can feast on top-notch, spanking fresh oysters – Wild Colchester, Carlingford Lough, Speciales de Claires – and wash them down with a glass of fine wine or, indeed, porter. Look up in Floral Hall and you'll espy Roast, looking out over the market – a smart establishment with a seasonally changing menu focussing on artisanal British food producers and offering dishes from salads to substantial eponymous roasts. For more down-to-earth fare, make your way to Maria's Market Café, a local institution where Maria dishes out generous portions of her legendary bubble-and-squeak.

Further transformations are afoot at Borough Market while a new railway bridge is built for London's Olympics in 2012. But the buzzy atmosphere and the incredible range of foods will remain, making this market one of the best in the world.

Billingsgate Fish Market

Formerly located on the north side of the Thames, London's historic fish market (which traces its roots back to the 16th century) is now to be found in the somewhat newer surroundings of Docklands, dwarfed by gleaming skyscrapers. This market is for early birds, so you'll need to set your alarm to shop here; the market ceases trading officially by 8.30am, and many merchants pack up well before that.

Once upon a time fishermen unloaded their catch on the banks of the River Thames to supply Billingsgate with the fish of the day; nowadays night-time sees a steady stream of lorries arriving with fresh seafood from as far and wide as Aberdeen, Newlyn and France. Once there, a host of 50-odd merchants waits to unload and sell these super-fresh catches to wholesalers, fishmongers, the restaurant trade and the general public.

Members of the public have a historic right to shop at the market, with Saturdays proving particularly popular with ordinary punters. But this is no pick-and-mix market; here you have to buy in bulk as many traders are wholesalers and consequently are reluctant to split a box. So make a trip of it with friends and divvy up the prize accordingly. The market heaves with life and noise, with porters steering loads through the narrow aisles, shouting out 'Mind your backs!' as they do so and bantering with the traders, who give as good as they get. The characteristic smell once you're inside Market Hall is a faint tang of the sea, rather than overwhelming fishiness, a sign of just how fresh the stock is.

To gain a fascinating and genuine insight into how the market operates, opt for one of the Billingsgate Seafood Training School's Billingsgate Market tours. Walk around the stalls with a guide offering a running commentary on everything you need to know about the wetfish trade. As well as identifying what's on sale – from shellfish (ridged-shelled cockles, scallops, mussels and clams) to the huge water-filled trays of wriggling, slithering live eels from Holland – the guides will teach you how to recognise seriously fresh seafood: from gleaming mackerel still stiff with rigor mortis to fish covered in clear slime, a visible sign of freshness. The guides don't duck the issue of fish sustainability either and are more than happy to point out the more sustainable species.

Upstairs in the cookery school proper, the emphasis is on practical, hands-on preparation, with Director CJ Jackson demonstrating clearly and expertly how to prepare an array of seafood before cooking it. Equipped with some seriously sharp knives, students gut mackerel or skin and gut a gurnard – a process not for the squeamish, but an empowering one. Students move on to cook and enjoy dishes ranging from fish soup (with freshly made fish stock) to roast sea bass.

Billingsgate Market 92
Trafalgar Way, London E14 5ST
020 7987 1118
www.billingsgate-market.org.uk
Open 5–8.30am Tuesday–Saturday.

Billingsgate Seafood Training School 92
30 Billingsgate Market, Trafalgar Way, London E14 5ST
020 7517 3548
www.seafoodtraining.org

Marine Ices

The Mansi family has been making and selling 'gelati' here since 1931, when Italian Gaetano Mansi, who ran a greengrocer's, decided to use up his excess stock of fresh fruit by turning it into sorbets. Demand blossomed and it's now Gaetano's grandsons that run this thriving ice cream business, supplying restaurants, shops and hotels, as well as their own relaxed, family-friendly Italian restaurant.

A trip to Marine Ices for ice cream has been a childhood treat for many generations of children in North London, and nowadays fine weather still sees a patient queue waiting in line outside the takeaway counter, enjoying the process of trying to decide which ice cream flavour to have. Customers can choose from classic Italian gelati (lighter than the dairy-rich American-style ice cream) in traditional flavours, such as coffee, mint chocolate chip and coconut, along with refreshing fresh fruit sorbets, such as lemon or raspberry.

If you're looking for a more indulgent treat then grab a seat in the ice cream parlour to partake of a sundae, ice cream milkshake or rum-flavoured *tartufo*.

Marine Ices 84
8 Haverstock Hill, London NW3 2BL
020 7482 9003
www.marineices.co.uk

Ottolenghi's Tasteful Takeaways

Passers-by strolling along the pavement past Ottolenghi's simple, white façade never fail to pause, their attention caught by the striking display of food in the window. Piles of trademark blowsy, pink-stained or cocoa-dusted raspberry or chocolate meringues sit alongside an array of goodies such as clementine and almond syrup cake or blueberry and vanilla cupcakes. On another counter, huge platefuls of vibrantly coloured, savoury dishes – from seared beef with horseradish sauce to salads of roasted sweet potato with pecans tossed with a maple syrup dressing – vie for attention. The food tastes as wonderful as it looks and consequently Ottolenghi has a devoted following in the capital.

Showcasing the considerable culinary talents of chefs Yotam Ottolenghi and Sami Tamimi, Ottolenghi's elegant food shops all offer food 'to go', while the Islington branch comes complete with a restaurant area.

One of the charms of the Ottolenghi food philosophy is that humble ingredients take centre stage. These are not dishes that rely on rich, luxurious or costly ingredients to make their mark, instead grains and pulses, such as quinoa, bulgur and chickpeas, are combined with simple vegetables – tomatoes, courgette and squashes – with such care and affection that they can't fail to create the most delicious of dishes.

Ottolenghi 86
287 Upper Street, London N1 2TZ
020 7288 1454
www.ottolenghi.co.uk

Also at:
63 Ledbury Road, London W11 2AD
020 7727 1121

1 Holland Street, London W8 4NA
020 7937 0003

13 Motcomb Street, London SW1X 8LB
020 7823 2707

Broadway Market

Broadway Market 87
London E8 4PH
www.broadwaymarket.co.uk
Every Saturday.

This flourishing, über-trendy community market in the heart of Hackney makes for a great Saturday day out. Dwarfed by tower blocks, the market stretches itself along a picturesque street of small, brick, terraced houses – Broadway Market – a traditional drovers' route.

Over 80 stalls line the street offering passers-by a tempting range of foods: hand-made chilli-spiced ketchups and chutneys, moreish biscuits, cheeses, good-looking fruit and veg, irresistible cupcakes and artisanal breads, to name but a few. Summertime sees locals and visitors alike stocking up here before heading off for a picnic at nearby London Fields.

Ready-to-eat food ranges couldn't be more cosmopolitan: from Ghanaian jollof rice or Jewish salt beef sandwiches to Portuguese salt cod rissoles and Gujurati thalis. On one corner, customers queue patiently at Ca Phe Vietnam's street café, waiting for caramel-flavoured Vietnamese coffee and freshly assembled *banh mi* – delectable, crisp Vietnamese filled baguettes. Cherished local deli-cum-café L'Eau à la Bouche – a popular meeting spot – does a roaring trade in coffees, sandwiches, salads and soups. Buskers gather an appreciative crowd; you may even see someone dancing. Customers range from veteran East Enders, chatting with friends and neighbours, to bright, young things, simply enjoying the buzz.

E Pellicci Café

E Pellicci 91
332 Bethnal Green Road,
London E2 0AG
020 7739 4873

On Bethnal Green Road you'll find this iconic, independent café, run by the Pellicci family since 1900, that's served generations of East Enders. At any time of the day, you'll find builders tucking into massive breakfasts alongside City gents enjoying a fry-up.

This is the place to come to enjoy a proper caff Great British Breakfast – bacon, egg, sausages, baked beans and Pellicci's renowned chips – all freshly cooked to order. Once you've ordered, sit back and enjoy the banter between the staff and the customers amid the background sizzle of frying food. And soak up your surroundings too; Pellicci's classic style (Art Deco-style marquetry and wooden panelling) was awarded Grade II listed status in 2005 by English Heritage.

Such is Pellicci's fame that a steady stream of celebrities eat here, from pop idols to soap stars. Pellicci's was run for many decades by the dapper, charming Nevio Pellicci (1925–2008), who had been born in a room above the café. Today, his son Nevio Junior continues the family tradition, hospitably greeting all customers, whether old-time regulars or first-timers, as though they are long-lost friends.

Bill's

Hit Brighton or Lewes hungry and the freshest, most individual place to eat is Bill's. Greengrocery has given way to produce – yes, it's the same thing but this is an irresistible mix of market stall and cool café. Eat in, take away or buy to cook it yourself: whatever your choice the Bill's experience feels like the best produce market with an exuberant eatery at its heart.

Bill is a tall, rangy man with a mop of grey hair – he's just a guy who was in the greengrocery business for 20 years or more on the site of his current store in Lewes. He's the third generation of greengrocers and appears keen not to be the last. To counter the attack of the supermarkets who moved into Lewes en masse, Bill set about reinventing himself and his store, cooking his fresh produce and creating a café culture based on fruit and veg. Lewes town was built in a strategic gap in the Downs to withstand attack from invaders, and Bill has done that too. Business is booming and with the second store now flourishing in Brighton, his is a real David and Goliath story of survival.

What the fruit and veg business in the UK lacks is passion, but Bill and his team have it by the basketload. Every member of staff exudes knowledge and a can-do attitude. The business has grown into a food-lovers' emporium. Provenance is the key to product selection – local is as important as organic and both are on offer, along with imported produce from artisan growers who, like the local suppliers, are paid a realistic price to keep them in business. This ethical philosophy results in quality produce, which Bill's many customers are happy to pay for. 'I don't think just local is enough,' explains Bill. 'People still want the stuff we can't grow here, especially from Europe. I try to offer the best of everything, and to make sure that everyone gets a fair deal.'

Bill's opened in Lewes in 2001, with the café open from breakfast through to tea. The store is in the lower part of town, in the picturesque Cliffe High Street, and has breathed life back into the community. In Brighton, Bill's sits in the newly fashionable North Lanes and stays open in the evenings too. It used to be that the onion-shaped domes of George IV's seaside palace were the most exotic thing in town, but they're now challenged by the thatch of berries, fruit and spikes of lavender or other seasonal decorations on Bill's irresistible gateaux and pastries. Surely, food that looks as good as this must be good for you.

Bill's 107
56 Cliffe High Street, Lewes,
East Sussex BN7 2AN
01273 476918
www.billsproducestore.co.uk

Also at:
The Depot
100 North Road,
Brighton BN1 1YE
01273 692894

Hogs Back Brewery

Beer enthusiasts Bill and Bridget Biddell farm the Hampton Estate at Seale on the straight-out-of-*Country-Life* southern slope of the Hogs Back ridge between Farnham and Guildford. Their land includes the last hop garden in Surrey – 14 acres of Fuggles, a traditional flavour-packed, tall hop that scrambles up poles and wires like runner beans to almost five metres.

Modern hops are short and easy to train, which makes them easier still to pick but that holds no sway with Bill and Bridget; they've kept faith with a traditional tall variety. Fuggles are the ultimate hops for craft brewers: they have big, bright green, open and clean flowers that have those high bitter factors sought after by brewers.

Hops are graded, like tea, for flavour and colour. 'Choicest' are the best and are favoured by all craft brewers. The nearby Hogs Back Brewery in Tongham takes as many of the (choicest) new season's pickings of Fuggles from Hampton as they can. The brewery uses mainly Surrey Fuggles (from Hampton) both for primary hopping (for flavour at the start of the brewing process) and for secondary, or late, hopping (for aroma, at the end of the boil-off).

'A few years ago there was a trend towards blends of hops in beers,' explains Tony, beer devotee turned brewery partner of Hogs Back. 'Now the move is back to bright, golden beers that are well-hopped with lots of flavour from single varietals. Our TEA, Traditional English Ale, is perfectly suited to this trend with a great big flavour from our very local hops.'

Hogs Back has been brewing for almost 30 years. It started with a couple of beer enthusiasts, an old Burco boiler and a happy determination to succeed. The Brewery remains in the 18th-century barns where it began, but now it takes up much more of them; though it is a wonderfully compact organisation, every inch of space is well used. The Surrey Fuggles are first added to a copper of hot liquor called 'sweet wort', which is strained from the mash tun after the barley malt has been 'mashed' or steeped. Flavour is extracted during a rigorous boil – American breweries call the copper a kettle, which gives a better idea of the process.

You can enjoy four different beers during the tour at the Hogs Back Brewery. Tasting stations are set up at various points around the barn and the brewery's 'tasters' bring brewing to life in the most refreshing way. The tours must be pre-booked and end up in the brewery shop, which is reason enough to visit in itself.

Favourites include BSA (Burma Star Association), a tawny-coloured and richly malted beer with a refreshingly bright bite, and OTT (Old Tongham Tasty), a chocolatey porter-style beer that is perfect with rich beef casseroles and shellfish. Seasonal beers can be bought on draft from the shop along with the brewery's main selection, which are also available bottled.

Hogs Back Brewery
Manor Farm, The Street, Tongham,
Surrey GU10 1DE
01252 783000
www.hogsback.co.uk
Tours 6.30pm Wednesday, Thursday and
Friday; 11am, 1.30pm and 3.30pm Saturday;
2.30pm Sunday. Cost £8 per person and
must be booked in advance.

Bill and Bridget Biddell
Hampton Lodge, Elstead Road, Seale,
Farnham, Surrey GU10 1JE
01483 810465
www.hamptonestate.co.uk

Sussex Cider

Drinking cider used to be a country-based pastime; for centuries people have been enjoying Sussex country life while sipping on a pint of this appley nectar. But recently 'townies' and city folk have realised they've been missing out and are now embracing cider-drinking wholeheartedly in a mission to make up for lost time.

Now, first things first. A good UK-produced cider with real depth and a true fruit flavour requires alcohol, at least 6% ABV, and no brew of less potency should really be classified as cider on our shores. It's easy to forget this potency when you discover a particularly gorgeous appley cider, tasting almost like fruit juice if made just from dessert apples, that's just too gluggable. 'Proper' ciders sometimes demand wine glasses rather than pint glasses.

Lots of apple orchards were planted in the Weald of Sussex after World War II and top (or tree) fruits became an important crop as the country struggled its way towards a varied, healthy and home-produced diet. Cider-making had long been a by-product of dessert- and cooking-fruit sales as windfalls and dropped apples could be picked up and juiced, minimising wastage. Merrydown vintage cider was first made in Sussex in 1946, but the mantle of craft of Sussex cider-making now rests firmly with husband-and-wife team James and Cathy Lane at Gospel Green.

Cider can be made from any apples: desserts, cookers or traditional cider apples, which fall into two kinds – bitter sharps and bitter sweets; both are virtually inedible because of their hard texture and bitterness. James and Cathy use only dessert and cooking fruit from their own orchards and the few local ones left, and always add apples from the ancient Mere de menage tree by their kitchen window to make their *méthode champenoise* cider.

The pair press or pulp the apples into a pomace, then wrap them in cloths to minimise oxidation and discolouration as they are layered into a cheese to be pressed to extract the juice in a press that James built himself. The cider then experiences its first fermentation in the vat before, six months later, it is siphoned off into champagne bottles and sealed with crown caps for a second (bottle) fermentation that takes a minimum of a year. Finally, some 18 months after the apples were pressed, the crown caps are removed and the cider is disgorged, removing any sediment that has built up during the fermentation and risen to the neck of the bottles. A 'dosage' may be added before the corks and wires are fitted, and the Gospel Green cider is then ready for sale. Cases of it fly out of the door. This clean, fresh cider has a good mousse and an elegant appley flavour; definitely one for flutes rather than pint pots.

For a double whammy of pleasure, you can stay in the barn once used by James and Cathy as a creamery to make cheese and enjoy Gospel Green cider on the smallholding on which it is made (see www.hideaways.co.uk). For the rest of us,

Gospel Green Cider 103
Gospel Green, Gospel Green Cottage, Haslemere, West Sussex GU27 3BH
01428 654120

The National Cider and Perry Centre 108
Middle Farm, Firle, Lewes, East Sussex BN8 6LJ
01323 811324
www.middlefarm.com

"Proper ciders sometimes demand wine glasses rather than pint pots."

the best chance of buying this sought-after cider and of tasting many others is at the shop at Middle Farm at Firle in East Sussex, which also houses the National Cider and Perry Collection.

Middle Farm has been a first-class farm shop for decades, specialising in local cheeses and meats with an onsite butchery. Now the farm encourages visitors to watch the cows being milked among all the other daily tasks with the animals. Cider-lovers can purchase Gospel Green, which rubs shoulders with about 100 other ciders and perries. Anyone wishing to take full advantage of the tastings should travel by bus from Lewes or descend from the South Downs Way at Firle Beacon; but be warned the return journey may be much harder.

The Goods Shed

Fast track to gastronomic delights through this goods shed in a railway yard in Canterbury. This six-days-a-week farmers' market has been housed for almost a decade in a beautiful brick-built shed with huge sliding doors, a high vaulted wooden ceiling and a buzz of culinary curiosity as shoppers wander the laden stalls.

Buy fish, fowl, game, meat and cheese at tile-fronted counters from knowledgeable vendors; fruits and veg arrive courtesy of a grower's cooperative. Wines and groceries, mixing Kentish with the best from the nearby Continent, remind food-lovers of the county's close links with Europe as the trains speed by.

The restaurant, raised for a bird's-eye view of the trading floor, offers coffee with pastries from the bakery, fresh vegetable juices (the apple, celery and ginger juice is superb) and seasonal lunches; and all the ingredients are available to buy downstairs. Those in a hurry in this cosmopolitan, student area can grab a takeaway from the fresh-to-order sandwich bar.

Evenings become somewhat more elegant affairs as candelabras and napery grace the scrubbed pine tables surrounded by an eclectic selection of dining chairs. But the food is the same: top-notch local fare.

The Goods Shed 114
Station Road West, Canterbury,
Kent CT2 8AN
01227 459153
www.thegoodsshed.net
Open 9am–7pm Tuesday–Saturday and
10am–4pm Sunday; closed Monday.

Wild Man, Wild Food

Fergus Drennan only does email, blogging and his website to feed his wild-food habit. 'I'd rather be outside but the electronic stuff allows me to share my passion,' he explains. A man of the wild, Fergus believes foraging has given him a sense of identity, and it's the perfect antidote to modern life.

An outing with him might last for 12 hours, involve a long walk, two three-course foraged meals and enough fresh air to put a city-dweller to sleep for several days. He leads courses in the countryside around Canterbury, come rain or shine, and has an encyclopedic knowledge of all things wild: fungi, berries, seashore plants and game. 'It started when I was seven years' old and is now my whole life, I forage full-time if there's any time left.'

Fergus cooks as few people are able to, with each ingredient being supremely fresh and at its best. His courses will have you eating things that would otherwise never pass your lips, and coming back for more. Not that it will just be given to you. It's a hands-on amazing food experience: find it, cook it, eat it.

Fergus Drennan 115
www.wildmanwildfood.com

Winterdale Cheesemakers

Winterdale Cheesemakers 112
Platt House Farm, Fairseat Lane,
Wrotham, Sevenoaks, Kent TN15 7QB
01732 820021
www.winterdale.co.uk
Open 11am–1pm Saturday.
Phone for course details and
before visiting at other times.

Robin and Carla Betts may be the new kids on the creamery block in the south-east but they produce some richly flavoured farmhouse cheeses from cow's, sheep's and goat's milk. They've even added a Cheddar-like cheese to their selection, as well as a Kentish Camembert.

You can visit Platt House Farm to buy cheeses direct and to talk 'fromagerie' with the people who really know their curds from their whey. You might also get to peep into the naturally cooled cellar, dug deep into the chalk, where Winterdale Shaw (the Betts' unpasteurised hard cheese) is matured for a minimum of six months. All natural cellars have their own microenvironments, imparting a unique flavour to the cheeses matured within, and the Betts are taking full advantage of theirs to develop their cheeses' rich, rounded taste. Think PDO Roquefort and you'll understand how special this is.

Winterdale Cheese Barn is open fleetingly on Saturday mornings – set the alarm or you'll miss it. Informal tours of the dairy and cheese room happen whenever possible, and there are plans to run what will no doubt be must-do cheesemaking courses, where you return months later to collect your matured cheese.

Kentish Cobnuts

Alexander Hunt 113
Apple Trees, Comp Lane, St Mary's Platt,
Near Sevenoaks, Kent TN15 8NR
www.kentishcobnuts.com
www.kentishcobnutsassociation.org.uk

If you find yourself in rural Kent between August and October, keep an eye out for nutters. It's the cobnut season and, yes, a nutter picks nuts.

Kentish cobnuts, a type of hazelnut, are moist, sweet and sold fresh in husks that quickly turn from green to gold. They're superb in a salad of watercress, early pears, blue cheese and an orange vinaigrette; the Victorians apparently adored them with port and cheese. They keep for months but need to stay in the fridge.

Cobnut orchards, or platts, have been mostly grubbed out to make way for lucrative, mechanised agriculture. Luckily, a six-acre orchard is being restored at Potash Farm in St Mary's Platt by Alexander Hunt. It survived, being a family's smallholding, but suffered neglect until Hunt started restoration, organic conversion and new plantings in 1995; there are now 500 newly planted trees to match the 500 original ones.

Despite developing a market with speciality foodshops and some supermarkets, Hunt's best outlet remains The Goods Shed in Canterbury (see opposite). He also sends cobnuts to Scotland for red squirrels. Now that definitely sounds a bit nutty.

West Dean Red Hot Chilli Fiesta

Gardening gurus Jim Buckland and Sarah Wain planted a seed of an idea and waited for it to grow. That seed has germinated and grown into the West Dean Red Hot Chilli Fiesta – the hottest destination for chilli-heads from around the UK and beyond. This annual must-do event offers a fabulous day out for food-lovers and gardening enthusiasts alike.

Chillies attract followers as few other foods do. Essential in cuisines that are spicy, exotic, mystic and a terrific foodie experience, chillies have become something of a gastro-cult. You won't see a finer collection of salsas, sauces and snacks laden with the vibrant green, red, orange, purple and yellow pods than at the West Dean fiesta. Some people even plan their summer holidays around it, returning year after year in August to buy yet another plant, to taste another sauce or just to lie on the grass after a chilli-laden snack, drinking beer and listening to the music. The more energetic try their hand (and hips) at dancing latino-style. But for some, their sole aim is to cruise the circuit of stalls on the ultimate chilli sensation mission; they will try anything that will make their eardrums throb and their noses burn.

Chillies are addictive. Start slowly with the milder varieties, but as your body builds up a tolerance you'll want more and more, and hotter and hotter. Really hot chillies are 'cooled' by the body's pleasure chemicals (endorphins), and that's how people get hooked: pain and pleasure. And it's not just the food that takes over, you'll see an incredible number of visitors arrive in shirts, shorts, hats and trousers made from chilli-print materials, previously restricted to the kitchens of fast-food chains.

This is not, however, just a 'beer and burn' event. Mike and Joy Michaud, breeders of the supremely hot Dorset Naga chilli, are gods to most chilli-heads. Great for business as the Naga has been, both these exceptional plant breeders and growers spend most of the show receiving the worship of their fans while trying to encourage them to experience not only the heat but the flavour of the chillies. They patiently explain to the crowds that, 'Heat alone is a man thing: heat and flavour is a pleasure to share'.

Cookery demonstrations and talks about choosing the right pepper and chillies for cooking take place on the gently sloping lawns amid the revellers. Purple and green are unripe colours, so the flavours of these chillies is milder and more grassy – herbaceous – even. Red, yellow and orange chillies sweeten and become rounder in flavour while ripening, but they get hotter too. Not all small pods are hot, some might even be sweet peppers with no heat at all; and it's not the seeds that should be removed for a milder flavour but the membrane holding them (though that's easier said than done). Did you know that chillies are hotter at the top than at the tip? If you want to learn more about chillies, then this is the place to do it.

West Dean Red Hot Chilli Fiesta 104
West Dean Gardens, Chichester,
West Sussex PO18 0QZ
01243 818210
www.westdean.org.uk/garden/home.aspx
Garden open 10.30am–5pm
March–October; 10.30am–4pm
November–February.
Fiesta is in early August.

> "Heat alone is a man thing: heat and flavour is a pleasure to share."

Chilli fans overwhelmed by eating, salsa and sunshine may never make it through the wrought-iron gate in the crinkle-crankle wall and into the kitchen garden, the inspiration for the fiesta. Here, amid figs, peaches and vegetables in serried rows, is a glasshouse (one of 13) containing the West Dean collection of some 200 chilli plants, all of which are carefully labelled and so make a great reference for buying the right seeds for a chilli with a difference.

This incredible fiesta is east meets west, pepper meets chilli and brash meets subtle. Like the chillies themselves, it's totally addictive.

Sustainable Sussex Fish

With plenty of well-stocked microfisheries around the south-east, it is day boats – fishing for a few hours at a time with traditional nets, lines and pots – that bring home the eco-sound catch.

'I get the pick of the best from guys who share my passion for sustainable local fish,' explains Robbie Phillips, a butcher-cum-fishmonger at Jordan in Bognor Regis whose counter is jammed with Dover soles, gurnard, local crabs and lobsters, plaice, bass and skate. There's huss (rock salmon) too, which comes right into the bay and is very popular, and the occasional porbeagle shark steak from the deeper waters at the back of the Isle of Wight. 'People come in here because fishmongers who can tell them where their fish comes from and how to cook it are almost a thing of the past.' It's an inspirational place to shop.

The dunes, cliffs, estuaries and islands of the coast provide enough microhabitats to keep even the most popular of fish slabs stocked with a huge variety of local fish. It's getting people to eat something other than cod that is challenging.

'We've always served local fish at the East Beach Café,' explains Sophie Murray, one half of the mother-and-daughter team using sustainable local fish in their architecturally amazing restaurant on Littlehampton's seafront. 'We've had to work hard with coley and pollack since day one, although they're both part of the cod family. It's just because they're not quite as bright-white and flaky but they taste great, and once they're in batter or diced in a fish soup or chowder the colour's not an issue. Gurnard is popular here, too; it's a great-tasting fish. Thank heavens it is enjoying a renaissance now and is no longer consigned to lobster pots as bait.' As you eat in this magnificently modern setting, you really connect with the sea – floor-to-ceiling windows open wide when the sun dances on the water.

Hastings, just along the coast from Littlehampton, is home to the largest beach-based fishing fleet in the UK. Guaranteed its use of The Stade shingle beach, free of charge and forever, the fleet is winched or moved by tractor to and from the sea, according to the state of the tide. The small boats supply the town's fish market, run by the Hastings Fishermen's Protection Society, which has a busy fish café upstairs with panoramic views of the sea.

Such small-scale fishing may have given way to industrial fishing in other parts of the country but in the south-east the fishing mantra is all about sustainability, not only of fish stocks but also of a way of life.

Jordan 105
Rose Green Road, Bognor Regis,
West Sussex PO21 3EU
01243 265551

East Beach Café 106
Littlehampton, West Sussex BN17 5GB
01903 731903
www.eastbeachcafe.co.uk

Hastings Fish Market 110
5 Rock-A-Nore Road, Hastings,
East Sussex TN34 3DW
www.hastingsfish.co.uk/fishmarket.htm

Save Our Sussex Eels

Smoked eel is a treat, meaty and richly flavoured. Eels were ubiquitous in the streams and rivers of the south-east for centuries. Come the autumn, on still nights with the moon obscured by cloud, fishermen would set their basketwork traps, ready to catch European eels *Anguilla anguilla* as they headed downstream to salt water. Traditional traps can still be seen on the River Test, just north of Stockbridge in Hampshire, although large modern traps feature further downstream.

Little is known about these mega-worm-like life-forms and it is hotly debated as to whether they all complete the mysterious migration, swimming up to 4,000 miles to the Sargasso Sea to spawn. What we do know is that more elvers, or young eels, need to make it back to our rivers to reach sexual maturity before beginning their own journey 'home' to reproduce. International pollution or the demands of the sushi industry may be affecting stocks Europe-wide. But there is good news in Sussex: larger than usual numbers have been reported in Chichester Harbour, so there is hope for more abundant local eel again soon.

More good news lies in the shape of The Weald Smokery, which smokes its own delicious fillets of eel. Swing by en route to a country spot and pick up lunch.

The Weald Smokery 111
Mount Farm, Flimwell, East Sussex TN5 7QL
01580 879601
www.wealdsmokery.co.uk

The Original Banoffee Pie

A blue plaque for the birthplace of a pie? You're joking! But when a pudding has been copied, translated, exported and drooled over as much as this one, why not celebrate at its birthplace?

'Born' in 1972, banoffee pie is a magical confection of shortcrust pastry, baked until golden, crisp and ready to receive 'the filling' (said filling should be started several hours ahead of the pastry). Cheats might now reach for a jar of conveniently pre-prepared toffee-like goo, but real dessert devotees think nothing of simmering unopened cans of condensed milk for three hours to achieve the darkly toffee-coloured filling that defines this pie. (Forgetting to keep the cans covered with water in the pan is a mistake you make only once.) Once spread over the pastry, the deliciousness is then hidden beneath bananas and whipped cream.

The Hungry Monk 109
Jevington, Near Eastbourne,
East Sussex BN26 5QF
01323 482178
www.hungrymonk.co.uk

Visitors to the Hungry Monk at Jevington, cult restaurant for almost 40 years for all its cuisine and olde worlde charm, will be among the few to know that it was here that banoffee pie was first created. The chef's secret is to add a little coffee to the cream, which discreetly subdues the sweetness of banoffee pie so that it is indeed possible to finish the whole dish.

Petersfield Farmers' Market

The throbbing success of Petersfield's Farmers' Market owes much to its confinement within the town's ancient square. Traders chat as they stand, cheek by jowl, touting for business from the quality-savvy customers, and the whole place simply buzzes.

Long Crichel Bakery bread (see page 45), Lyburn cheese, Hampshire-grown watercress and fish from river and coast jostle with microbreweries and veg growers keen for your custom and all will lure money willingly from your wallet. And in among it all are a surprising number of meat stalls, each doing well selling meat that has been bred, reared and butchered within miles of the market.

'We bring our finest downland meat here, lamb and mutton, knowing that Petersfield shoppers really appreciate the trouble we take. People walking in the countryside nearby will see our sheep grazing on permanent pastures and helping downland conservation,' explain John and Kate Olphert of Harting Farm Produce, who also make home-made wild fruit jellies to accompany their meats.

At the right time of year it is impossible to leave the square without a blueberry pie, or at least a huge punnet of these trendy superfruit. Ancient and modern local produce – this market has it all.

Petersfield Farmers' Market
The Square, Petersfield, Hampshire GU32
01420 588671
Open 10am–2pm, first Sunday of the month.

Vatika and Wickham Vineyard

Mock and you will miss out on eating at this English vineyard restaurant. Vatika – vineyard in Hindi – is an ultra-chic gastro-temple nestling right into the vines on one of the oldest wine estates in Hampshire. Owned by Michelin-starred chef Atul Kochar, Vatika's food is all about flavour; here restaurant favourites are given a subtle yet brilliant Indian twist while celebrating the local produce crafted dexterously in the kitchen.

Spicing is low-key and creative, extracting the best flavours from countryside favourites such as pigeon breasts; cooked in Vatika's tandoor oven these become perfectly pink. Kochar is masterful with fish: the roasted sea bass with coconut beurre blanc is to die for. But, this place is not a cheap pop-in diner, you'll need to book ahead; in fact, why not make a day of it?

The vineyard's own wine, Row Ash Dry, light and crisp and made from 100 per cent Seyval Blanc grapes, is a great accompaniment to the subtle spiciness of Vatika's food. It's also affordable enough for you to take a good few bottles home. Time your visit for lunchtime and you can take the excellent audio tour around the vineyard, vines and winery. In the evening, with the vineyard illuminated, this is a magical food experience.

Vatika 100
Botley Road, Shedfield,
Hampshire SO32 2HL
01329 830405
www.vatikarestaurant.co.uk

Wickham Vineyard 100
Botley Road, Shedfield,
Hampshire SO32 2HL
01329 834002
www.wickhamvineyard.com

Minghella ice cream

Ice cream: the most licked and loved of all Italy's exports. Dreaming of Italy but ending up on the Isle of Wight, you'll be consoled to know that the island's first family of ice cream has its tastebuds very firmly rooted in gelato know-how. This is Minghella home territory and has been since 1950.

For years the Brits didn't really know the taste of good ice cream – like our chocolate, the manufactured norm was bulked out with sugar and, in the case of frozen 'delights', water and air. Then came the revolution, usually led by an artisan *gelatiere* of Italian descent, setting out to make the ices 'like Moma used to make'.

Now Gioia, the daughter of founders Edward and Gloria, is MD at Minghella's and there are two generations of this ice cream-addicted family working side by side to develop their iconic ice cream business. The island's own Channel Island cattle provide the whole milk and rich cream that has always formed the basis of the ices. Other flavour-rich ingredients include unrefined sugars with the deep sweetness of molasses, great-quality alcohols and local fruits in season, including tomatoes for the delicious Bloody Mary Sorbet, and plums and apples from the family's own orchard. Minghella's is all about pleasure; they even make ice cream-eating as guilt-free as possible with their low-fat, low-sugar DolceVita range.

Minghella's quickly established its ice creams as among the best and, from an island-based enterprise where the products were served as desserts in the family café, it soon became celebrated at Fortnum & Mason's famous Fountain Restaurant and Ice Cream Parlour.

Anthony Minghella, the eldest of Edward and Gloria's five children, brought international fame to his family's name directing films such as *The English Patient* and *Truly, Madly, Deeply.* Ice cream-lovers have been treated to Minghella's at premières and awards ceremonies while small cinema clubs like the New Park Cinema in Chichester sell Minghella's mini-tubs to its discerning audiences.

The Isle of Wight might not seem an obvious foodie destination, but things are changing. You might catch a film of delicious places to visit while on the ferry across The Solent. Arriving at Yarmouth from Lymington, Minghella fans should celebrate with a visit to Gossip's Café for a scoop or two. If you're travelling from Portsmouth, turn right at Fishbourne and head round to the Solent Ice Cream Parlour at Cowes for a first lick.

Anyone with hiking boots and the determination to climb Brading Down will be well rewarded at the Minghella's van with ice creams and the most fantastic views over Sandown and the east of the island. The Minghella's ice cream van is on Brading Down every day, weather permitting, between noon and 5pm.

Minghella's Ice Cream Van 99
Brading Down, Isle of Wight
www.minghella.co.uk

Gossip's Café 97
The Corner, (Flat) The Square, Yarmouth,
Isle of Wight PO41 0NS
01983 760646

Solent Ice Cream Parlour 98
12 Bath Road, Cowes,
Isle of Wight PO31 7RH
07821 067784

> "The island's own cattle provide the whole milk and rich cream that is the basis of the ices."

The New Forest Marque

The smallest and most accessible of our National Parks – the New Forest – is fast becoming a culinary hot spot. Few places have such a living tradition of food and rural life, but the New Forest has been as guilty as anywhere of providing tourists with fast and uninspiring grub. Now, though, that's all set to change with the growing awareness that New Forest food is good for tourism, the natural ecosystem and the economy.

The New Forest is common ground for food-lovers. It has been pretty well preserved since William the Conqueror's time, when the hunter king set up a system of verderers, agisters and commoners – literally the judges, stockmen and land-users of the forest – to conserve the animals and the environment for his sport. The same hierarchy now jealously guards the forest as a wild workplace.

Open heathland and woods are maintained by grazing for which the commoners have the rights. Pigs are put out during the pannage season, in the autumn, to gorge on beech mast and acorns – a traditional last supper. Pannage pork draws food-lovers to the New Forest at a time when the keen-eyed might also gather a pennybun mushroom or two.

The New Forest Marque promotes the foods of this ancient place. The White Buck at Burley has joined the growing numbers of pubs and restaurants with Forest Marque produce on their menus, and many food shops use ticketing with the logo to draw attention to these foods. 'Our aim is to make it really easy for everyone to recognise and buy forest food. Eating and enjoying it – and then buying more – keeps this place alive,' explains Sarah Richards, the force behind the scheme.

There are plenty of butchers in the New Forest – not surprising as there is so much grazed and wild meat to be enjoyed. Honeyford's Country Butchers on the High Street in Lyndhurst makes its own venison sausages and burgers, and sells roasting joints and fore-quarters, diced for slow cooking. Such low-fat, high-flavour wild meat is what visitors and locals come to the forest for. You'd travel miles, and people do, to SW Pickles & Son in New Milton's Fernhill Lane. It specialises in venison and game and, what's more, hand-slices all of its bacon.

Just outside Lymington is the Heathcote family's Warborne Organics, an award-winning farm shop offering almost as many varieties of fruits from their own orchards as you'd see in an RHS garden, as well as vegetables galore. Everything is freshly picked from the fields when it's needed in the shop. This field-to-shop approach is key to offering organic produce in top condition. Lamb and poultry is from the farm too; you'll probably see chickens roaming around the orchards.

'We set out to produce great food for our local community and it has just gone on from there. We originally only opened at the end of the week and not at weekends, but now we're a seven-day business. The organic method is essential

The White Buck 93
Bisterne Close, Burley,
Hampshire BH24 4AT
01425 402264

Honeyford's Country Butchers 94
54 High St, Lyndhurst,
Hampshire SO43 7BG
02380 282637

SW Pickles & Son 96
3 Fernhill Lane, New Milton,
Hampshire BH25 5JN
01425 614577

Warborne Organic Farm 95
Warborne Lane, Boldre,
Lymington, Hampshire SO41 5QD
01590 688488
www.warbornefarm.co.uk
www.newforestproduce.com

"Our aim is for everyone to buy forest food. Eating and enjoying it keeps this place alive."

to the way we farm as it fits in with my views about human health, animal welfare and care for our environment,' explains George Heathcote, who is a great advert for organic growing and responsible land stewardship. The shelves in the shop are laden with preserves made from the farm's own fruit, cooked in small batches when perfectly ripe for maximum flavour. Bread arrives from Long Crichel Bakery (see page 45) and is displayed alongside local fish, organic wines and cheeses, and blooms grown at Warborne. If you're self-catering in the New Forest why not phone ahead and order a mighty fine veg box?

Central England

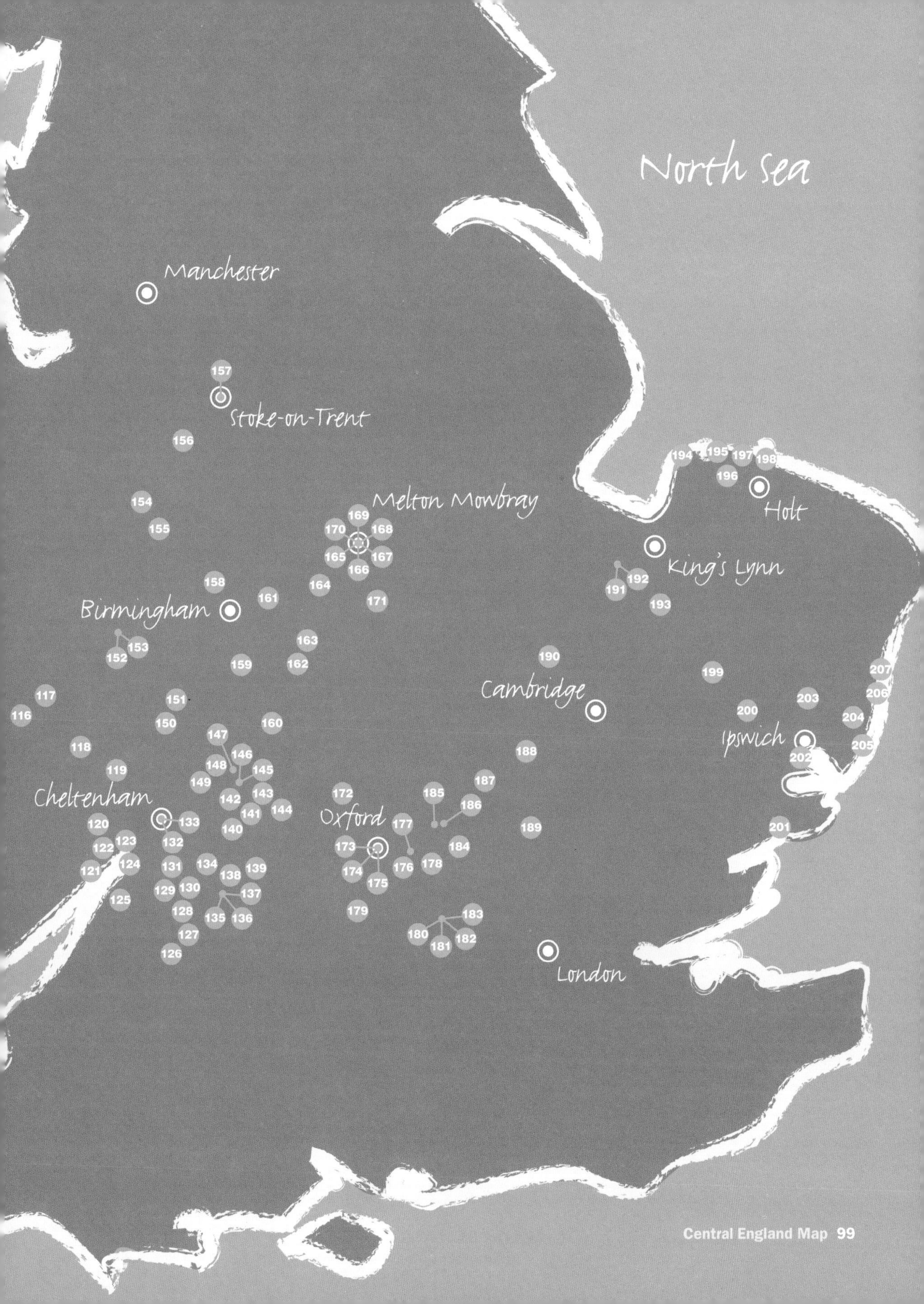

North Sea

Manchester

157
Stoke-on-Trent

156

154
155

Melton Mowbray

169
170   168
165   167
166
164
171

158
161

Birmingham

153
152

159   162   163

Holt

194 195 197 198
196

King's Lynn

191 192
193

117
116

151
150

160

190

Cambridge

199

207
206

200   203
204
205

147
118

146
148   145
149

Ipswich

202

Cheltenham

120

133
132

142   143
141   144
140

Oxford

172

185
177
186

187

188

189

201

122 123
121 124
119
131 134
125   129 130
128   138
127   135 136
126

139
137

173
174   176
175

184
178

179

183
180   182
181

London

The Cotswold Chef

Some people want to parachute out of planes or paraglide from cliffs; others try white-water rafting or scale impossible-looking crags. But for those wanting an altogether different form of extreme experience, Rob Rees (aka The Cotswold Chef) is your man. His food tours give people the chance to see every aspect of food production – right down to a morning at Ensors, a top abattoir, in the picturesque Forest of Dean. 'Very few people get to see a pig being slaughtered,' he says. 'It can be a challenge, but there are those who feel it's an important aspect of knowing where their food comes from.'

Rob's moniker of The Cotswold Chef is more than just a trademark name. He has spent the last decade celebrating food producers throughout the region. 'They're my inspiration,' he says. He incorporates many of them into his food tours, offering opportunities money can't normally buy. Participants can spend a day making chutney with award-winning Kitchen Garden Preserves in Stroud, taste beer at Wickwar Brewery, or join Danielle Slatter, making fair trade ice cream on the family dairy farm at Farmington, a village near Cheltenham.

Originally from Essex, Rob studied to be a chef at Westminster College before working at Le Gavroche in London and Hyatt Regency in the Grand Cayman Islands. But it was at the Royal Crescent Hotel in Bath in the 1980s that he was introduced to the concept of local food. 'The head chef, Michael Croft – now at Calcot Manor in Tetbury – was the first to give me artisan British cheeses and to make me think about the provenance of food.'

Rob's passion for good regional food has defined his style since, and many producers are indebted to his advice. He has travelled the world – Australia, India and America – promoting Cotswold produce, and was awarded an MBE for services to the food industry in 2006. You can get up close with this food hero at one of his cookery demonstrations at Cirencester Farmers' Market, which take place from 9am till 1pm on the second and fourth Saturdays of each month.

But it's not just a case of preaching to the converted. In 2008, he set up the charity The Wiggly Worm to help 'failing' youngsters and their parents. Over a course of six weeks, he and his team transform teenagers who have never boiled an egg into confident 'chefs' who provide a full meal for tables of invited guests – often including their own parents.

'These children have dealt with so many difficult things, perhaps looking after a disabled parent or being surrounded by drugs and alcohol. Seeing them achieve professionally is fantastic – as is seeing them smile at their own achievements,' he says. 'It's a case of let's use food to make a difference to the world.'

Rob Rees 130
01453 840885
www.thecotswoldchef.com

Cirencester Farmers' Market 135
Market Place, Cirencester, Gloucestershire
GL7 2NW
www.cirencesterfarmersmarket.com
9am–1pm, second and fourth Saturdays of
each month.

"Rob's passion for good regional food has defined his style..."

Stroud Farmers' Market

The Hairy Bikers have visited it, it's featured on *Rick Stein's Food Heroes* and *Blue Peter*, and it's even been the setting for a book by romantic novelist Katie Fforde. Stroud Farmers' Market is widely considered to be one of the best in the country, with its eclectic collection of between 45 and 60 stalls – and it has the awards to prove it. Moreover, it's one of the few farmers' markets outside London to run every single Saturday.

Stroud Farmers' Market 🔢131
Cornhill Market Place and surrounding streets, Stroud, Gloucestershire
9am–2pm, every Saturday.

Depending on the time of year, you'll find fresh asparagus, sunflowers, sweetcorn, hop vines and Christmas trees. Plus, there are exotic snacks made with local produce – such as Niang's chicken saté made from Madgett's superb free-range chicken from Tidenham Chase – and organic producers such as Adeys Farm attend regularly and cook up burgers and sausages onsite. There's also a market café and even a buskers' corner.

Opened in 1999 by Jasper Conran and the late Isabella Blow, the market recently celebrated its 10th anniversary. And one of its biggest fans was there to celebrate: food writer Matthew Fort. 'I always go in with a clear mind of exactly what I want to buy from each stall, and then I lurch away with five times the amount of food I intended,' he says.

One of the elements behind its success is undoubtedly the vision of organiser Clare Gerbrands. It was in 1992 that Clare and her husband, Kardien, decided to take a year out when they left their home in Stroud to travel across Europe with their children. 'I was particularly impressed with how well we all ate,' says Clare. 'The markets in Italy were amazing. There would be 100 stalls with fish, seasonal fruit and vegetables – absolutely fresh food. Then, in Spain, I had loads of apricot trees and almonds around, and I got into making jams and marmalade.'

When they arrived back in Stroud, they discovered that two out-of-town supermarkets had opened with, Clare felt, potentially disastrous results. So she approached the council with plans for a market featuring local artisan goods. And thus, Stroud Farmers' Market was born.

Ask Clare why Stroud is so successful and her answer is succinct: 'The market is so good because the food and drink on sale is exceptional, there is a great atmosphere and there is a different mix of stallholders every week, offering a fresh shopping experience for customers'. But as she also points out, it's not just the producers who benefit: 'Farmers' markets draw people in, and they have highlighted how many independent retailers there are in small towns. On market days in Stroud, trade in general goes up by about 25 per cent.'

The Butts Farm Shop

When *Cotswold Life* magazine – the region's leading glossy – awarded The Butts Farm in South Cerney its 'Farm Shop of the Year' award, it stated that among the cornucopia of local produce there was 'the most fabulous butchery where fresh meat is served by welcoming staff who are delighted to share their hands-on knowledge with their customers'.

The farm itself could also win awards in offering the perfect place to educate children about ethical food production. At various times of the year, young visitors can watch chicks hatching, cuddle the bunnies, feed the Gloucestershire Old Spots pigs, see the rare Norfolk Horn sheep and give lambs and kids their bottles. The shop is not huge, but the stock is superb, including vegetables grown by the Drinkwater family at Ebrington in the North Cotswolds and Netherend Farm butter, which was served at 2009's G20 summit. And Butts' own frozen pies are particularly good.

You won't have to venture too far to find another fabulous farm shop. The Organic Farm Shop at Abbey Home Farm is run by Hilary and Will Chester-Master, winners of the Soil Association Organic Trophy for lifetime achievement. As well as a first-rate café and all-organic shop, there are lovely woodland walks.

The Butts Farm Shop 136
South Cerney, Cirencester,
Gloucestershire GL7 5QE
01285 862224
www.thebuttsfarmshop.com

The Organic Farm Shop 137
Abbey Home Farm, Burford Road,
Cirencester, Gloucestershire GL7 5HF
01285 640441
www.theorganicfarmshop.co.uk

Royal Produce

The Princess Royal is well known for hosting Gatcombe Horse Trials on her rolling estate on the edge of Minchinhampton, but her interests in a rare-breeds farm on her estate are less well known. Gloucestershire Old Spots pigs, White Park cattle and Wiltshire Horn sheep roam the 500 acres of wood and grassland that make up Gatcombe Park estate. 'I went for rare breeds because they mind their own business and they're pretty efficient,' the Princess said. Their excellent meat is available from traditional butchers, Taylor's, just down the road in the centre of Minchinhampton.

To keep things in the family, shop for organic produce at the Veg Shed, a barn on her brother Prince Charles's Highgrove estate. It was in 1986 that the Prince decided to convert this land, on the edge of Tetbury, to an organic system. Depending on the season, you'll find such delights as soil-covered beetroot, crisp onions, piles of spring greens and creamy-white parsnips, all grown sustainably, with minimal impact on the environment. Displays remain colourful and varied year round with tables of organic produce such as red peppers, lemons and bananas from sunnier climes.

Taylor & Sons 128
West End, Minchinhampton, Stroud,
Gloucestershire GL6 9JA
01453 882163

The Veg Shed 127
Broadfield Farm, Tetbury,
Gloucestershire GL8 8SE
Open 8am–5pm Wednesdays, Fridays
and Saturdays and can also be found at
Cirencester Farmers' Market.

Pubs with Cotswold Charm

If there's one name indelibly associated with the Cotswolds, it's that of Laurie Lee, whose *Cider with Rosie* immortalised the glorious slopes of the Slad Valley. In life, Laurie was often to be found holding forth in his beloved Woolpack Inn; in death, he was buried between the church and the pub. Laurie may be here in spirit only, but the pub is 'haunted' by actor Keith Allen who loves the atmosphere, character and glorious views of Slad.

Today, the inn is a mecca for Lee fans, but it's also earned a name for itself for food and drink. Chef Michael Carr has won favourable reviews for his well-executed, unfussy British cuisine; and the beer is straight from the excellent Uley Brewery a few miles down the road.

Then there's Old Spot Inn in Dursley, a CAMRA 'Pub of the Year' thanks to its magnificent real ales and described as 'a pub of a thousand locals'. The Green Dragon Inn at Cockleford is another award-winner, with a delightful location, 17th-century charm, open fire and beamed ceilings. Prue Leith favours the Fox Inn at Lower Oddington for its good, simple, fresh food.

The Woolpack Inn 134
Slad Road, Slad. Gloucestershire GL6 7QA
01452 813429
www.thewoolpackinn-slad.com

The Old Spot Inn 125
www.oldspotinn.co.uk

The Green Dragon Inn 140
www.green-dragon-inn.co.uk

The Fox Inn 143
www.foxinn.net

Cotswold Fine Dining

Within the space of 30 miles or so you can find no fewer than three Michelin-starred restaurants: it seems the Cotswolds are home to some of the brightest chefs around.

'Bold' and 'brilliant' are epithets applied to two-star chef David Everitt-Matthias, who runs Le Champignon Sauvage in Cheltenham with his wife, Helen. Heston Blumenthal and Gordon Ramsay are admirers of his uncompromising vision: seared scallops; carpaccio of pig's head and pickled pear purée; and rabbit tortelloni with turnip and vanilla purée, radish and apple are recent examples of dishes on offer. Expect to book a couple of months ahead for a primetime seat.

Talented Marcus Ashenford gained his first Michelin star at the tender age of 25. He and wife Kate run 5 North Street, which is small but bursting with age-old character, in pretty Winchcombe. Treat yourself to the special set menu based around lobster, scallops and venison. And in a 17th-century former rectory in breathtakingly beautiful Upper Slaughter, Matt Weedon heads the team at the Lords of the Manor, which gained its first star in January 2009.

What's more, award-winning chef Michael Bedford runs classes on everything from al fresco dining to fish preparation at the Chef's Table in Tetbury – a deli, bistro and cookery school all rolled into one.

Le Champignon Sauvage 132
www.lechampignonsauvage.co.uk

5 North Street
Winchcombe, Gloucestershire GL54 5LH
01242 604566

The Lords of the Manor 142
www.lordsofthemanor.com

The Chef's Table 126
www.thechefstable.co.uk

Cotswold Cheesemakers

It would no doubt amuse farmers of yore to think that hand-made cheese is now considered a luxury, artisan product. Making cheese used to be simply a way of using up spare milk; now, it's often a way of enabling hard-pressed dairy farms to control the money they can make, rather than having milk prices dictated to them. Yet that only tells a part of the story. For the cheesemakers of Gloucestershire, Herefordshire and Worcestershire are among the best in the world, and they create their products with passion, commitment and consummate skill.

Single Gloucester is one of relatively few cheeses with a protected designation of origin (PDO), meaning the cheese can be made only in Gloucestershire by someone who owns a Gloucester cow. Single Gloucester is made from a combination of semi-skimmed and full-cream milk. Traditionally, the farmer would skim the evening milk for butter, then mix it with the full-cream milk the next morning to make cheese. The result is a light, creamy interior, encased in a mouldy, natural rind, with a mildly tangy flavour.

You can count the makers of Single Gloucester on one hand. One of them, Diana Smart of Churcham, near Gloucester, is an award-winning cheesemaker who also supplies the seven-pound Double Gloucester cheese for the cheese rolling event that takes place on Coopers Hill each Spring bank holiday Monday in May.

Charles Martell is the man who rescued Single Gloucester from extinction in the late 1970s. He also makes the famously pungent Stinking Bishop at his farm in the Forest of Dean, a cheese beloved of Wallace and Gromit: it featured in *The Curse of the Were-Rabbit*. Another of his is Hereford Hop coated in lightly-toasted hops.

While you're in this neck of the woods, don't miss out on the award-winning range of cheeses from Daylesford Organic, Lady Bamford's farm shop and creamery on the Gloucestershire/Oxfordshire border, known as the 'Harrods' of the Cotswolds. And Lady Angus of Cerney House is famed for her fresh Cerney goat's cheeses.

In Worcestershire, the Stacey family of Gorsehill Abbey Farm produces St Eadburgha, a Camembert-style cheese named after the great granddaughter of Alfred the Great, to whom a local church is dedicated. Made from the milk of Montbeliarde and Friesian cows that graze in pear orchards and on lush, grassy pastures, it's perfect eaten with pear and a full-bodied red wine.

Delia Smith favours Perroche, a mousse-like, almondy goat's cheese that grills beautifully. It hails from the talents at Neal's Yard Creamery, perched on Dorstone Hill with views down the Wye Valley and over to the Black Mountains.

Smart's Traditional Gloucester Cheese [120]
Old Ley Court, Chapel Lane,
Birdwood, Churcham, Gloucester,
Gloucestershire GL2 8AR
01452 750225
www.smartsgloucestercheese.com

Daylesford Organic [144]
Daylesford, Near Kingham,
Gloucestershire GL56 0YG
01608 731700
www.daylesfordorganic.com

Cerney Cheese [138]
Cerney House Gardens, Cerney Lodge,
North Cerney, Cirencester,
Gloucestershire GL7 7BX
01285 831300
www.cerneycheese.com

Gorsehill Abbey Cheese [148]
Collin Lane, Broadway,
Worcestershire WR12 7PB
01386 852208
www.gorsehillabbey.co.uk

Neal's Yard Creamery [116]
Caeperthy, Arthur's Stone Lane,
Dorstone, Herefordshire HR3 6AX
01981 500395
www.nealsyardcreamery.co.uk

Cheese Works [133]
www.thecheeseworks.co.uk

Mousetrap Cheese [117]
www.mousetrapcheese.co.uk

Woefuldane Organic Dairy [129]
3 Market Square, Minchinhampton,
Gloucestershire GL6 9BW
01453 887065

Try before you buy these cheeses from farm and specialist food shops, such as Cheese Works in Cheltenham, considered one of the UK's finest cheesemongers. Mousetrap Cheese shops in Leominster, Hereford and Ludlow, owned by cheesemaker Mark Hindle, also have excellent ranges.

But there's one family that has gone a stage further. Melissa and Jonathan Ravenhill have opened Woefuldane Organic Dairy in the small Cotswold town of Minchinhampton, selling only their cheeses, milk, butter, cream, home-made salad dressing and free-range eggs from the family's 110-acre organic farm, which lies just half a mile down the road. The family's herd of dairy Shorthorns graze on the rare unimproved limestone grassland of Minchinhampton Common, high up in the hills above Stroud. The milk is used to create cheeses such as Blue Heaven, a semi-soft mould-ripened blue. Their range may be small but fans would say it's pretty near perfect.

Day's Cottage Apple Juice

Apples aren't just for autumn – you can eat fresh apples from Cotswold orchards from late July until December. With such wonderful names as Beauty of Bath, Taynton Codling, Severn Bank and Arlingham Schoolboys you'll ponder why you don't see much more of such varieties. And your apple-munching can continue late into the year, finishing off with Ashmead's Kernel, created by Dr Ashmead in the 18th century, which is still crisp, firm and russetted into early December.

That these varieties still exist is a testament to the work of individuals such as Helen Brent-Smith and Dave Kaspar of Day's Cottage Apple Juice. The couple once worked in London, but when they got the opportunity to take over part of the family farm in Brookthorpe, Gloucester, they jumped at the chance.

In 1992, they started to make and sell apple juice: today, they produce around 30,000 bottles of apple and pear juice a year, as well as cider and perry made from fruit gathered on the farm and surrounding orchards, including one planted by Helen's great aunt in 1912. Not only have Helen and Dave followed age-old traditions when making their juice, but they've also planted more than 500 trees of old apple varieties and formed a Gloucestershire Museum Orchard to preserve the county's indigenous varieties; in fact, Dave helped found the Gloucestershire Orchard Group. 'Traditional orchards are so important,' Dave says. 'They're on unimproved grassland so they provide a unique habitat for flowers and wildlife. We see green woodpeckers, little owls and fieldfares on a daily basis – they feed on the dropped fruit. There are butterflies, like red admirals and commas, bats, which live in the hollow trees, and the noble chaffer beetle, specific to the rotting heartwood of fruit trees.'

Once upon a time, landowners up and down the country would each make their own 'cyder' – a full-bodied drink from the first pressing of apples. Then, the pulp would be re-pressed and mixed with water and given to agricultural labourers free of charge, thereafter known as cider with an 'i'. Kevin Minchew is a true cyder-maker who founded Minchew's Real Cyder and Perry in 1993 at Aston Cross, Tewkesbury. 'Cyder is made from a single pressing of vintage fruit, rather like extra virgin olive oil,' Kevin explains. 'That first pressing gives a concentrated intense liquid.' In other words, Kevin's award-winning drinks – created on a simple second-hand press – come straight from apples newly picked from local orchards. His is the world's largest range of single-variety cyders and perries.

Like Gloucestershire, Herefordshire has a long history of cider-making, which pre-dates the Romans. At The Cider Museum in Hereford, you can learn about the processes and try the cider brandy – one of only two places to make it in Britain.

Day's Cottage Apple Juice
Upton Lane, Brookthorpe,
Gloucester, Gloucestershire GL4 0UT
01452 813602
www.dayscottage.co.uk
Helen and Dave are happy to show visitors around as long as they phone ahead to arrange a day and time. Ask them about the orchard events they regularly run.

Gloucestershire Orchard Group
109 Orchard Way, Churchdown,
Gloucester, Gloucestershire GL3 2AP
01452 855677
www.orchard-group.uklinux.net/glos

Minchew's Real Cyder and Perry
Rose Cottage, Aston Cross,
Tewkesbury, Gloucestershire GL20 8HX
07974 034331
www.minchews.co.uk

The Cider Museum 118
21 Ryelands Street, Hereford,
Herefordshire HR4 0LW
01432 354207
www.cidermuseum.co.uk

Three Choirs Vineyards

On a sun-kissed day, its picturesque 100 acres have a look of Provence about them, so you could easily be forgiven for thinking you'd stepped into a magical portal of some kind. But the south-facing slopes of the Three Choirs Vineyard are firmly rooted in Newent in the Forest of Dean.

About 20 different grape varieties grow on these free-draining sandstone soils. Wine buff Oz Clarke considers it one of his favourite vineyards – and it is, in fact, England's most awarded single-estate vineyard. Although Three Choirs is most celebrated for its very palatable reds, Mr Clarke favours the 'light, fragrant Bacchus or the surprisingly exotic Siegerrebe'.

It's a glorious place to visit – guided tours and wine tastings are available – but it's also a place to dine, and even rest your head if need be in their B&B. The restaurant is first class, with its doors opening out on to those grape-laden trellises. Modern English food is on the menu, conjured from fresh, seasonal ingredients; in early summer, you might be dining off asparagus grown down the road in Newent; or whatever the time of year, you'll find tasty locally smoked salmon.

Each and every current estate wine – white, red, rosé and sparkling – is available in the well-stocked shop.

The Three Choirs Vineyards 119
Newent, Gloucestershire GL18 1LS
01531 890223
www.threechoirs.com

Juri's Bakery and Tea Shoppe

Japanese visitors love coming to the Cotswolds for a quintessentially English afternoon tea; but for the Miyawaki family a visit simply wasn't enough. Instead, Iwao and Junko and their daughter Juri – a Cordon Bleu-trained cook – opened Juri's, The Olde Bakery Tea Shoppe, in a honey-stoned building in Winchcombe High Street in 2003. And not only have they taken on the English at their own game: they've won – in 2008, Juri's was named 'UK's Top Tea Place' by the Tea Guild.

Juri makes everything herself, which means she will often get up at 4am to bake scones (always served warm), delicious cakes and lunches. 'In Japan, tea is more of a mental and spiritual experience. Whereas in England, it's a social event: a way of getting together and celebrating, or simply enjoying life,' she says.

The family welcomes visitors from all over the world, including Japan, especially since the local newspaper in Mr Miyawaki's home region of Hokkaido ran an article on them. Iwao has also trained as a Blue Badge Tourist Guide – the only Japanese person to do so in the Cotswolds.

'The Cotswolds are important for Japanese people,' he says, 'because they have the right values: heritage and nature.'

Juri's – The Olde Bakery Tea Shoppe 149
High Street, Winchcombe, Near Cheltenham,
Gloucestershire GL54 5LJ
01242 602469
www.juris-tearoom.co.uk

Cotswold Fish

Donnington Trout Farm 146
Upper Swell, Stow-on-the-Wold,
Gloucestershire GL54 1EP
01451 830873

Bibury Trout Farm 139
01285 740215
www.biburytroutfarm.co.uk

Severn and Wye Smokery 121
01452 760190
www.severnandwye.co.uk

You might not associate this landlocked region with fish, but you'd be wrong. Gloucestershire plays host to fantastic trout farms: fish thrive in the cool, clear waters of the streams that cascade down hillsides and hug the valleys.

One such farm lies at picturesque Donnington, near Stow-on-the-Wold. You can buy fresh or smoked trout at the farm shop or fly-fish on their small, secluded lake.

One of the oldest trout farms in the country – founded in 1902 – Bibury Trout Farm sits in the centre of England's 'prettiest' village. Here, children can feed the trout or try the beginners' fishery.

The River Severn, of course, is famous for elvers and salmon. Elvers cross the Atlantic and swim into the Severn on the spring tide at the end of February. Their aim is to reach the river above Worcester where they can grow into eels and their means of transport is the Severn Bore, the river's famous tidal wave.

Today, the elvers are dwindling but the salmon are thriving. For local fish at its best, visit the Severn and Wye Smokery where you can buy fresh and smoked salmon, grab a bite in the restaurant or watch smoked fish being processed.

'White Gold' Asparagus

Over Farm Market 122
Over, Gloucester, Gloucestershire GL2 8DB
01452 521014
www.over-farm-market.co.uk

The Fleece Inn 151
The Cross, Bretforton, Near Evesham,
Worcestershire WR11 7JE
01386 831173
www.thefleeceinn.co.uk
www.britishasparagusfestival.org

Any number of succulent vegetables can be pulled from the fertile earth of the Vale of Evesham in southern Worcestershire. Sheltered by the Cotswold escarpment, this flood plain of the River Avon is richly agricultural: affectionately known as England's market garden.

But it's the 'white gold' for which it's best known. Asparagus has the shortest of seasons, lasting from Shakespeare's birthday on April 23 to Midsummer's Day on June 21. Half the pleasure lies in its rarity, and only two things will kill it, say the growers: one is weed and the other is greed. If you try to cut spears too late into the summer, the crown won't have a chance to recover for the next year.

During the season, you'll find farmers' markets, farm shops and restaurant menus full of asparagus from renowned growers, such as Bangrove Farm near Tewkesbury or Over Farm, which has its own farm shop just outside Gloucester.

Each year, an asparagus auction is the 'crowning' event of the season. It's traditionally held at one of the country's oldest inns, The Fleece Inn at Bretforton, on Whit Sunday, with a festival on the Monday with asparagus tastings, farmers' market, craft fayre and rural skills demonstrations.

Cotswold Farm Park

High up in the Cotswold Hills in Guiting Power sits the picturesque Cotswold Farm Park, a family-run farm where you can feed the animals, see the sheep being sheared and the cows milked and pet the newborn lambs each spring.

But this is a farm with a difference, for it's home to more than 50 breeding flocks and herds of British rare-breed farm livestock. Indeed, it was set up in the late 1960s by an expert, Joe Henson, founder chairman of the charity the Rare Breeds Survival Trust. He deeply loves farming and was horrified that certain farm breeds were in danger of becoming extinct. But after setting up the farm, he and his business partner, John Neave, quickly realised these rare breeds were not commercially viable in themselves. As a result, the Cotswold Farm Park was opened to the public in 1971, as a way of making ends meet.

It has proved a happy decision all round. Thousands of children come here each year with their schools and their families to meet and learn about animals such as the Golden Guernsey goat, which might not exist were it not for people like Joe. Some visitors will already have seen the farm on the BBC's *Countryfile*, for it's now run by Joe's son, the television presenter Adam Henson.

The Cotswolds have three traditional breeds: the Gloucestershire Old Spots pig, the Gloucester cow and the Cotswold sheep. And you can gaze upon fine examples of all of them at the Cotswold Farm Park.

The Old Spots are firm favourites with visitors of all ages because they're such a pleasure to meet. The clue is in their lop ears, which farmers will tell you is an indication of docility. (Apparently, prick-eared pigs can see too much.) A few weeks after the piglets are born, you'll see them tearing about the place in gangs like mischievous teenagers.

On any one day you can enjoy watching a selection of each of the cattle breeds, and do look out for the Gloucesters. They're easily spotted because of their black-brown colour – people refer to it as mahogany. But most important are the white tail and the white stripe down the back, which usually starts at the hips. They're very strong animals, which was necessary for their one-time walk to Smithfield Market, and they were also used as draught oxen. Of course, the Cotswold sheep – originally bred for their wonderful wool – come into their own at lambing time.

You can taste some of this rare-breed meat at the farm park's own café. It's also on sale at Lambournes Butchers in Stow-on-the-Wold and from the Cotswold Food Store in Longborough. If you haven't tried rare-breed meat before, you'll be in for a treat; many gourmands describe the taste as a return to the past. Old Spots, for example, have a layer of fat that has been bred out of many modern animals; but within that fat lies a superb flavour. While the Cotswold is a mutton sheep, this meat is coming back into fashion. Food champions, such as Prince

Cotswold Farm Park 141
Guiting Power, Near Cheltenham,
Gloucestershire GL54 5UG
01451 850307
www.cotswoldfarmpark.co.uk

Lambournes Butchers 145
Digbeth Street, Stow-on-the-Wold,
Gloucestershire GL54 1BN
01451 830630
www.lambournesbutchers.co.uk

The Cotswold Food Store 147
Longborough, Moreton-in-Marsh,
Gloucestershire GL56 0QZ
01451 830469
www.cotswoldfoodstore.co.uk

"A few weeks after the piglets are born, you'll see them tearing about in gangs like mischievous teenagers."

Charles, are trying to persuade people to give mutton another go. The difference between mutton and lamb, they say, is like that between beef and veal.

'For me, it's vital that we keep these breeds going,' Joe Henson says. 'For one thing, they're part of a "living museum" to enable people interested in our heritage to come and see the types of animals our ancestors farmed.'

'But if you're interested in saving them, the best way you can help is to eat them.'

Fine Dining in Bray

Bray in Berkshire is a village with far more impact in the culinary world than its small size would imply. Seemingly sleepy, it boasts not one, but two three-Michelin-starred restaurants and other top-notch eateries besides, making the postcode of SL6 one of the world's hottest destinations for diners and food critics alike.

Best known of the restaurants are The Waterside Inn, these days run by Alain Roux, who took over the helm from Michel and Albert – his father and uncle respectively – and The Fat Duck, the restaurant that offers a less-than-traditional gourmet experience, owned by chef-patron Heston Blumenthal.

If you find yourself nearby there are other fine eating establishments where you might be able to get a table without booking ahead. Caldesi in Campagna, a welcoming family restaurant, run by Giancarlo and Kate Caldesi, serves unforgettable Italian food. The Hinds Head hotel has experienced chef Clive Dixon (well known to foodies in the Thames Valley and Cotswolds) in charge of the kitchen, though the place is owned by Mr Blumenthal.

Blumenthal has been called a chef-alchemist and, given that part of his education took place at one of Buckinghamshire's technology-specialist grammar schools, it may not be surprising to some that his interest in cooking has a scientific bent. His wizardry is often summed up by the mention of one or two headline-grabbing dishes, such as snail porridge or bacon-and-egg ice cream, but he prefers to consider what he does as an eating experience of the senses, more simply described as modern cooking than as molecular gastronomy.

He has become renowned for collaborating with experts in science, engineering and psychology as well as musicians, perfumiers and DJs, as part of his quest for better cooking, and has a science laboratory of a kitchen in which to research and develop his dishes. Historic British gastronomy is another of his passions and he is working alongside food historians researching our celebrated gastronomic heritage. Influences of this work can be found on the menus of both The Hinds Head and The Fat Duck restaurants.

There can be no doubting Heston Blumenthal's credentials or his cooking genius: The Fat Duck was voted the UK's best restaurant in the *Good Food Guide 2010*, scoring 10 out of 10 from judges and diners despite a food scare in 2009, caused by its oyster suppliers. But if you don't like to plan your life weeks in advance (there's a two-month waiting list for just 15 tables), opt for his pub instead.

The Hinds Head offers a little of the Blumenthal magic without the long waiting lists – or the hard swallow at the size of the bill. The inn dates back to Tudor times and while Heston's approach is still in evidence, so is Clive Dixon's love of British seasonal cooking and ingredients. Expect the extraordinary along with the more

The Waterside Inn
Ferry Road, Bray, Berkshire SL6 2AT
01628 620691
www.waterside-inn.co.uk

The Fat Duck
High Street, Bray, Berkshire SL6 2AQ
01628 580333
www.fatduck.co.uk

Caldesi in Campagna
Old Mill Lane, Bray, Berkshire SL6 2BG
01628 788500
www.caldesi.com

The Hinds Head
High Street, Bray, Berkshire SL6 2AB
01628 626151
www.hindsheadbray.com

FEAR KNOCKED AT THE DOOR FAITH ANSWERED
NO ONE WAS THERE

ordinary fare. Heston and the experts at Hampton Court Palace's Tudor kitchens have rediscovered British traditional historic fare to offer rabbit brawn, cuttlefish and powdered duck to diners as well as shepherd's pie, blade of beef and sausages with mash. Here are chances aplenty to satisfy an adventurous palate without straying too far from your comfort zone. Oak beams and bulging walls are testament to the building's age, while comfortable ladderback and leather chairs and polished tables take The Hinds Head well beyond gastro-pub status.

Whichever establishment you plump for and whatever style of cooking takes your fancy, if you're in Bray, you're spoilt for choice.

The Pouget Dynasty

Tucked away in the heart of the city of Oxford is a collection of fine food establishments run by what could be called the city's food aristocrats – the Pouget family.

Entrepreneur Will Pouget is the dynamo behind The Vaults and Garden Café, located under the dreaming spire of St Mary's Church between the High Street and Radcliffe Square. The vaults' garden faces the Radcliffe Camera in one of the best-known and most photographed parts of Oxford, but the café still remains a relative secret from the thousands of tourists who flock to the city each year. Will's food pedigree couldn't be finer, since his father is Baron Robert Pouget de St Victor, the man behind Oxford Blue cheese, which was created and introduced to the nation in 1995; Will's brother Harley produces Oxford Isis cheese, sold through the Oxford Cheese Company.

Not content with pleasuring fromage-o-philes, the family also runs various businesses: an organic takeaway and restaurant – The Alpha Bar – in Oxford's famed Covered Market; an unusually healthy burger and salad trailer that trades near the Ashmolean Museum (6.30pm–3am Thursday–Saturday); Woodstock Road Delicatessen; and the Oxford Provender Company, which produces another of Baron Pouget's essentials – Original Oxford Sauce.

The Vaults and Garden Café 🔵173
Radcliffe Square, Oxford, Oxfordshire
OX1 4AH
01865 279112

Oxford Cheese Company 🔵174
17 Covered Market, Oxford, Oxfordshire,
OX1 3DY
01865 721420

Woodstock Road Delicatessen 🔵175
Woodstock Road (Near Little Clarendon Street), Oxford, Oxfordshire OX2 6HA
01865 316228

Waterperry's Orchard Fruits

So many visitors to Waterperry Gardens don't even realise it has acres of productive orchards alongside the incredible gardens of this former horticultural school for ladies. Some 60 apple varieties grow under the watchful eye of Chris Lanczak, who trained in the days of Waterperry's founder, Miss Beatrix Havergal.

Chris and his team preserve the heritage of rare varieties such as Ashmead's Kernel, Orleans Reinette and Kidd's Orange. You can sample the fruits of their success at the garden shop – pop any of the exotically named apples as well as old favourites, such as Cox's Orange Pippin and Bramley, in a basket along with seasonal plums, greengages and rare pear varieties. Waterperry's apples are on sale from August until January.

Waterperry Gardens 🔵177
Near Wheatley, Oxford, Oxfordshire
OX33 1JZ
01844 339254
www.waterperrygardens.co.uk
Open daily 10am–5.30pm in the summer,
10am–5pm in the winter.
Closed between Christmas and New Year.

But there's much more to the orchards' production besides simple fruit. Using 22 different varieties Waterperry also produces its own unrivalled apple juice. You can buy cases online or single bottles from the shop and selected local outlets.

Time your visit to coincide with the October Apple Weekend or an open weekend in January when there are orchard tours. Whatever time of the year you visit, you'll find Waterperry inspiring – and if you want to create an orchard of your own, they'll even sell you a tree or two to take home.

The Chiltern Brewery

Using a combination of centuries-old traditional techniques and state-of-the-art equipment, the Chiltern Brewery produces fine-quality beers along with its wonderfully named Bodgers Barley Wine at a former farm close to the Prime Minister's retreat, Chequers.

In 1980 Richard Jenkinson swapped his city job for a hobby he turned into a business. Keeping it in the family, the brewery is now run by his sons, Tom and George, together with Tom's wife Charlotte and their dedicated staff. Book yourself on to one of the brewery's popular tours and then head to the onsite shop for some beer retail therapy; you can also indulge at home in their online shop.

The former cowshed and outbuildings that house the brewery and shop now have wide polished boards and a counter created from barrels and old brewery equipment, evoking the industry's charms and history; all the while there's a delicious aroma of hops in the air. The shop sells not only a range of Chiltern Brewery's chandlery products, created with their beers and ales, but also complementary foods sourced from local small-scale producers.

You can sup a pint or two of their hoppy nectar during a trip to Aylesbury town centre, since the brewery now runs the Farmers' Bar at the National Trust's ancient inn, the King's Head.

The Chiltern Brewery 178
Nash Lee Road, Terrick, Aylesbury,
Buckinghamshire HP17 0TQ
01296 613647
www.chilternbrewery.co.uk
Shop open 9am–5pm Monday–Saturday.

The King's Head 186
King's Head Passage, Market Square,
Aylesbury, Buckinghamshire HP20 2RW
01296 718812
www.farmersbar.co.uk

Whitwell Watercress

Mention watercress in Hertfordshire and you'll evoke one of two responses: a sigh for the demise of an industry that once thrived in the county or the name of Sansom.

Five generations of Sansoms have farmed watercress in Whitwell, with twin brothers Derek and Patrick (known as Ron and Pat) now at the helm, keeping what was their grandfather's farm at Nine Wells, near Hitchin, in full production. There are nine boreholes at the farm, hence its name, that provide the vital water. Eschewing too much technology, the brothers still have their watercress knife-cut by hand and prefer not to use expensive electric pump extraction, but to rely on rainfall for enough pure water to bubble up around the watercress beds.

Watercress is very high in iron, calcium and folic acid as well as other essential nutrients, hence its superfood status and recent revival of interest in its production.

In its heyday, Nine Wells Watercress Farm's highly sought-after harvest was taken to Hitchin railway station by horse and cart before being packed off to Birmingham, London, Leeds and Manchester. Today you'll find the Sansom's watercress at farmers' markets in Bedfordshire and Hertfordshire, as well as Cambridgeshire. You can also buy direct from the farm during the cutting seasons, which are in spring and from September until Christmas.

Nine Wells Watercress Farm 189
Lilley Bottom Road, Whitwell,
Hertfordshire SG4 8JP
01438 871232

The Old Farmhouse Bakery

As a steady stream of cyclists and walkers make their way over Steventon Green to By The Meadow Farm you might wonder what they're buying from the farmyard buildings beyond. Follow your nose and you'll be led to The Old Farmhouse Bakery, set up more than 25 years ago by Kate Bitmead when her children were small and the village baker retired. Frustrated she couldn't find a good enough alternative, she took on the role herself, converting a Shire horse cart shed and stables in the process.

The Old Farmhouse Bakery 179
By The Meadow Farm, Steventon,
Oxfordshire OX13 6RP
01235 831230
www.theoldfarmhousebakery.co.uk

But charming though the buildings are, they would be nothing without the products, which are as enticing as their surroundings. Besides bread, Kate sells cheeses from British artisan makers and other local foodstuffs, such as preserves, honey and eggs. Long-standing suppliers have become friends and she delights in introducing customers to new finds.

As the dairy and beef herds have gone and demand for the bakery is ever-increasing, Kate has been joined by her farmer husband Rodney – though they're determined to stay true to their roots and not expand beyond what's manageable. Their daughter Beccie is also a mainstay of the business and its offshoots, having given up her city marketing job to join the family firm and offer it her expertise, as well as her willingness to work long and irregular hours. A small team of dedicated bakers work alongside them and the family are regulars at local farmers' markets in the area – and award-winners to boot.

The secret to their success, say Kate and Rodney, is their oven, which came from the other side of the village. Formerly coal-fired, it was cooled for the first time and moved, brick by brick, to its new site – along with the original peels (the long paddles used to place the dough in and to bring the loaves out), the bread racks and the dough trough with its gorgeous patina. You might suspect, however, that there's more to their success than their 1939 Collins Tridex brick oven (though it's a thing of beauty in itself) and you'd be right. Kate is fussy in the extreme about sourcing her raw ingredients, trying, testing and tasting not just new products, but the existing supplies too – and rejecting when necessary.

The Old Farmhouse Bakery fills your senses from the moment you draw up in your car or wander through from the village green. The converted buildings offer glimpses of pies and tarts being made, the aromas of bread and cakes waft from the racks and, once you're inside, the samples set temptingly on boards and in baskets offer you no chance of redemption. As one long-standing customer explained, as she selected her day's purchases: 'I come with a limited amount of cash in my purse otherwise I'd buy up the whole shop.' That said, she carried on buying, producing a debit card as if to emphasise the point.

"The secret to their success, say Kate and Rodney, is their oven."

Outside, cars crunch their way over the gravel, disgorging eager passengers and drivers who, if they are new to the experience, enter the bakery with eyes wide and mouths wider as they take it all in. Parents push their prams over the threshold and show toddlers the way bread used to be made, retired couples ooh and aah over the selections – some long-forgotten by commercial bakeries and only half-remembered by the customers themselves.

Across the courtyard Beccie and Kate have a newer venture, a gallery where everything that's sold is UK sourced and created, but the main attraction, most people would agree, is the bakery itself.

Raymond Blanc

Any foodie worth their salt will know that Oxfordshire is home to one of the nation's flagship restaurants, Le Manoir aux Quat' Saisons, and the inimitable Raymond Blanc. Largely self-taught, he's a man who has changed British attitudes to food. His opinion is sought by politicians, food producers and retailers, his influence is undeniable and, fuelled by the best nutrition, he's a human dynamo, vigorous and vibrant, with sharp eyes that take in everything.

From his adopted home city of Oxford, where he opened his first restaurant, Raymond Blanc's effect on Oxfordshire and the shires has spread, like ripples in a pond. Little gastro-pubs pepper the region, opened by RB protégés who have been trained by their mentor and inspired by his values to move on to their own ventures. The television show *The Restaurant* ensures the counties of Berkshire, Buckinghamshire and Oxfordshire host many of the contestants' establishments, creating a buzz in the area as the man himself judges and assesses their efforts. The winning couple from each series gets to open its own restaurant, backed by Raymond Blanc's wisdom and experience.

At the top of the Raymond Blanc tree, Le Manoir celebrated its 25th anniversary in 2009, and since it first opened its doors critics have been raving about it – it has held two Michelin stars from the word go and one visit is enough to see why. It's not just the location or the house, which are pure English village; it's not the staff, who are infused with French panache and pride for jobs seriously undervalued in this country; it's not the beautiful gardens, particularly the vegetable garden, though you'll be bowled over by those too; it's not even, let it be said, solely the food. It's a combination of everything, tiny details and huge differences, that ensure Le Manoir's reputation and status.

It's not cheap to savour the full Manoir experience (though it's worth every penny), and there are other ways to enjoy the benefits of Monsieur Blanc's brilliance without blowing your annual dining-out budget. Watch his website for special deals and offers; you can have a splendid lunch at Le Manoir and enjoy the legendary surroundings without splashing out on a five-course dinner; Maison Blanc patisseries in Henley, Burford and Oxford are undeniably worth a visit; and don't underestimate the value of eating at Brasserie Blanc – less salubrious than its haute cuisine cousin, but offering high-quality home cooking that is informal and local. Raymond is a regular for Sunday lunch at the Oxford Brasserie Blanc, so don't be surprised if you find an animated Frenchman on the next table, enjoying being cooked for rather than doing the cooking.

Le Manoir aux Quat' Saisons 176
Church Road, Great Milton, Oxford,
Oxfordshire OX44 7PD
01844 278881
www.manoir.com

Maison Blanc
136–142 High Street, Burford, Oxfordshire
OX18 4QU
01993 823457
www.maisonblanc.co.uk

Also at:
1–3 Duke Street, Henley on Thames,
Oxfordshire RG9 1UR
01491 577294

3 Woodstock Road, Oxford, Oxfordshire
OX2 6HA
01865 510974

Brasserie Blanc
71–72 Walton Street, Oxford, Oxfordshire
OX2 6AG
01865 510999
www.brasserieblanc.com

Rumsey's Chocolateries

Stepping into either of the Rumsey's shop-cum-cafés is like walking on to the film set of *Chocolat* – and that's exactly the experience Mary and Nigel Rumsey want their customers and clients to enjoy when they sit down and take a break from the world outside.

Their attention to detail shows in everything, from the uniformed staff and the old-fashioned counter to the carefully sourced original (and very ornate and heavy) tills. Even the floor tiles were chosen to echo those in Joanne Harris's fictional French village premises.

Each and every chocolate on display is hand-crafted and beautifully presented; you definitely don't want to scoff these – take your time and enjoy the indulgence. In 2009 the Rumseys opened the Cocoa Pod School of Chocolate where they can pass on all the skills, pleasures and artistry behind chocolate-making.

The Rumsey's little empire started when professional patissiere and chef Nigel was asked by a colleague to hand-make chocolates as gifts one Christmas. Enamoured by the idea, Nigel created extra for his own family and friends. These proved such a hit that Nigel found himself making ever more of them and the couple's home kitchen soon became such a chocolate-making centre that Nigel decided to give up his day job.

Nigel travelled to the finest chocolate-making centres of Europe to perfect and enhance his skills and the reputation of his cocoa creations spread far and wide. Soon he was supplying restaurants and high-class retail outlets and the kitchen became a professional unit. As customers had to come to the house to collect their purchases, a shop of some sort became a must.

'We decided if people were travelling to us we had to offer them somewhere they could have a coffee, especially as some were coming quite some distance and if we were to open up a retail outlet people needed to see the chocolates being dipped,' explains Mary. 'Just at that time I watched the film *Chocolat*...'

The film set the perfect scene with Juliette Binoche playing a rebellious French *maman* who stirs up a sleepy French village, transforming a run-down shop into a café and chocolate-making paradise.

Appropriately, on Valentine's Day 2004, Nigel and Mary opened their first café in a former bank in the Buckinghamshire village of Wendover, after kitting it out with finds from auctions, architectural salvage and reclamation yards. Three years later, the Georgian town of Thame was also boasting its own Rumsey's café.

Rumsey's Chocolateries 184
The Old Bank, 26 High Street, Wendover, Buckinghamshire HP22 6EA
01296 625060
www.rumseys.co.uk

Also at:
8 Upper High Street, Thame, Oxfordshire OX9 3ER
01844 260303

The Cocoa Pod School of Chocolate
74 Oxford Road, Stone, Buckinghamshire HP17 8PL
01296 747531

"Stepping into either of the Rumsey's shop-cum-cafés is like walking on to the film set of *Chocolat*."

At either café you are guaranteed a treat, regardless of whether or not you plan to buy chocolates. A glass wall separates onlookers from the theatrical work of the chocolatiers, (passers-by can also look in but they don't enjoy the heady smell of cocoa) and the aroma of roasted coffee enhances the experience. As you might expect, Nigel's background as a patissiere ensures that delicious tarts, pastries and gateaux are plentiful, and there are also ice creams made to Nigel's secret recipes. Salads, soups and other savouries may well tempt you to stop for lunch.

At their chocolate school in Stone, Nigel designs fun and informative workshops aimed at whoever's attending. Pupils vary in age and skill set: professional chefs come along to brush up their techniques, amateur cooks come to learn the basics, and hen parties and kids come to get messy.

But one thing's for sure – after a visit to Rumsey's you'll be a chocolate devotee.

Afternoon Tea

It may seem as quintessentially English as summer rain, but the tradition of taking afternoon tea with friends and family dates back only to 1840. It was Anna Maria, the Duchess of Bedford, who first admitted to being peckish in the long hours between breakfast and dinner. With no fridge to raid and no snacks to enjoy, she asked her butler to bring tea, bread and cakes up to her boudoir at her husband's country seat of Woburn Abbey in Bedfordshire.

After a little spell of subterfuge Her Grace started inviting equally famished friends to join her, and before long, thanks to the fact she started the custom up more overtly in London (she was lady-in-waiting to Queen Victoria, so definitely in with the 'in-crowd'), getting an invitation to Woburn Abbey's Blue Drawing Room for afternoon tea was quite the thing.

These days you can only visit the Blue Drawing Room, sadly no more scoffing takes place in this delightful space. Instead you'll be directed over to the Duchess Tea Room for a spot of afternoon tea; you may feel you have to dress up to match the auspicious surroundings, but it's not obligatory. And if you'd like even more finesse with your cup of rosy lea then prebook the indulgent Duchess Anna Maria afternoon tea – all with delicacies made by the staff rather than bought in. Depending on your taste, and whether you book here or the neighbouring Inn at Woburn village (also part of the estate), you can choose an afternoon tea of finger sandwiches, scones, cake and tarts or toasted teacakes and dare we say it – even coffee and champagne. The Georgian inn offers a quiet retreat from the hustle and bustle of people browsing the delightful little shops that line the high street – very evocative of a period drama rather than 21st-century England.

For the most gracious of surroundings, the Jacobean-Georgian splendour of Hartwell House (top right) is hard to beat. Hartwell has been home to many a historical figure – William the Conqueror's son; Richard the Lionheart's brother, John; the Hampden family and Thomas Cook. Here, in one of the house's sumptuously ornate and elegant drawing rooms, your afternoon tea arrives with cute little cucumber sandwiches and a wondrous selection of miniature cakes on cake stands along with a fine bone china tea service.

For a more exotic setting, take your afternoon tea in the India Room at Winston Churchill's birthplace, Blenheim Palace (bottom right). Sip your tea (stick out your pinky) and savour your sandwiches while being surrounded by scenes of India. Take a glance out of a window at the amazing water terraces. History buffs will delight at this Palladian mansion and World Heritage Site but all visitors will marvel at the sandwiches and top-notch cakes, making it everyone's cup of tea.

The Duchess Tea Room
Woburn Abbey, Woburn Park,
Bedfordshire MK17 9WA
01525 290333
www.woburn.co.uk
Open March–October but phone ahead to check tea is being served.

Hartwell House
Oxford Road, Near Aylesbury,
Buckinghamshire HP17 8NR
01296 747444
www.hartwell-house.com
Open for afternoon tea 3.30–5.30pm Monday–Friday, 4–5.30pm Saturday and 4.30–5.30pm Sunday; best to book in advance.

Blenheim Palace 172
Woodstock, Oxfordshire OX20 1PP
01993 813874 (for booking afternoon tea)
www.blenheimpalace.com
Open daily February–December. Afternoon teas are served 3–5pm whenever the palace is open and should be booked in advance.

Mrs Jordan's Mill Shop

One whiff from Mrs Jordan's Mill Shop is enough to take you back to a time when it was possible to buy boxes of broken biscuits and have a pound of brown sugar weighed out on brass scales. You may find yourself magically transported back to an era when you could breathe in the aromas wafting from open hessian sacks of coffee beans lying on the beeswax-polished wooden floors of such a Mill Shop.

Mrs Jordan's Mill Shop 188
Holme Mills, Biggleswade,
Bedfordshire SG18 9JY
01767 318222
www.jordanscereals.co.uk
The shop is closed lunchtimes, Saturday
afternoon and Sunday.

Not that there are open boxes of anything on the shelves at Mrs Jordan's shop, since we live in more regulated times, but the items sold recreate those heavenly scents once so familiar. Mrs Jordan (Pamela, but she is never known by her first name: friends and family call her Whizzer, everyone else calls her Mrs Jordan) sells all kinds of goodies here, from red lentils and rolled oats to jars of honey and malt extract, packing the dried goods from big sacks into smaller bags to sell to her regulars, who drop by and collect their weekly or monthly shop, picking up their favourite breakfast cereals as they do so.

The Jordan family have been milling near Biggleswade for five generations, and it was Mrs Jordan's son, Bill, who asked her, about 30 years ago, to open up and run a shop. He and brother David had started creating breakfast cereals, rather than milling animal feed and flour, as previous Jordans had done, and a whole new business was taking off. Now internationally adored, their wholesome cereals and muesli were then beginning to cause quite a stir on British breakfast tables and Bill wanted an outlet onsite at Holme Mills that sold the ingredients they used, as well as boxes of the cereals themselves, to the public.

'But he never gave me a brief, dear,' says Mrs Jordan, from the family home she has lived in for 60 years. 'So I ended up selling what I liked.'

You'd have to be a tough man to tell Mrs Jordan not to sell what she liked, and she might not listen to you anyway, so beside the bags of familiar Jordans Crunchy Oats and Frusli Bars and the bagged up raisins and flaked almonds that Bill had in mind, Mrs Jordan sells birthday cards and gifts, photo frames and fancy pens. There are soft toys on the top shelves, with kidney beans and pulses, dried apricots and apple rings on the shelves below. Bottles of cider vinegar vie for space with fruit juice and bags of those delicious dried strawberry pieces that your children pick out of your muesli to eat like sweets. Using ingredients from the shelves, you can even create your own muesli if you prefer a recipe other than Bill and David's – though you'll have to do it in the privacy of your own home.

In the run-up to Christmas, the shop becomes a hive of activity, as people pop in to buy the ingredients for their cakes and puddings, paying by cash or cheque, as Mrs Jordan isn't into new-fangled credit and debit card machines.

"One whiff is enough to take you back to a time when a pound of brown sugar was weighed out on brass scales."

The business at Holme Mills is a far cry from 150 years ago, when the first of the Jordans started milling on the banks of the River Ivel, and from the days when Bill and David experimented with muesli recipes on the kitchen table of their mum's home. Bill also runs a wildlife sanctuary besides maintaining the family business interests, and David has plans to turn the Holme Mills site into a heritage centre. Mrs Jordan, meanwhile, still sells from her old-fashioned shop, aided by a loyal posse of assistants – and long may she flourish.

Alder Carr Farm Shop

From Needham Market's high street, the charming Alder Carr Farm is just a minute's drive past a smartly converted mill or a 10-minute walk across the pretty River Gipping. The Hardingham's family farm business in the agricultural heartland of Suffolk seems even more locally rooted than most farm shops, with a crowded community noticeboard and an invitation to local allotment growers with gluts to sell their produce in the shop. And yet it is also patronised by foodie celebrities, such as local resident Delia Smith, who says that she no longer bothers to make her runner bean chutney when the one sold at Alder Carr is just as good.

Alder Carr Farm Shop 200
Creeting St Mary, Needham Market,
Ipswich, Suffolk IP6 8LX
01449 720820
www.aldercarrfarm.co.uk
Open 9am–4.30pm Tuesday–Saturday
and 10am–4pm Sunday.
Farmers' market held on the third
Saturday of the month.

The onsite Alder Tree dairy run by one of the Hardingham daughters makes outstanding ice cream. The list of contents is a joy to read: fruit (comprising at least a third and mostly grown on the farm), cream and sugar (but not too much). Irresistible flavour combinations such as rhubarb with stem ginger and gooseberry with elderflower have been praised variously by Nigel and Nigella (Slater and Lawson). The label 'prize-winning' can be used indiscriminately, but the Alder Tree gooseberry ice cream is truly deserving – last year it earned a rare three stars at the Guild of Fine Foods Great Taste Awards, the 'Oscars of the Food Industry'. Buy a small tub in the shop to enjoy in the lovely, laid-back courtyard, whose atmosphere is so mellow that even the wasps seem benign.

The first thing you see on arrival is the base of an 18th-century Suffolk postmill, which is now a florist's studio. Beyond that you can follow a permissive path – courtesy of Natural England, at least until 2017 – over a wobbly bridge to a wetland wood (carr) of alder and elder, which produce the flowers for the ice cream. Wander back across the rough grass and wildflower meadow and you're sure to pass some Highland cattle, whose superb meat is sold in the shop, along with free-range eggs gathered from the farm's hens.

The friendly staff in the shop, tea room, bakery and deli care more about quality than about turning a profit. The place urges participation, not just consumerism. Extensive fields are planted with fruits and vegetables for picking yourself. Punnets are freely available and a big blackboard in the entrance of the shop shows which fruits are ripe and ready that day; expect fruits other than the usual strawberries and raspberries, there are tayberries, gooseberries, blackcurrants and rhubarb. What's more, the shop sells Kilner jars and posts notices encouraging home bottling and preserving, which may just prompt someone to head down the road of becoming a domestic god or goddess.

Jimmy's Farm

Pig farming is hardly a natural bedfellow with celebrity, but the engaging Jimmy Doherty has managed to combine the two. The BBC2 series *Jimmy's Farm* brought to the small screen Jimmy's struggles to reinvent himself as an organic farmer. In 2003 he bought a run-down farm near Ipswich with a loan from that other Essex James, his schoolmate Jamie Oliver, and now everyone can enjoy the fruits of his labour.

The small child who on arrival says 'What's that smell?' quickly unwrinkles his nose when he gets to feed the sheep, pat a ferret or build a den in the hazel and chestnut wood. Grown-ups, more than likely, will take more pleasure in feasting their eyes (and emptying their wallets) in the farm shop. The counters are bursting with trays of rare-breed Essex and Saddleback pork from pigs free to roam the farm's pastures and forage in the woodland.

Jimmy's Farm 202
Pannington Hall Lane, Wherstead,
Near Ipswich, Suffolk IP9 2AR
08444 938088
www.jimmysfarm.com
Farm shop open daily year round.
Farmers' market on the first Saturday
of the month.

Various types of sausage abound: choose from the classic Essex pork sausage or something more unusual such as the Stilton and garlic sausage named 'Super Blue' to honour Ipswich Football Club.

On leaving the shop you'll no doubt sniff another more enticing smell – some of the tastiest hot dogs ever – coming from Jimmy's Field Kitchen, just next to his wife Michaela's pride and joy – the herb and vegetable gardens.

Richardson's Smokehouse

The 'No Smoking' sign at Richardson's Smokehouse in Orford must surely be a joke. The evocative smell of oak smoke lures many daytrippers down Baker's Lane to a mountain of oak logs and the brick kiln whose interior literally drips with black tar. From the smokehouse emerges a heavenly range of smoked foods for sale in the small shop.

Not content with the mackerel he started with two decades ago, Steve Richardson experiments with a vast array of slow-smoked foodstuffs, from bloaters and ham hocks to garlic bulbs and chorizo. Some products are seasonal, such as the prized smoked eel and wild duck, but most are available every day of the year. Steve takes whole ham hocks, blackens them with smoke and smothers them in honey and mustard or molasses and cider to create the most irresistible cut of meat, all for just over a fiver. The smokehouse is especially popular in the run-up to Christmas, so plan your trip accordingly.

Richardson's Smokehouse 205
Baker's Lane, Orford, Suffolk IP12 2LH
01394 450103
www.richardsonssmokehouse.co.uk
Open daily 10am–4pm(ish).

Butley Orford Oysterage 205
Market Hill, Orford, Suffolk IP12 2LH
01394 450277
www.butleyorfordoysterage.co.uk

Richardson's is located virtually in the backyard of the celebrated Butley Orford Oysterage, an entirely separate business. If you want to dine at this restaurant famed for its fresh fish and unpretentious presentation, book well in advance.

Suffolk Food Safari

A swathe of East Suffolk has resolutely kept the major supermarkets away. As a result an astonishing diversity of independent and, some would say, quirky food producers has flourished in the region. The new mantra of tracking food and drink from plough to plate, field to fork and grape to glass prompted Tim and Polly Robinson to launch Food Safari.

Food Safari
26 Double Street, Framlingham,
Woodbridge, Suffolk IP13 9BN
01728 621380
www.foodsafari.co.uk
Events cost from £75 per head for a half day
to £195 for a full day.

The Anchor 206
Main Street, Walberswick, Suffolk IP18 6UA
01502 722112
www.anchoratwalberswick.com

The company's innovative series of food events, farm visits and hands-on workshops go behind the scenes of Suffolk's farmers, fishermen, artisan bakers, butchers and cheesemakers. Clients have a chance to explore the origins of their favourite foods and to meet the characters who cultivate the plumpest oysters, raise the free-est-range pigs, forage for wild food and make wine or brew beer, all within a confined area of Suffolk's river valleys from the Blyth to the Orwell.

The half- or full-day events often involve a cookery demonstration and inevitably culminate in a feast using the day's featured food, usually at Food Safari's partner gastro-pub – the Anchor in Walberswick.

Specialist interests can be customised for small groups, so if you have always yearned to pluck and prepare a pheasant, just find a few friends who share your interest and escape on your own Food Safari.

Houghton Mill

Unlike Chaucer's ribald miller, the two chaps bagging up stoneground flour at Houghton Mill appear to be stone-cold sober. Stone being the operative word here, since these millers have to make sure that the water-powered stone millwheels turn the wheat grown at Wimpole Hall Farm 20 miles away into the nutty wholewheat flour you can take away or consume in the delicious scones served in the mill café and garden.

Houghton Mill 190
Houghton, Near Huntingdon,
Cambridgeshire PE28 2AZ
01480 301494
www.nationaltrust.org.uk/main/w-houghtonmill
Open Monday–Wednesday afternoons
late April–late September and weekends
late March–late October.
Milling demonstrations on Sundays and
bank holidays.

Of the hundred watermills that once lined the banks of the River Great Ouse, Houghton is the last one still operating. When it was threatened with demolition in the 1930s, the Youth Hostels Association stepped in and installed bunk beds among the wooden mill fittings. Later, care of this most strikingly picturesque timber-built and boarded mill passed to the National Trust.

On milling days, when the water level is suitable, cogs, gears and wheels whir away. Flour is such an unsexy staple for Anglo-Saxons that it is startling to see what sophisticated engineering went into producing it before steam power arrived.

After a leisurely stroll across the water meadows or a little trip on the Great Ouse by rowboat, nothing could be nicer than returning for a spot of afternoon tea in the glorious garden beside the mill's tearoom.

Snape Maltings Farmers' Market

The sound of sizzling sausages, the smell of fresh baking, the quack of ducks on the pond and the smiles of the stallholders combine to create an irresistibly cheerful and welcoming atmosphere at the Snape Maltings Farmers' Market.

The medley of Victorian buildings, once used for malting Suffolk's best-quality barley for beer, makes a charming backdrop for this monthly market. After accepting offers of free tastings from the two-dozen East Anglian producers who set out their stalls every month, you may not have enough room for the barbecued bangers or the delicious cakes served by the Metfield Bakery's Café and Deli.

The market is bustling without being so busy that the producers don't have time for a chat. Susan Adams, for example, regularly brings her free-range wild boar joints, sausages and bacon. She may look more librarian than farmer with a Dangerous Wild Animals Licence, but she takes quiet pleasure in talking about her animals kept at Brampton near Beccles. For those new to wild boar cuisine, she gives out slips of paper with recipe ideas, for example, slow-cooked shoulder of wild boar steak with a honey and vinegar glaze.

Other producers who are likely to be on hand at Snape are the colourful Bhaji Man with his spice kits, Katharine and Jason Salisbury who make rich and creamy farmhouse cheese from the milk of their Guernseys (one of the few cheesemakers in Suffolk), Piers Pool from High House Fruit Farm patiently defending his samples of cloudy apple juice from the wasps, two smiling chaps who make cupcakes (currently so fashionable) and Karoline Newman, a cheese-straw specialist, offering samples of marmite or pesto-flavoured nibbles.

Snape Maltings is well known as the home of the Aldeburgh Music Festival held every June, started by Benjamin Britten just after World War II. It's less well known for hosting the Aldeburgh Food and Drink Festival – one of the most significant food events in the East Anglian calendar. The list of traders reads like a who's who of local food heroes, all of them battling to preserve the distinct food culture of Suffolk towns and villages. The centrepiece of the festival is the last weekend in September when chefs such as Mark Hix and Thomasina Miers come to the Maltings. But the fringe events stretch over a fortnight and involve 70 producers in various venues offering everything from chocolate-tastings to masterclasses on East Anglian charcuterie.

The opening in 2008 of the Metfield Bakery's Café and Deli has brought sophisticated eating but without pretension. The mezzanine café with its stripped pine and exposed rafters is unashamedly Clerkenwell in ambience, but offers intriguingly old-fashioned English dishes such as ox tongue with summer beets

Snape Maltings Farmers' Market 204
Snape Maltings, Near Aldeburgh,
Suffolk IP17 1SR
01728 688303
From 9.30am on the first Saturday of the month (ample free parking). There's an additional summer market in August. Aldeburgh Food and Drink Festival takes place on the last weekend of September.

Metfield Bakery's Café and Deli 204
Snape Maltings, Near Aldeburgh,
Suffolk IP17 1SR
01728 687980
Open daily from 10am till tea-time, plus Friday and Saturday evenings.

"The market is bustling without being so busy that the producers don't have time for a chat."

and lemon posset with shortbread. Family groups in search of brunch come for blueberry pancakes or rarebit and apple chutney, while concert-goers opt for oysters and grilled rabbit with fennel and aioli. Metfield's owner, Stuart Oetzmann, is the enterprising young chef-cum-baker-cum-organic farmer who has brought his artisan breads, famous rare-breed-pork pies and sticky cakes over the border from deepest Norfolk. Naturally the coffee is triple-certified – organic, fair trade and Rainforest Alliance.

After any predictable overindulgence, a walk along the tidal estuary is called for. From the Maltings car park, a boardwalk follows the edge of the River Alde, perhaps past a rigged sailing barge or two, to the picturesque little thatched church at Iken. Watching the long-billed curlews and other waders pecking the mudflats for their tea might put you in mind of another snack, assuming you've worked up enough of an appetite before your return to Snape.

Wyken Vineyards

Hidden in a testingly remote corner of East Anglia, the Wyken Estate offers a tantalising glimpse of the region's elusive rural beauty. At its centre sits a charming Elizabethan manor house where the grounds, including a herb garden, formal knot garden and maze, are open to the public. But it's to the barn that foodies flock, where the 16th-century structure has been transformed into an elegant and airy space comprising a café and the Leaping Hare restaurant, highly regarded for its careful and distinctive but unpretentious cooking. All ingredients are seasonal and many are sourced locally; the changing menu might include Wyken-Estate-raised pigeon with wild mushrooms or lambshank from Stowlangtoft, a few miles south.

The wine list couldn't get much more local since the grapes for Wyken's prize-winning white and rosé wines grow right here. Wyken Moonshine is a refreshing sparkling wine, while the Bacchus and Madeleine Angevine whites pack full-on lychee and gooseberry flavours. It's not just wines, either; they sell a chocolatey beer called Good Dog Ale made from their own barley.

A stroll to and around the vineyard allows you to absorb the peace of this rural seclusion. First, find the fingerpost at a gate, then follow a mown path into a tangled fairy-tale wood. Soon you emerge into the light not to find a gingerbread house – gingerbread is back at the café – but to discover row upon row of neatly trailing vines on a carpet of golden grasses, with the gently rolling Suffolk countryside forming the perfect backdrop. Even the houses on the estate and the corrugated-iron-roofed huts are painted in tasteful hues to complete the picture.

Back at the pantiled barn, there's the café and the shop to explore; enjoy coffee and carrot cake on an outdoor terrace beside a lush espaliered fig tree before browsing in the Leaping Hare Country Store. Its colourful array of designer garden and interior accessories, vintage clothes, toys and seldom-seen crafts are sure to find their way into your basket, along with some wine from the estate.

The 'lady of the estate' is Carla Carlisle, an expat American. She's now more huntin'-and-shootin' English than the English; she even writes a column in *Country Life*. Yet her origins peep out in unexpected places, for example in the home-made blueberry pancakes served with bacon and maple syrup on the café breakfast menu and the woollen rugs from North Carolina on sale in the shop.

A visit on Saturday mornings will reward you with a small but perfectly formed farmers' market. Expect to find just-picked fruit and veg, bread and baked goods, local meat, cheeses and even mushrooms and unusual herbs. But if you spot a cake you fancy at the bakery stall, buy it when you see it, because they almost always sell out by lunchtime.

Wyken Vineyards and Leaping Hare 199
Wyken Road, Stanton,
Bury St Edmunds, Suffolk IP31 2DW
01359 250287
www.wykenvineyards.co.uk
Restaurant, café and shop open daily
10am–6pm; dinners on Friday and Saturday
only (booking often necessary).
Gardens open daily 2–6pm Sunday–Friday
April–September.
Farmers' market 9am–1pm every Saturday.

Pick Your Own Samphire

Known as the 'poor man's asparagus', samphire is freely available from tidal flats along the East Anglian coast in summer. The emerald green shoots rising from wetlands and mud are not difficult to recognise, so coastal walkers should keep a sharp eye out and a plastic bag in their pocket. If you're not the kind to search along the edges of tidal creeks, pools or salt marshes for this prized delicacy, you can simply buy it from a fishmonger.

If you're keen to pick your own, promising places include the vast salt marshes along the North Norfolk Coastal Path between Thornham and Salthouse, especially around Brancaster and Stiffkey. A less-discovered place is on the Suffolk Coast and Heaths Path, where a tidal pool about a 10-minute walk north of mysterious Shingle Street is fringed with the edible plant throughout July and August.

When samphire is young and fresh, a few inches of the tops can easily be snapped off to enjoy for supper, rinsed of its salt and lightly steamed with butter and a drop of balsamic vinegar. Local chefs, such as Galton Blackiston from the Michelin-starred Morston Hall near Blakeney in North Norfolk, love to use it in season as a briny base for seafood salads and fish dishes.

Morston Hall Hotel & Restaurant 197
Morston, Holt, Norfolk NR25 7AA
01263 741041
www.morstonhall.com

Head to Wisbech Saturday market or fishmongers throughout the region to buy samphire.

Walsingham Farms Shop

Not many people know that England's answer to Lourdes is tucked away in rural Norfolk. Little Walsingham was second only to Canterbury as an English destination for pilgrims in the Middle Ages; today, its shrines continue to attract believers by the coachload. In the centre of the village, secular devotees come on a more materialist pilgrimage to the innovative Walsingham Farms Shop, where the splendid range of foods produced in North Norfolk is something of a revelation.

Produce such as juicy apple and cinnamon loaf cakes made by the Riverside Bakery in King's Lynn, goose eggs from Top Farm in Great Snoring, Mrs Temple's artisan cheeses and organic flour milled nearby at Letheringsett simply spill from the shelves of this well-designed shrine to good food, housed in a converted stone and brick grain store. The shop and kitchen combi – the only farm shop in Norfolk to make the *Telegraph*'s 50 best in 2009 – sells delicious home-made pies, soups and puds every day.

While devout Catholics walk barefoot along the mile to the tiny Slipper Chapel, food-lovers merely stroll 100 paces to the Norfolk Riddle. Disguised as a humble chippy, this well-priced restaurant comes with its own French chef and all ingredients are sourced from the farm shop.

Walsingham Farms Shop Partnership 196
Guild Street, Little Walsingham,
Norfolk NR22 6BU
01328 821877
www.walsinghamfarmsshop.co.uk
Open 9am–6pm Tuesday–Friday, 9am–5pm
Saturday and 10am–4pm Sunday.

Norfolk Riddle 196
2 Wells Road, Little Walsingham,
Norfolk NR22 2DJ
01328 821903
www.walsinghamfarmsshop.co.uk
Open daily for lunch and dinner.

Whin Hill Cider

Whin Hill Cider 195
The Stables, Stearman's Yard,
Wells-next-the-Sea, Norfolk NR23 1BW
01328 711033
www.whinhillcider.co.uk
Open Tuesday–Sunday in July and August;
weekends only Easter–June and
September–October.

You wouldn't normally expect to uncover treasure in a busy resort car park, but at Whin Hill Cider that's just what you'll find. In a converted 18th-century barn next to the main seafront car park in bustling Wells-next-the-Sea you can taste and buy an enticing range of locally grown cider and apple juice.

Generous tastings are cheerfully dispensed by Jim or Pete, the two partners who fled their office jobs to plant 1,000 apple trees by hand in 1994 and who still do all the picking, pressing and bottling. After choosing between their mouth-puckering Extra Dry and the rosy-coloured sweetish effervescent Browns, or one of the six full-bodied ciders in between, it is difficult to resist buying one or two or a dozen bottles to take away. But don't rush off; there's a peaceful vine-bedecked courtyard that offers the perfect place to linger over a pint, provided you don't mind returning the friendly overtures of Fred the resident chocolate Labrador.

Two kinds of perry are also available, made from eight varietals of pear also grown at Jim and Pete's orchards 10 miles inland. Their neat 13-acre orchard on Station Road, just north of Stanhoe, is especially pretty in the blossom season and well worth a visit.

Burnham Market Gastronomy

Grooms Bakery 194
01328 738289
www.groomsbakery.co.uk

Gurneys Fish Shop 194
01328 738967
www.gurneysfishshop.co.uk

Humble Pie 194
01328 738581
www.humble-pie.com

Arthur Howell Butcher 194
01328 738230

The fiercely independent food culture of the ultra-chic village of Burnham Market invariably wins plaudits from Sunday supplement reviewers. Once you have feasted your eyes on the wares on offer at the village deli, bakery, butcher and fishmonger, you may be more than willing to overlook the disadvantages of the Chelsea invasion.

There is nothing *nouveau* about the collection of first-class gastronomic shops crowded round the oh-so-attractive village green. Grooms Bakery is run by a fourth generation of the Groom family; Arthur Howell's butchers business was established in north Norfolk in 1889; and the Gurney family sends out a couple of boats into the Wash to catch some of what they sell in their fish shop.

The marvellous yet friendly delicatessen Humble Pie is a relative newcomer, opening in 1980. At busy times you will have to join the queue of linen-clad sophisticates patiently waiting outside to choose from its imaginatively crammed shelves, but the wait is well worth it.

Burnham Market is the ideal place to stock up for a lavish picnic – perhaps a wedge of Norfolk Dapple cheese from the deli, sea-salt focaccia from the baker and Gurneys' famous potted shrimp or irresistible Thai fish cakes – before heading down to nearby Brancaster Beach at low tide.

Fish Sheds

Fish sheds are to restaurants what Ryanair is to airlines – cheap and frill-free. But whereas Ryanair seems to attract nothing but complaints and venom, the unpretentious fish shacks along the East Anglian coast elicit wonder and delight from locals and holidaymakers alike. Who needs polished service and fancy sauces when you can be served a platter of seafood of unimpeachable freshness for less than a tenner?

Cookie's Crab Shop on the north Norfolk coast is longest in the tooth. Fifty-three years ago, a small fish shop opened on the Green in the tiny village of Salthouse along the coast from the honeypot resort of Cley-next-the-Sea. Eventually it spawned a sort of café, whose fame spread, so that more tables had to be crammed into a jerry-built gazebo and shed in the yard. Nowadays crowds happily brave the chaos of the queue-to-order, then queue-to-pay system, necessary even if you have reserved a table, which at most times is pretty much essential.

The huge blackboard menu over the counter prominently features Cookie's signature royal salads. Plates are piled high with dressed crab, smoked mackerel, chunky hot-smoked salmon, anchovy fillets, cockles and prawns, plus beetroot (unfashionably pickled) and cucumber salad – all for an astonishing £6.50. The absence of all fripperies means that if you want a glass of wine, local cider or beer to accompany your meal, you will have to bring along not only the grog but the glasses as well.

At the opposite end of the bulbous coastline of East Anglia is another long-established seafood shack with the unglamorous-sounding name of The Company Shed. Hovering at the water's edge of West Mersea, an island connected to the rest of Essex by a causeway prone to flooding at high tide, is an unadorned plank-clad shed, easily spotted by the length of the queue stretching out the door. You won't wait long to be served prawns, cockles, fish terrines and baked eel from the colourful takeaway counter; but if you want a table, you will have to queue. However, any queuing time allows your dining companion plenty of time to set off in search of bread, wine and mayonnaise if you happen to have come unprepared. The Company Shed is best known for its fresh oysters, gathered from Mersea's muddy creeks almost within shell-shucking distance of the shed.

About equidistant between these two lies the enchanting resort of Southwold, at times quaint, at other times swanky, which boasts the newest must-visit fish shed. In 2006 a fisherman from Mersea Island saw that the idea of a fishmonger-turned-eatery would transplant easily to Southwold. So Darren and his wife Caroll moved up and acquired their first ramshackle black-tarred fishing shed on the River Blyth and started selling fish through a hatch window.

The Sole Bay Fish Co is now four semi-derelict fisherman's shacks knocked together but it still sells the daily catch of wetfish and shellfish that Darren brings

Cookie's Crab Shop
The Green, Salthouse, Holt,
Norfolk NR25 7AJ
01263 740352
www.salthouse.org.uk
Open daily 9am–7pm in summer,
10am–4pm in winter;
discretionary hours on cold, wet days.

The Company Shed
129 Coast Road, West Mersea,
Essex CO5 8PA
01206 382700
Open 9am–5pm Tuesday–Saturday and
10am–5pm Sunday.

Sole Bay Fish Co
Shed 22e Blackshore, Southwold,
Suffolk IP18 6ND
01502 724241
www.solebayfishco.co.uk
Restaurant open 12–3pm Tuesday–Sunday;
fish shop open daily.

> ## "Unpretentious fish shacks elicit wonder and delight from locals and holidaymakers alike."

in on *Our Caroll II*. And, for three hours in the middle of the day, you can nab one of the eight tables and order from a sublime selection of lobster and crab platters. Both bread and wine are on a BYO basis, though Caroll will happily supply glasses so that you can linger either at the single table at the front watching the comings-and-goings of the harbour or in the back with a view over the fields to Southwold. If you are lucky enough to be there at fish-feeding time, you can experience the unexpected excitement when Darren feeds the lobster, crabs and fish in his giant aquarium.

Elgood's Brewery

Often used as the setting for costume dramas, the sweeping Georgian terraces of Wisbech in the fenlands of north Cambridgeshire reveal a remarkable throwback to a golden age of British brewing. Elgood's Brewery occupies its original 18th-century buildings proudly overlooking the River Nene to the front, and hiding secret gardens behind.

First recorded as a brewery in 1795 and now run by the fifth generation of the same family, Elgood's is completely independent. The hour-long brewery tour is of historic as well as brewing interest. In the large upstairs room, you can admire a stepped pair of room-sized copper cooling trays resembling shallow swimming pools, the only such pair left in Britain, though health and safety regulations now forbid their use. The hops and premium Maris Otter barley from East Anglia are all English; it's only the sugar that's imported from Barbados. Elgood's use highly roasted malt (almost like coffee beans) to achieve their beautifully treacly Black Dog mild.

Tours of the brewery are naturally rounded off with a tasting of up to three ales and, depending on the weather, you can choose to sup these in the brewery's own bar or in the seating area overlooking the expansive gardens. Black Dog and Cambridge Bitter (voted Champion Beer of Britain by CAMRA a couple of years ago) are always on tap and interesting seasonal beers change: Golden Newt is a deliciously floral summer drop. Nothing beats drinking the ales from the cask, but they do sell bottled versions in the Visitor Centre shop.

The whole place is quintessentially English. Historic pub signs adorn the entrance hall and the charming little museum, including the rules of Lemuel Cox's Inn stipulating that boots not be worn in bed and organ grinders must sleep in the washhouse. The brewery's logo – a black dog with a castle key in its mouth – represents Black Shuck, who for centuries has been chasing visitors and locals alike from the ghost-trodden fens into the nearest pub. So, do as the fenlanders do and happily be chased into the homely Rose Tavern a short stroll along the North Brink for a hand-pulled pint of Elgood's ales or to one of the many rural gems tied to the brewery, such as the Lamb & Flag Inn in Welney.

Outside the brewery buildings you're greeted by an unexpected and peaceful four-acre garden, designed over the last decade by one of the Elgood daughters to show off the superb mature trees including a 200-year-old English oak and a bizarre monkey puzzle shaped like a tall toadstool. Although contemporary in feel, the tranquil garden incorporates Georgian and Victorian features – there's a rockery, a statue of a beloved pet dog long deceased and a hedge maze in which you are guaranteed to get lost, especially after a few of Elgood's delicious ales.

Elgood & Sons 191
North Brink, Wisbech,
Cambridgeshire PE13 1LN
01945 583160
www.elgoods-brewery.co.uk
Open late April–late September; brewery tours 2pm Tuesday–Thursday; open one pre-Christmas weekend.

Rose Tavern 192
53 North Brink, Wisbech,
Cambridgeshire PE13 1JX
01945 588335

Lamb & Flag Inn 193
Main Street, Welney, Wisbech
Cambridgeshire PE14 9RB
01354 610242

Melton Mowbray Pies

As you drive into the Leicestershire market town of Melton Mowbray, the boundary sign reads 'Rural Capital of Food'. The automatic association of pasties with Cornwall and lamb with Wales refers to a vague region. But the name Melton Mowbray is, and always will be, synonymous with pork pies. So, it is no surprise that the authorised bakers of hereabouts object strenuously to any old manufacturer taking their name in vain for inferior pork pies, much as French champagne producers ensured that Australian bubbly was not allowed to be labelled 'champagne'. So convinced are the nine members of the Melton Mowbray Pie Association of the special qualities of their pork pies that they lobbied the European Union to grant Protected Geographical Indication status to their product, and in 2008 they won.

Few British foods are as iconic as the pork pie. A proper pork pie comprises delicious, cubed 'roast' pork (rather than minced cured meat), with pepper seasoning and jelly, all encased in a hand-raised pastry before being formed by hand and baked without using moulds or hoops. As a result the shape of these artisan pies is charmingly irregular.

One of the best places to see the pies in the making is Brockleby's Farm Shop less than two miles from the pie capital and well within the borders of this sacred borough. On baking days, hot, buttery pastry smells assault your nostrils on entering the shop. Brockleby's makes and sells the only certified organic Melton Mowbray pies in the area, and therefore the world. And, what's more, it's a totally local affair: the pies are made behind a counter at one end of the shop from rare-breed pork raised at another Leicestershire farm, flour milled at Whissendine Windmill in Rutland and even home-produced lard and jelly, from the trotters.

Brockleby's produces many other pies in addition to pork ones, and much else besides. The farm shop's owner, Ian Jalland, is primarily a sheep farmer as his forebears were, and the first pie he sold was a Moroccan lamb and apricot one. These pies are still made from Hebridean or Jacob sheep raised at his other farm near Loughborough, and they are superb. Brockleby's strapline is 'Food with Provenance' and the care with which so many products on the shop's shelves are traced to their origins is mightily impressive.

The meat used in the pies and prepared dishes is exactly the same as you'll find at the farm shop's butchery counter. When Ian was establishing the shop in 2005, he had trouble recruiting butchers and pie-makers with traditional skills. He managed to entice a local butcher out of retirement long enough to train a willing candidate, who just happened to be a trained chef.

Rather than drive to Brockleby's, walkers may prefer to amble through this beautiful countryside; follow the circular walk along the valley of the River Wreake from neighbouring Kirby Bellars, and back again, taking less than an hour.

Brockleby's Farm Shop 170
Asfordby Hill, Melton Mowbray,
Leicestershire LE14 3QU
01664 813200
www.brocklebys.co.uk
Open Monday–Saturday.

Ye Olde Pork Pie Shoppe 169
10 Nottingham Street, Melton Mowbray,
Leicestershire LE13 1NW
01664 482068
www.porkpie.co.uk
www.mmppa.co.uk

"A proper pork pie is encased in hand-raised pastry so these artisan pies are charmingly irregular."

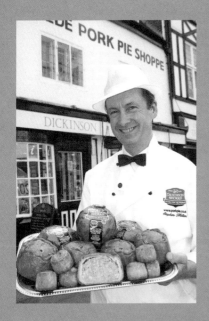

Back in the market town of Melton Mowbray, Ye Olde Pork Pie Shoppe – despite the off-putting name with its guaranteed appeal to coach parties – produces pies of such quality that they consistently win competitions. This bakery was established in 1851 about 10 years before Charles Dickens published *Great Expectations*, in which young Pip steals a 'beautiful round compact pork pie' from home to give to the terrifying Magwitch. So, the pie is undoubtedly a part of England's culinary heritage, and that's no porky pie.

Stilton Cheese

Only six dairies are licensed to label their blue cheese as Stilton, and all must be located in Leicestershire, Nottinghamshire or Derbyshire, according to EU classification. Sadly, though, this means that Stilton cheese can no longer be made in the pretty village of Stilton, which sits on the edge of Cambridgeshire.

The story goes that the Leicestershire farming folk who invented Stilton in the early 18th century linked up with the landlord of the Bell Inn in Stilton (about 40 miles away), who sold it in quantity since his village had become a busy staging post on the Great North Road. Controversy still rages over the origins of Stilton, with letters in obscure libraries being trawled for early references and recipes. The Stilton Cheesemakers Association jealously guards its monopoly of the name but has acknowledged that cheese was certainly made in Stilton at an early date, though probably not the blue cheese we know today.

Because of the scale of the demand – 100,000 8kg Stilton cheeses are exported each year, and this is just one-tenth of the total output – most Stilton dairies operate on a massive scale. The only one that welcomes passing visitors is the smaller Websters Dairy located in the secluded Wolds village of Saxelby. Drive along tree-lined lanes across rolling hills and you'll see fields full of dairy cows. The heavy clay over limestone found in this part of the world is ideal for supporting rich grassy meadows.

Architecturally speaking, Quenby Hall is the grandest Stilton producer. The hereditary owner of this well-proportioned Jacobean house, set in a 1,400-acre estate, reintroduced Stilton cheesemaking in 2006 after a lapse of about 200 years. Alas, you can't visit the hall unless you hire the whole place for a wedding or to shoot a film, but you can admire it from afar.

The specialist cheese shop in nearby Melton Mowbray, the Melton Cheeseboard, is one of the best local places to find more than one kind of Stilton. The primary allegiance of this fromagerie is to the Long Clawson Dairy and it carries their complete range, including fruit blends such as white Stilton with cranberries. Another recommended outlet to sample a range of Stiltons, over the border in Rutland, is Hambleton Farms Fine Foods shop in Oakham.

The characteristic crumbly texture and tangy flavour of Stilton mellows over time into a creamier and less-sharp-tasting cheese. Unlike some cheeses, Stilton is not pressed; instead the curds are allowed to drain naturally, giving it its unique texture. Stilton purists believe that the curds should be hand-ladled, which is done at Quenby. Some go further and maintain that true Stilton should be made with unpasteurised milk, but alas the EU definition means that this is no longer allowed.

The four Leicestershire members of the Stilton Cheesemakers Association (www.stiltoncheese.com) are:

Quenby Hall [164]
Hungarton, Leicestershire LE7 9JF
0116 259 5403
www.quenbystilton.co.uk

Long Clawson Dairy [165]
Long Clawson, Melton Mowbray,
Leicestershire LE14 4PJ
01664 822332
www.clawson.co.uk

Tuxford & Tebbutt [166]
Thorpe End, Melton Mowbray,
Leicestershire LE13 1RB
01664 500555
www.tuxfordandtebbutt.com

Websters Dairy [167]
Saxelby, Near Melton Mowbray,
Leicestershire LE14 3PH
01664 812223
www.webstersdairy.co.uk

Recommended retail outlets for Stilton include:

The Melton Cheeseboard [168]
8 Windsor Street, Melton Mowbray,
Leicestershire LE13 1BU
01664 562257
www.meltoncheeseboard.co.uk

Hambleton Farms Fine Foods [171]
Knights Yard, Gaol Street, Oakham,
Leicestershire LE15 6AQ
01572 724455
www.fcphipps.co.uk

Garden Organic, Ryton

It is hard to imagine how something that for many years was known as the Henry Doubleday Research Association could transform itself into a jolly family day out. But that is exactly what Garden Organic has done at Ryton Gardens. Ten acres of 30 individual organic gardens in the heart of rural Warwickshire are organised according to themes, from orchards of old plum and damson varieties to a demonstration garden for aspiring allotment gardeners (now so fashionable) on the best ways to train runner beans. Interest in organic growing and eating has become mainstream only in the past decade or two, fuelled partly by anxiety over the potential dangers of genetically modified foods and pesticide residues in the soil and rivers. Yet Britain's primary charity devoted to organic horticulture has been patiently championing the cause for more than half a century.

Garden Organic at Ryton Gardens (163)
Wolston, Near Coventry,
Warwickshire CV8 3LG
024 7630 3517
www.gardenorganic.org.uk
Open daily 9am–5pm; the restaurant is open
weekends only, 9am–3pm.

Food-lovers will enjoy surveying the Herb Garden and the Cook's Garden, located next to the garden's restaurant. In one garden you will see bizarre foods like *achocha*, considered to be the 'lost crop of the Incas' and tasting a bit like a cross between a cucumber and a green pepper. Nearby 'heritage' vegetables are grown with colourful names such as Mr Stiff's Bunching Onions and Cherokee Trail of Tears climbing beans. Another area is devoted to biodynamic gardening which, despite sounding a bit lunatic (literally, since it can involve planting by the phases of the moon), produces many flourishing plants without any Miracle-Gro.

The Vegetable Kingdom is aimed at children. If Hollywood can give cars the Disney treatment, why not vegetables? The interactive displays and cartoon storyboards focus on how people learned to turn wild plants into tame vegetables. Historical events are brought to life, such as the Dig for Victory campaign of World War II and the Irish Potato Famine, where vegetables take a starring role.

Preservation of old strains of plant lie at the core of the charity. Just one letter separates GO from GM but they are mortal enemies. Garden Organic battles to preserve genetic diversity in its Heritage Seed Library, so that archaic strains of food plants and so-called heirloom vegetables won't vanish from the world forever. When European legislation was introduced in the 1970s to regulate seed sales, seed merchants were forced to register each separate variety, at considerable expense. So, they didn't bother with thousands of old varieties such as the Afghan purple carrot, black sugarsweet turnip, colossal leek and lazy housewife's climbing French bean; now it's against the law to sell such seeds. Eight hundred rare varieties are stored in the Heritage Seed Library from which members can choose six a year to propagate for free.

Those who may not feel inspired by displays about composting and companion planting might be tempted by the spacious shop, which carries every conceivable organic product. Surplus fruit and veg harvested from the gardens are sold here or are incorporated into the daily menu of the cheery café. Plants and herbs can be

"Heritage veg have colourful names: Mr Stiff's Bunching Onions and Cherokee Trail of Tears climbing beans."

bought in season, including vegetables grown from heritage seeds. After exploring these gardens, even the most reluctant gardener might decide to have a go.

Special events focus on particular foods. For example the charity's famous Potato Day held every January offers tastings of many potato varieties, plus cookery demonstrations and planting advice. Chefs such as the charity's Vice President Raymond Blanc and high-profile cookery writers such as Sophie Grigson endorse the place and occasionally put on demonstrations here.

Voted Britain's Best Organic Restaurant by the Soil Association in 2007, the Garden Restaurant is open at weekends, serving fully organic meals including fabulous Sunday roasts. Or book ahead for the once-a-month evening where the restaurant opens its doors for a Diner's Club.

Hilltop Farm Shop

Set atop a hill with stunning views of grazing animals and a gently rolling landscape extending to Leamington Spa, Hilltop Farm Shop has successfully turned itself into a one-stop-shop for food-lovers.

The destination café-restaurant on two levels of a converted brick barn lures yummy mummies in school holidays, ladies who lunch (or breakfast) and locals attracted by the prizes that Hilltop has won for 'Best Sunday Lunch' in the *Observer Food Monthly* Awards and 'Best Locally Sourced Dish' in the Warwickshire Food and Drink Awards. On occasional Saturday nights, the café even offers a three-course posh-nosh menu.

In addition to the farm's own beef and lamb, local products range from home-grown asparagus to chocolate brownies baked by Sarah Edwards' Cakery, six miles away. Water buffalo burgers and ice cream made from buffalo milk hail from Napton, where the Alsop family maintains a herd of water buffalo. The pure buffalo milk ice cream (in toffee, coffee and banoffee) has a lighter texture and boasts 50 per cent less cholesterol than ice cream made from cow's milk. After cake and ice cream, choose the seasonal soft sheep's cheese favoured by Rick Stein from Berkswell near Coventry, made for just a few months after the lambing season.

Hilltop Farm Shop 162
Fosse Way, Hunningham, Near Leamington Spa, Warwickshire CV33 9EL
01926 632978
www.hilltopfarmshop.com
Open 9am–6pm Monday–Saturday and 9am–5pm Sunday.

Taste of the Country Deli

Of all the useful training grounds for deli owners, farming must rank highly. Jim and Helen Cherry started out as farmers selling their meat the hard way, at farmers' markets. They decided they liked selling food even more than producing it and opened a shop in the South Warwickshire village of Long Compton. Four years later they started another more ambitious deli less than six miles away in the village of Shipston-on-Stour, a Cotswold village as pretty and prosperous as any other.

The deli is modelled on a farmers' market, meaning that the vast majority of stock has travelled no more than a few miles – from Matthews Cotswold Crunch flour to Spot Loggins ice cream. Jim can tell you who makes any particular product; for example, most of the bread is supplied by a French couple (Patrick and Patricia Valentin) baking less than three miles from Shipston. As you read the product labels, you get the impression that many of these lines have grown out of tiny home-kitchen enterprises.

The full-service in-house kitchen produces about half of what the deli sells, from sublime lime cheesecake to the more mundane but delicious oatcakes and cheese straws. Tracy the baker also does a marvellous line in gingerbread men: while the road outside was dug up for a long time, she created a wonderful tableau of lazy British workmen.

Taste of the Country, Shipston 160
2–4 Market Place, Shipston-on-Stour, Warwickshire CV36 4AG
01608 665064
www.tasteofthecountry.co.uk
Open 9am–6pm Monday–Friday, 9am–5pm Saturday and 10am–4pm Sunday (Easter–Christmas).

Henley Ice Cream Parlour

The much-loved half-timbered ice cream shop on Henley-in-Arden's architecturally rich high street refrains from parading its heritage credentials. Mercifully there is no plaque claiming that 'Shakespeare Ate Ice Cream Here'. The grannies with their pre-school charges, the children in school uniform and even the droves of summer tourists at the outside tables do not come because of the 16th-century low-beamed ceiling or the long and colourful history of the dairy on this site. They come, summer and winter, for an old-fashioned smooth-textured treat.

Henley Ice Cream Parlour & Tea Rooms 159
152 High Street, Henley-in-Arden,
Warwickshire B95 5BS
01564 795172
www.henleyicecream.co.uk
Open daily till 6pm or 7pm in summer, 4pm or
5.30pm in winter.

Henley ice cream used to be made behind the shop but now it is manufactured on farms in Staffordshire and Worcestershire. All the traditional flavours feature (vanilla, rum and raisin, and mint choc chip) among the 20 or more on offer, with a few experimental ones such as kirsch cherry or lime and ginger.

No better testimonial to the superiority of the ice cream is needed than the hand-printed letters displayed on the wall from a class of junior school children from Birmingham. Hassan Iqbal enthuses: 'Dear all the ladies of the Ice Cream Shop, It was delicious, lovely and tastey, It was biggiest ice cream I ever had'. High praise indeed.

Church End Brewery

Stewart Ellis, owner and chief brewer at Church End Brewery, is a self-confessed beer snob. No macro lagers are served in this tucked-away north Warwickshire village. Hard-working brewery equipment can be seen through a glass wall producing dozens of real ales, from dark roasted porter to a pale ale made with honey named Pooh Beer.

Church End Brewery 161
109 Ridge Lane, Near Nuneaton,
Warwickshire CV10 0RD
01827 713080
www.churchendbrewery.co.uk
Open 6–11pm Thursday, 12–11pm Friday–
Saturday and 12–10.30pm Sunday.

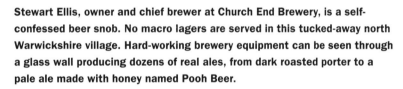

The friendly folk serving in the Tap Room and the Vestry bars will willingly give you a taste of whatever is on tap, just like in an old-fashioned cheese shop where slivers of cheese can be sampled before selecting. Another option is to order the 'coffin', the publican's answer to a tasting menu. Named for the coffin-making factory where the brewery started in 1994, the coffin looks more like a wooden muffin tray and holds eight glasses of beer, each a third of a pint, all for £8.50.

Defying current trends, Church End concentrates on beer not food. But when customers do get peckish, they can tuck into some Fowlers of Warwickshire Sage Derby, a truckle of oak-smoked Cheddar or proper pork pies supplied by a local butcher. A spacious garden overlooks the Warwickshire countryside, which can be explored on foot using a free map of local walks produced by one of the brewery's regulars.

Ludlow Food Festival

This gloriously historic market town (population 10,500, with 500 listed buildings) was declared 'the most perfect town in England' by John Betjeman and that was before it became an unrivalled centre of gastronomy. Ludlow's unspoiled hinterland is thick with farms and rural enterprises producing free-range eggs, honey, damsons, exotic mushrooms, Barbary ducks, charcuterie, goat's cheese and so on. One game dealer even markets squirrel.

Ludlow Marches Food & Drink Festival 152
Ludlow Castle, Castle Square,
Ludlow, Shropshire SY8 1AY
01584 873957
www.foodfestival.co.uk
Held Friday–Sunday on the
second weekend of September.

The mark of a superlative food culture is how many butchers and bakers there are, and how easy it is to obtain locally traceable beef and eggs. So, the Ludlow Food Festival has grown naturally out of the town's longstanding love affair with seriously good food and with the 'slow food' movement. The mid-September festival creates a huge buzz in the town and makes wonderful use of the grounds of medieval Ludlow Castle. Marquees and stalls take over the Inner and Outer Baileys, and café tables are set up in the now-grassy moat.

Food producers and gastro-pioneers of all descriptions thrust miniature pots of ice cream with fruit sauces at you, offer you sips of cider or slivers of farmhouse Cheddar, even kernels of sweetcorn. Some stalls are peddling recherché products (smoked seeds, elderflower vodka) while others offer unreconstructed traditional fare such as lemon drizzle cake and fresh raspberries available from Country Markets (the re-branded WI markets).

Free cookery demonstrations, talks and debates take place on three stages throughout the weekend. Specialist workshops, for example to see a Michelin chef demonstrating six ways to cook mutton, can also be joined for a fee.

The castle grounds are not large enough to contain the festival, which in 2009 attracted twice as many visitors as there are Ludlow residents. Satellite events include pudding tastings (four for £2) in the Methodist Church and several festival trails to sample and rank sausages from the town's four butchers, loaves from three bakers and beer from a dozen pubs and one brewery. So popular are these tasting trails around the town that cries of 'Blimey' and 'My word' are frequently heard when an unsuspecting participant bowls up with a sausage trail card (£3.50) and sees the length of the queues lining up to taste a sausage. Adjudicating among sausages is as impossible as judging the Leeds Piano Competition – they're all bloody good.

Despite the crowds, the festival atmosphere remains chilled. Jazz saxophonists, clarinet and guitar duos and Welsh brass bands entertain around the town. Local shops show off their home-grown ingenuity in a window-dressing competition. Apparently really nice people, most of them volunteers, run the festival, at least according to the mother of one of the stall-holders serving crèpes and coffee. Unlike some high-profile food festivals, this one is child-friendly with a circus skills area in the gardens. There is even an RSPCA-run dog crèche.

Ludlow Food Centre

The Ludlow Food Centre feels almost utopian in its vision of what food shopping should be. Located within an ancient 8,000-acre estate, this clean and spacious food emporium stocks nothing but the finest produce. Around the edges of the food hall, behind plate-glass windows, experts are at work making cheese and butter, roasting coffee, preparing cuts of meat, and producing a vast array of wonders from chutneys to chocolate brownies.

Ludlow Food Centre 153
Bromfield, Near Ludlow, Shropshire SY8 2JR
01584 856000
www.ludlowfoodcentre.co.uk
Open daily 9am–5.30pm Monday–Saturday
and 10.30am–4.30pm Sunday.

The atmosphere in the Centre is contemporary and progressive. The food production areas have state-of-the-art equipment, all clean and glistening, and the utilitarian building has all the latest environmental features. Just outside the dairy window, a powerpoint presentation runs on a laptop about some of the onsite food-making processes, such as churning and hand-salting butter.

The people who work at Ludlow Food Centre – 80 in all – give the impression of enjoying their jobs to the full, and not being mere cogs in a machine. They have names: Dudley is the cheese supremo, Viv makes the pure fruit ice cream, John just won the overall title of best regional butcher at a meat expo and Sandy is the MD who personally responds to comments on the website TripAdvisor.

The knowledgeable staff are more than happy to engage in conversation about what they are selling, just as you would expect to find at a farmers' market. There is not a whiff of mass-production; for example, some of the carrot cakes sold in the vast bakery section are decorated with little icing carrots, whereas others sit beneath a generous scattering of chopped walnuts. Perhaps this is the modern equivalent of medieval masons putting their discreet stamp on church carvings.

The range of produce is astonishing, vast and – unfortunately for anyone on an economy drive – irresistible. Certain items are exclusively available from the delicatessen counter. Take the cheeses for example: the resident cheesemaker, Dudley Martin, has been given carte blanche to experiment and produces seven different cheeses (including soft, hard, Cheddar and blue), but you have to be lucky to find them all available. When cheeses are hand-made in small batches and left to mature over months, demand often outstrips supply. Shropshire Blue is a nationally recognised cheese, and yet has nothing to do with Shropshire, having been first made in Scotland in the 1970s by a cheesemaker from Nottinghamshire. Unfazed, the Ludlow Food Centre dairy now makes a deliciously creamy Ludlow Blue, the only Shropshire Blue made in the county.

Something that probably did originate locally is Shropshire fidget pie, which is a staple at the deli counter but not widely made even by other specialist pie-makers in the region. Fidget pie is made from chunky gammon, apple and cheese with mashed potato mixed with mustard piped on top, so as to look almost like a cupcake. It's a unique foodie treat, and too good to miss.

At the adjacent Conservatory Barn Café you'll see the same attention to detail, extending to heating the milk to just the right temperature whenever a white coffee is ordered. Naturally the cheeseburgers are made from home-reared beef topped with a slab of Dudley's Oakly Park Cheddar served in a bun from the bakery. And a welcome throwback to a more golden age is the working post office next door.

After a surfeit of delightful things, you might be tempted further by the five-mile circular walk past Priors Halton farm (where the organic meat is produced) through the valley of the River Teme into lovely Ludlow itself.

The MD's ambition to 'create an experience rather than just somewhere you pop in for the grocery shop' has borne fruit. After a shopping spree here, a supermarket shop will be very hard to bear.

Essington Fruit Farm

You do not expect to find a 50-acre farm on the outskirts of Wolverhampton, almost within earshot of the M6, but here it is and, what's more, it's good enough to have been in the national finals for Best Farm Shop, Farm Tearoom, PYO and Farm Butchery.

The posted list of fruits and vegetables at harvest time is impressively long: from beetroot to blueberries, cabbages to currants, leeks to loganberries, sugar peas to shallots and an unsurpassable variety of strawberries; though, of course, they're not all ready at the same time. A blackboard indicates which crops are in such plentiful supply that they are being offered at a discount.

If you don't have time to locate the autumn raspberries behind the runner beans, you can buy them in the appealing farm shop that also carries home-baked cakes from the Essington kitchen, home-butchered meat, local honey and so on.

As you pay for your virtuous punnet of plums, cinnamon-scented smells may drift from the nearby warming oven, making it impossible to resist adding a slice of bread pudding to your already laden basket.

Essington Fruit Farm 156
Bognop Road, Essington,
Wolverhampton, West Midlands WV11 2BA
01902 735724
www.essingtonfarm.co.uk
Open daily 9am–8pm in summer; 9am–5pm
Tuesday–Saturday and 10am–5pm Sunday
for the rest of the year.

Wroxeter Roman Vineyard

Wroxeter Vineyard is a neighbour of Viroconium, the fourth largest city in Roman Britain. Today all that remains are the spectacular second-century baths, from which the neat rows of grape vines are visible on the nearby slope. Evidence of vine-growing in Roman times has been found here, so the vineyard follows in venerable footsteps.

Vineyard tours must be pre-booked but anyone is welcome to drop by and stroll around or use the picnic tables alongside the vineyard. The labels at the end of each row evidence that German grape types are favoured here, while tastings in the shop reveal that the Regner Shropshire Dry is a most acceptable drop, though it's the rosés that win more prizes. Bravely, Wroxeter also makes red wines and is the most northerly vineyard to do so.

The Millington family who created the vineyard work tirelessly, though they must feel quite worn out after labelling by hand 20,000 or so bottles every year. Future plans include a glassed-in café, not to mention making their own olive oil. Visit the grove of olive trees brought from Italy in 2007; you may find it hard to believe but these spindly plants should start to fruit in 2012.

Wroxeter Roman Vineyard 155
Wroxeter, Near Shrewsbury,
Shropshire SY5 6PQ
01743 761888
www.wroxetervineyard.co.uk
Open 9am–5pm Monday–Saturday and
10.30am–4.30pm Sunday.

Fordhall Community Farm

From one point of view Fordhall Farm is just an organic farm with a small farm shop and a unisex compost toilet. From another, its story contains all the elements of a gripping drama – youth and old age, love and death, and heroes triumphing against the odds.

The late father of the young brother and sister who now manage the farm was a true English eccentric – an early practitioner of organic farming, inventor, live yogurt entrepreneur, chef and raconteur. Arthur Hollins (1915–2005) spent decades tirelessly building up the farm that he took on at the age of 14.

Just before he died, a letter came from a remote landlord giving him notice to quit. His two children Ben and Charlotte, still in their 20s, mustered a terrific campaign to save the farm, by persuading 8,000 people to buy shares for £50. And thus was born The Fordhall Land Initiative, now dedicated to connecting people, especially children, with their natural environment and the sources of their food.

The farm's shop occupies a converted milking shed. Both this and its online cousin stock Fordhall's farm-reared beef, lamb and pork.

Fordhall Farm 156
Tern Hill Road, Market Drayton,
Shropshire TF9 3PS
01630 638696
www.fordhallfarm.com
Open 11am–4pm Wednesday, Saturday and Sunday; 11am–6pm Friday.

Staffordshire Oatcakes

Famed throughout the county, but sadly not the country, Staffordshire oatcakes are prized as a speciality and a treat by locals. The chapatti-like oatcake has nothing in common with the Scottish hardtack variety, and Staffordshire natives insist theirs has more flavour than Indian chapattis made from wheat flour, Mexican maize tortillas, Sri Lankan rice-flour dosa or French buckwheat galettes.

Dozens of neighbourhood bakers in the Potteries centred on Stoke-on-Trent still griddle-bake oatcakes made from a batter of oatmeal, flour, yeast, sugar, salt, milk and water. When eaten hot and filled with cheese, bacon or sausage, they are quintessential comfort food and cost less than half the price of a supermarket sandwich. Or buy them by the half-dozen for home-freezing and reheating.

You can track down one of about 40 remaining oatcake emporia in Hanley, Burslem and other residential areas of Stoke-on-Trent and Newcastle-under-Lyme. One of the most authentic places, though, is the end-of-terrace Hole-in-the-Wall, which narrowly escaped demolition in 2008 as part of an urban renewal scheme and whose future remains uncertain. So, don't delay in sampling their superlative fresh oatcakes cooked in full view and served through a window to the waiting crowd on the pavement outside.

The Hole in the Wall 157
62 Waterloo Street, Hanley, Stoke-on-Trent,
Staffordshire ST1 3PW
01782 261883
www.oatcakes.org
Open, like many oatcake shops,
6am–12.30pm Thursday and Friday,
6am–1pm Saturday and 6am–12pm Sunday.

Another place to try Staffordshire oatcakes is:
www.hollybushinn.co.uk

Battlefield 1403

The foodie credentials of this new visitor attraction just north of Shrewsbury may not be obvious from its name. The bloody Battle of Shrewsbury was fought in 1403 on the surrounding fields. So when coming to choose a name for their new farm shop venture in 2008, in once derelict farm buildings, on the land they had farmed for six generations, the Jagger family thought it an obvious choice. According to history, and to Shakespeare, it was here that Henry IV turned Henry Hotspur (a rebel nobleman) into 'food for worms'.

Food for people is the focus now. And no expense has been spared in the design and execution of the centre three miles north of Shrewsbury, consisting of farm shop, café and museum. This textbook case of rural regeneration is a good example of the new breed of smart, well-lit farm shops that take design seriously and provide aesthetic as well as gastronomic satisfaction. One end of the shop consists of a picture window framing a lovely view of the countryside. The style of text stencilled on the walls wouldn't look out of place in the Tate Modern, yet you are in the middle of a Shropshire field.

The onsite butchers and pie-makers create a mouth-watering display, with beef roulades in pastry a speciality and superb original pies, for example chicken, pear, Stilton and walnut. Only the peacocks, larded capons and almond milk soup on which King Henry indulged at feasts are lacking.

Little evidence remains that Sparrow's Café, now spilling out on to the stylish courtyard, once consisted of cattle cubicles, though it is possible to see that the mezzanine level was originally a hayloft. Having spotted at the deli counter next door what most appeals – perhaps chicken liver and brandy parfait sprinkled with green peppercorns – you might be lucky enough to find it on the café menu, served with toasted granary bread and red pepper chutney, for less than a fiver.

The other strand of Battlefield 1403's appeal to visitors is the historical display, imaginatively set out in a long, low farm building, renovated thanks to a Redundant Building Grant. A suit of armour includes an ungainly pig-faced visor, which you can imagine Hotspur lifting to get some air and, in that fatal moment, receiving an arrow in the mouth. Other cases display less-bloodthirsty artefacts such as a ladle for pottage and a medieval hunting horn. Cartoon panels of historical goings-on keep the children entertained.

From the south-west corner of the site, a short signposted footpath leads alongside a couple of fields to the isolated church of St Mary Magdalene. Built in 1406 as a memorial to the estimated 1,600 men who fell on the surrounding battlefield, it is atmospheric despite having been heavily 'Victorianised'. You can borrow a key from the farm shop if there is no volunteer from the Churches Conservation Trust on hand and step inside to see for yourself.

Battlefield 1403 **154**
Upper Battlefield, Near Shrewsbury,
Shropshire SY4 3DB
01939 210905
www.battlefield1403.com
Open 9.30am–5.30pm Monday–Saturday
and 10am–4pm Sunday.

North England

Edinburgh

285

North sea

287
286
288

289
290

Carlisle

283
282
284 Newcastle-upon-Tyne

281

250
251
249
253
254
252 Keswick
256
255
248
260
257
247
258 259
246 245
244
243
265
262 263
261 264
Staveley

Barnard Castle

270
271
273
272 274
269 Ripon

240-241 242
239
236
237 235
238 234
233

232

rish sea

275
277
276

280
279

Leeds
278

215
213 214
216

217

212
Manchester

227
228

225
218 219 226 224 229 231
221 223 230
220 222
Bakewell

211
210

208

209

Stichelton Cheese

Since it was first made in 2006, Stichelton has been big news in the world of blue cheese. Derbyshire, Nottinghamshire and Leicestershire are the traditional, protected home of Stilton – the majestic blue that is, sadly, no longer made with raw, unpasteurised milk. But just north of Sherwood Forest, on an organic farm on the historic and extensive Welbeck estate, American-born cheesemaker Joe Schneider produces a raw-milk version – Stichelton, which has won the hearts and tastebuds of many a cheese fiend.

Stichelton
www.stichelton.co.uk

Buttery, rich and thoroughly veined, with a long finish with nary a trace of bitterness, Stichelton is a premium product named after the ancient word for Stilton. It's more likely to be prized by the customers of Borough Market (see page 70) and Neal's Yard Dairy (see page 68) than to be found in Peaks supermarkets, but a salty, creamy Stichelton fix is an excellent reason for a visit to the Welbeck Farm Shop, which also sells meat, game and bread produced on the estate.

The Welbeck Farm Shop **231**
Welbeck, Worksop,
Nottinghamshire S80 3LW
01909 478725
www.thewelbeckfarmshop.co.uk

While you're there take in the Harley Gallery, which celebrates the best of British craft, the Dukeries garden centre and the fledgling School of Artisan Food, which will soon offer a degree course in artisan food production as well as shorter courses, and you've made a day of it.

Coghlans Cookery School

Janet and Andrew Coghlan have been in the hospitality industry all of their working lives, and their cookery school, near Chesterfield, hints at this shared five-star background.

Coghlans moved to specially designed premises in 2005, and in these sleek, capacious and modern surroundings, Head of School Janet supervises courses in everything from lads-and-dads dinners (demos with a cold beer and lots of chilli) to hands-on eight-week courses that move from soups and bread to grand chocolate centrepieces. New enterprises include a foraging course with Miles Irving, author of *The Forager Handbook*.

Coghlans Cookery School **229**
Unit 5b Broom Business Park,
Bridge Way, Sheepbridge, Chesterfield,
Derbyshire S41 9QG
01246 453131
www.cookingexpert.co.uk

The aim is to inspire confidence and foster skill; and the school's doors are also opened to disadvantaged local youngsters or keen young sportspeople who need to acquire kitchen skills and a grasp of home cooking and healthy eating. Lessons are given in what amounts to a dream domestic kitchen, accessorised with snazzy equipment from Rangemaster, Le Creuset and cutlers Richardson Sheffield.

Once you've finished peppering your tutor with questions (you'll have chances aplenty as the staff-to-student ratio is impressively high), be sure to have a good look around: there are 200,000 bottles of wine onsite, as well as a cook shop, chocolate shop and free mini-demos, which pop up when you least expect them.

Chatsworth Farm Shop

Lesser farm shops quake at the prospect of Chatsworth's tasteful, efficient and strikingly large operation. Founded by the Dowager Duchess of Devonshire – the youngest of the Mitford sisters – in 1977, Chatsworth Farm Shop has always been ahead of its time. Manager Andre Birkett has been instrumental in making sure the shop, a few miles from the house on the Chatsworth estate, stays that way.

The sourcing policy at Chatsworth is admirably local: when finding products, Andre and his team look first to the estate, then the tenant farmers, followed by Derbyshire producers and then small-scale British ones.

The busy onsite bakery, cheese counter and new fishmonger all have their regulars but, not surprisingly given the quality of the local meat, the fully fledged butchery counter remains the big draw. Any important festive orders – perhaps a turkey or one of the well-loved hams – are best made early. While the rest of the Peaks shiver under winter skies, the run-up to Christmas is one of the busiest and jolliest times to visit the shop and the huge, heated Christmas marquee put up to accommodate extra visitors. Throughout the year, events, fairs and dinners in the onsite restaurant keep things lively – and the Dowager Duchess still does occasionally step behind the counter to serve her customers.

Chatsworth Farm Shop ②
Pilsley, Bakewell, Derbyshire DE45 1UF
01246 583392
www.chatsworth.org

Derbyshire Oatcakes

Peter Oldfield has been making Derbyshire oatcakes since he was 11, and produces thousands every week at his bakery in the village of Calver. With a note of resignation in his voice, he acknowledges that not everyone knows what a Derbyshire oatcake is any more. But those who do also know that these flat, round oaty griddle cakes are an integral part of a Derbyshire breakfast and, toasted, a fine carriage for melted cheese, jam, a fried egg or a baked filling of chilli-spiked beans.

Made with oatmeal flour, sugar, salt and yeast, fermented for four hours and then cooked on a searing hotplate until they're as bubbly as a crumpet, Derbyshire oatcakes are thicker than their better-known Staffordshire cousins and don't contain the bicarbonate of soda that often crops up over the border. They're sold by the dozen in local bakers' shops, bagged up in unassuming plastic and often tucked quietly away behind the fancy cakes and crackle-topped loaves, but worth seeking out as one of the region's last truly distinctive foods.

Asked about his favourite way to prepare a Derbyshire oatcake, Peter nominates his father's method: fry the oatcake, fry an egg, fold one inside the other and eat with a sprinkling of salt. Without the egg, the salt, and the frying, they are a virtuous and nutritious food. It's your call.

On sale across the Peak District, including:
Chatsworth Farm Shop (see above),
Ibbotson's of Ashford (see page 168) and
Bloomers Original Bakewell Puddings
(see page 164).

Authentic Bakewell Pudding

As its name might suggest, Bakewell is a town where the bakers' ovens are put to continual good use. But they're not crowded with what many visitors expect. The Bakewell tart, an almost-dainty thing composed of shortcrust pastry, jam, almond frangipane, thick icing and a glacé cherry, is what you get in packets at the supermarket. It is not what you get – at least if you've any sense – from bakers in Bakewell.

This bustling town at the heart of the Peaks has something stodgier, and altogether more delicious, as its best-loved taste. The Bakewell pudding is a low-rise, circular affair – a puff-pastry shell, strawberry jam and an egg-and-almond topping with a secret ingredient that gives it a rich, sturdy texture; most people guess at apple, but they're wrong. The puddings are sold in three sizes to take away from bakeries across the town, and tourists can be seen grappling with their paper bags of crumbly stickiness on every corner. For those with more decorum, The Old Original Bakewell Pudding Shop, which shares the secret 'original' recipe with Bloomers bakery, does a roaring trade in its restaurant, serving fresh-from-the-oven puddings with custard or wonderfully cold cream.

There's barely a tea towel or postcard in Bakewell that doesn't relate the story of the pudding, created by accident in the 19th century. The accepted version has Mrs Ann Greaves, wife of the innkeeper of the Rutland Arms Hotel (which is still going strong), instructing a flustered cook to produce a jam tart for some important guests. The cook singularly failed in her task, but since the confusion resulted in a delicious alternative pudding, she was forgiven. The pudding has, apparently, been made in the town ever since, and its dense almond flavour and buttery pastry has certainly become something that ex-Bakewell dwellers hanker after. Several makers in the town now post their puddings to far-flung locations, with customers in Germany particularly keen to get their hands on them.

For our money, the best pudding in town is to be found at the Old Original Bakewell Pudding Shop, and its owner Jemma Pheasey is at the forefront of an effort to have the puddings recognised by the EU alongside Cornish clotted cream, Welsh lamb and Melton Mowbray pork pies. If Bakewell puddings were awarded a PGI (Protected Geographical Indication), only products made from an agreed recipe and in the Bakewell area would be able to carry the proud name of Bakewell pudding. The process is admirable, but it can be contentious and extremely time-consuming; it took Melton Mowbray (see page 142) a decade to get their accreditation. If only Ann Greaves and her cook knew what a fuss their harried afternoon of baking would still be causing all these years on.

The Old Original Bakewell Pudding Shop 222
The Square, Bakewell, Derbyshire DE45 1BT
01629 812193
www.bakewellpuddingshop.co.uk

Bakewell Pudding Parlour 223
Wye House, Water Street, Bakewell,
Derbyshire DE45 1EW
01629 815107
www.postapudding.com

Bakewell Tart 224
Matlock Street, Bakewell,
Derbyshire DE45 1EE
01629 814692
www.bakewelltartshop.co.uk

Bloomers Original Bakewell Puddings 225
Granby Cottage, Water Lane, Bakewell,
Derbyshire DE45 1EU
01629 814844

Thornbridge Brewery

Thornbridge Brewery is a huge success story that started with a bloke who wanted to brew some beer in his back garden. Granted, that man is Jim Harrison and his back garden is part of the estate at his home, a Jacobean manor house called Thornbridge Hall, near Ashford-in-the-Water.

Alex Buchanan of Thornbridge Brewery takes up the story. 'Jim had always liked his beer and dabbled in home brew when he was a kid. The brewery was established in the grounds of Thornbridge Hall, using second-hand equipment, and we were very fortunate that we employed two young brewers who had fantastic ability and great passion for brewing good beers.'

2005 was a year of firsts. Jaipur IPA, which remains Thornbridge's best-selling beer and is a favourite of Oz Clarke, won the brewery's first award at the first beer festival it entered. The awards now tally around the 100 mark; it seems that the house policy of allowing brewers to travel, research and expand their experience pays off in fine beers and coveted prizes.

It's an international team with five brewers, Alex explains. 'We have an Italian (head brewer Stefano Cossi), a Kiwi, a bloke who was born in Staffordshire but grew up in New Zealand, a guy from Leeds and a guy from Norfolk. It sounds like the start of a joke! It's a bizarrely large number of brewers for a firm our size, but one of the reasons is that they go off to universities in Sardinia to look at yeast, or go and judge in competitions. Brewing is fantastic, but you stand still if you spend all your time doing it.'

This sense of adventure has led to more local collaborations, too, with a light beer inspired by Castleton chocolatiers Cocoadance (see page 169) and a summer beer laced with elderflowers from the verdant Thornbridge Hall estate. Experimentation with wood-aged beers, which spend time in old whisky or sherry casks, and harvest ales using green, just-picked hops show just how creative Cossi's team can be. The brewery's location has an impact, too. 'When Jaipur started to do well, someone suggested we reduce its strength,' Alex says. 'At 5.9% ABV it's quite a hefty beer, but that's what it should be. We haven't changed it, but we've got to have lower-strength beers like Wild Swan, which is 3.5% ABV, because in the Peaks people want to go for a walk and have a beer.'

Success has also led to expansion. The new Riverside Brewery, which required a £2m investment, is a far cry from the Thornbridge site, set up in what was a stonemason's shop. In Bakewell, plans are afoot for a shop, brewery tours and even a line of Thornbridge Brewery T-shirts. Nevertheless, the old and arguably more romantic site will keep going. 'After a little bit of refurbishment, Thornbridge Hall will be used for research and development, and Stefano will be happy there because he loves to experiment and try things,' says Alex. 'We've always been brewery-led, it's been very successful and we would never want to stifle that.'

Thornbridge Brewery 226
Thornbridge Hall, Ashford-in-the-Water, Derbyshire DE45 1NZ
01629 641000
www.thornbridgebrewery.co.uk

Thornbridge Riverside Brewery
Buxton Road, Bakewell, Derbyshire DE45 1GS

Thornbridge Brewery beers are available across the Peak District, including:

Rowley's 230
Church Lane, Baslow, Derbyshire DE45 1RY
01246 583880
www.rowleysrestaurant.co.uk

Ibbotson's of Ashford

Ken and Kathryn Ibbotson haven't even been running their exemplary village deli for a decade, but already Ashford-in-the-Water, just up the road from Bakewell, wouldn't be the same without them. At a time when many local shops are sadly under threat, Ibbotson's succeeds with a unique combination of the prosaic and the foodie. Run out of loo paper? No problem. Looking for baby artichoke hearts, American marshmallow 'fluff', smoked chillies, tinned anchovies? That's no problem either. City-dwellers holidaying at the campsite over the hill, excitedly buying provisions considerably more exotic than they expected, wonder why their urban corner shop can only manage brown sauce and Special Brew.

Ibbotson's of Ashford 220
1 Church Street, Ashford-in-the-Water,
Derbyshire DE45 1QB
01629 812528
www.homemadepickles.co.uk

Papers, cards, fruit, vegetables, even flowers and freshly brewed coffee are Ibbotson's stock-in-trade, but they also have an award-winning sideline: pickles. Ken's own crisp, hot pickled onions are legendary, perhaps bought to be served on the side with a meat pie from Bakewell, one of Ibbotson's hot pork sandwiches or a slab of veggie pâté. To follow, home-made cakes include a gooey caramel slice and chewy Florentines.

There's been a shop on this site for generations – in fact, the great-grandson of a former shopkeeper currently does the Ibbotson's paper round – but it may only be now that the shop on Church Street has really come into its own.

Great Peak District Fair

Held annually since 2002 in Buxton's elegant Pavilion Gardens, the Great Peak District Fair is chief among the crowd-pulling events that give visitors their much-relished taste of the Peaks. Over one weekend every October, around 12,000 visitors mill about in splendid Victorian surroundings, and while they might stop at a craft stall or admire the work of a local painter, the universally acknowledged purpose of a visit is to stock up on local produce, and perhaps snaffle a few samples on the way round.

The Great Peak District Fair 219
The Pavilion Gardens, St John's Road,
Buxton, Derbyshire SK17 6XN
01298 23114
www.paviliongardens.co.uk
Held every October.

Admission to the fair is free, and the atmosphere is as far from the slick corporate nature of the big food shows as it's possible to be. The exhibitors vary from year to year, but the air is always gently fragranced with conflicting aromas; perhaps the rich smell of smoked fish and pâté from the Derbyshire Smokery, sizzling water buffalo steaks from the unlikely but thriving herd reared by Richard Gill and his family near Chesterfield, or bread and cakes, made with locally milled flour, from the St Clements Bakery not far away.

Recognisable faces include the Castleton chocolatiers Cocoadance (see opposite), butcher John Mettrick (see page 172) and the Marsdens of Hope Valley Ice Cream (see opposite); if you can't visit each of them individually, the Great Peak District Fair offers a rare chance to catch these local characters all together.

Hope Valley Ice Cream

Hope Valley Ice Cream 🔵
Thorpe Farm, Hathersage,
Hope Valley, Derbyshire S32 1BQ
01433 650659
www.hope-valley.co.uk

The Marsden family offer their customers a 'taste of Hope' at their dairy farm near Hathersage. Armed with a gelato machine and a sense of adventure, the Marsdens, whose family has been farming in this beautiful valley for 300 years, began making ice cream with the milk from their dairy cows in 2007.

Although the ice cream is sold at farm shops across the Peaks, it's much more enjoyable when you've had to work up an appetite for it. Consequently, walkers make a beeline for Thorpe Farm's tiny ice cream parlour, across the yard from the milking shed, and perch on the stone wall outside to enjoy apple sorbet made from the farm's own fruit or perhaps Camilla's Vanilla, Maisy's Mint Choc Chip or Rosemary's Raspberry Pavlova. Who are these ladies? The cows, of course. Each Italian-style ice (made with eggs, milk and a little cream, and boasting a lower butterfat content than the overwhelming American-style stuff) is named after one of the farm's Friesians.

The flavour that stands alone, without a cow's moniker, is also the purist's choice – Marsden's Dairy Ice Cream is made without vanilla or other flavouring and tastes simply of the farm's pure, sweet milk; it's definitely worth walking uphill for.

Cocoadance

Cocoadance 🔵
Mam Farm, Castleton, Hope Valley,
Derbyshire S33 8WA
01433 621334
www.cocoadance.com
A chocolate experience lasts over three hours and costs £28 per person.

Self-taught chocolatiers David Golubows and Bridget Joyce have one of the prettiest workshops in the land. They're to be found tempering, dipping and moulding chocolate in a National Trust farmhouse below the majestic Mam Tor, and the view from the Cocoadance window is over the stark but striking High Peak landscape.

Access to this chocolate-scented little world is by appointment only, and visitors come as part of one of the couple's exclusive 'chocolate experiences'. An afternoon is spent learning about the origins of chocolate and the Venezuelan bean-drying shuffle that gives Cocoadance its name, with plenty of chocolates to taste before students start to make their own.

Bridget and David use a vast array of ingredients, including local hedgerow finds and Thornbridge Brewery's beers (see page 166), to create their award-winning chocolates, which are sold in grand department stores as well as local delis and online. At the first attempt to enrobe, roll and dip their chocolates and get to grips with piping bags and dipping forks, visitors may have less lofty ambitions for their own finished products. Thankfully they're able to pick up a little something more professional – rhubarb and nettle truffles, oozy chocolate and chilli 'lips' or just very good chocolate-dipped fudge – before they leave what must be the Peaks' most picturesque chocolate factory.

Leah Stevenson

Leah Stevenson has known since she was a little girl that she was going to do 'something foodie'. For a while, that something was done in London: she trained at Le Cordon Bleu, worked as a food buyer for Harrods and ran a deli for the convivial chef Mark Hix, a family friend. But the allure of the countryside was too strong to resist, and in 2008 she returned to the family farm perched above Macclesfield, on the borders of the Peak District, and launched a cookery school called Leah's Pantry.

Harrop Fold Farm is already a busy, industrious place. Leah's parents run a multi-award-winning B&B and there's a thriving art school based here, too. The outbuildings have gradually been converted by her builder father and one of the barns has become the kind of kitchen foodies dream of: cool granite surfaces, a shiny red range, stunning views over Cheshire and, for the ultimate warm welcome, a Cath Kidston teapot and a huge jar of buttery, home-made jammy dodgers.

Leah gives cookery demonstrations and small, exclusive classes in this glamorous kitchen and lives above it. In a few hours on a sunny Wednesday, our class of five learned how to make and decorate a huge variety of cupcakes, studded with raspberries and white chocolate, blackberries and almonds or zingy lemon zest. After a light lunch, including cauliflower cheese soup and bubbly cheese scones spread with Leah's favourite Shropshire butter, we got to grips with the sugarcraft skills she learned from John Slattery, the master cake-decorator based over the hills in Manchester. The cupcakes were topped with surprisingly elegant sugar roses and dusted with edible glitter or, in the case of the lemon cakes, topped with Leah's home-made lemon curd and a swirl of crisp meringue. None of us knew we had it in us.

'Demo and dine' evenings are another popular way to spend time at Harrop Fold. Four courses, made with seasonal Peak District and Cheshire produce, are interspersed with champagne and demonstrations aimed at demystifying the task of putting a smart dinner together. 'People who don't cook sometimes have a perception that a meal for friends takes ages and it's so difficult,' says Leah, 'but I like showing people how easy it is to impress people with a dinner party. One of my favourite recipes, for example, is slow-cooked lamb with tomatoes, apricots and onions, and things like that aren't hard to achieve.' What is hard to achieve is the relaxed atmosphere and attention to detail that helps Leah's students absorb some of her casual confidence – and all for the price of a modest dinner out.

Leah's Pantry 218
Harrop Fold Farm, Rainow,
Macclesfield, Cheshire SK10 5UU
01625 560085
www.leahspantry.co.uk

JW Mettrick & Son

Reece Shearsmith, Steve Pemberton, Mark Gatiss and Jeremy Dyson have a lot to answer for round Glossop way. Their successful BBC comedy, *The League of Gentlemen*, thrust an unassuming locale into the cult spotlight from 1999 onwards, and three series, a movie and a stage show have ensured that it has stayed there.

JW Mettrick & Son 217
20 High Street, Glossop, Derbyshire
SK13 8BH
86 Station Road, Hadfield, Glossop,
Derbyshire SK13 1AJ
01457 852239
www.mettricksbutchers.co.uk

Royston Vasey, the fictional small town where the League's gents pursued their eccentric interests, is based on Hadfield, near Glossop. Royston Vasey's butcher's shop, H Briss & Son, purveyors of that addictive 'special stuff', is based on Mettrick's Hadfield shop. Along with Royston Vasey's pub and snack bar, it features on the volunteer-run League of Gentlemen tours that still entice the series' fans. But it's good to know that the real Mettrick's sells nothing more sinister than exceptionally good meat.

Mettrick's started life in Hadfield in the late 19th century, as George Woolley's butcher's shop. As the younger men of the family came into the business, the name changed, and it's now led by the devastatingly knowledgeable and passionate John Mettrick. His gentle demeanour is not to be confused with a lack of enthusiasm for the best local meat, and Mettrick's longstanding links to the Derbyshire farming community stand the business in good stead against any competition the big shops can muster. Many suppliers have been sending meat to Mettrick's for more than 20 years; at the last count, the longest-serving supplier was a Mr WH Evans, a 96-year-old farmer on Anglesey, who had been supplying salt marsh grazed beef for an impressive 70 years.

Having brought together sheep farmers from the Peak District according to a strict assessment process, Mettrick's sells their meat as the trademarked High Peak Lamb. 'We've got the High Peak farmers geared up for year-round supply of lamb,' says John, 'so we don't need to supplement it with lamb from New Zealand. In the summer we're drawing the Texel lambs off the lower fields, and in the winter we'll be taking Gritstone lamb that are born on the moors, where they have a long time on the vegetation and therefore a great flavour.'

Grown chefs, including many in Manchester's most prestigious restaurants, weep with delight at the prospect of a delivery of this very special stuff. The quality is due in part to rigorous farming standards, but also to the fact that the lamb is processed at Mettrick's own abattoir in Glossop and so never travels further than 10 miles to get there. The only abattoir of its kind in the county, run by John's brother Steven, the Mettrick's slaughterhouse enables full traceability. 'We can give the customer a whole history of the meat that they're eating, right from the farm to the plate.'

The abattoir is the setting for the BBC's guts-and-all series *Kill It, Cook It, Eat It*, in which meat-eaters and vegetarians alike are asked to consider the realities of

J.W. Mettrick & Son Ltd. - Family Butchers

Locally Produced Meat - completely traceable produce - fr

Chicken BBQ ~ Cooked Meats ~ Confectionery ~ Sandwiches ~ Homemade P
Tel: 01457 852239   Speciality Sausages ~ Quality Fresh Meat

"We can give
the customer
a whole history
of the meat
that they're
eating, right
from the farm
to the plate."

eating meat by witnessing the abattoir process. It also shows off the old-fashioned butchery skills of the Mettrick's staff – and their extremely sharp knives.

Back at the shops, it seems customers' tastes are changing. 'Mutton has seen a bit of a renaissance and we're selling as much Peak District mutton now in a week as we used to in a month,' says John. 'We're dead chuffed about it. It's better for the customers and it helps to keep the balance. A few years back the older animals were worthless, so it's a great change. People are mainly going for diced mutton, for stews and curries, although the odd one is brave enough to do a leg.' If you want to impress JW Mettrick & Son, you've got to buy a leg o' mutton.

Low Sizergh Barn

Serious foodies travelling from the south should swing off the M6 en route to the Lakes and take a break at Low Sizergh Barn – one of Cumbria's flagship farm shops. The shop is housed in an 18th-century Westmorland stone barn and every inch of its quirky food hall is packed with produce from regional suppliers. Take time to browse through its myriad selection of cheeses, vast array of cakes and ample choice of meats from nearby farms. The shop's shelves are stuffed with jars of local jams, relishes and pickles.

And the list doesn't stop there. A highlight of Low Sizergh's stock is its fantastic range of organic vegetables grown onsite through the Growing Well scheme – a project that offers people recovering from mental health issues the chance to regain confidence and learn new skills by working the land. Take time to explore the two-mile-long farm trail on which you'll encounter sheep, chickens and a herd of cows whose fresh milk is transformed into smooth ice cream and organic cheese.

Time your trip to the barn's rustic café to coincide with afternoon milking when you get a bird's eye view through an enormous window of the Low Sizergh herd being milked in the dairy below. Then head downstairs to the barn's old 'shippons' (areas where animals lived during the winter) to browse through a tempting range of Cumbrian crafts from local artists and potters.

If your tastebuds are left wanting more, then head west along the A590 to the Cartmel Peninsula to Holker Hall. This stately home of Lord and Lady Cavendish sits in a tranquil expanse of scenic countryside and is home to one of Cumbria's finest and grandest food halls. The Holker estate has a long history of farming and its produce, which includes cheese, salt marsh lamb and seasonal venison, is for sale alongside other regional fare and top-quality continental foods. Holker is most famous, though, for its salt marsh lamb reared on the swathes of salt marshes that fringe the edges of the Cartmel Peninsula and that are washed daily by the waters of Morecambe Bay.

Further north, on the outskirts of Kendal, lies Plumgarths, where you can buy prime beef, free-range pork and Cumbrian chicken as well as a selection of some of the tastiest beers brewed in the county. Plumgarths also stocks the full range made by Strawberry Bank Liqueurs (see also page 176) – a local company who creates the lip-smackingly good damson gin. And if you can't make it to the shop in person, just order on the phone or online.

Low Sizergh Barn Farm Shop 265
Low Sizergh Farm, Sizergh, Kendal,
Cumbria LA8 8AE
015395 60426
www.lowsizerghbarn.co.uk
Open daily 9am–5.30pm Easter–December;
9am–5pm January–Easter.

Holker Hall 240
Cark-in-Cartmel,
Near Grange-over-Sands, Cumbria LA11 7PL
01539 558328
www.holker.co.uk
Open daily 10.30am–5.30pm (till 4pm out of season). Closed January.

Plumgarths 264
Crook Road, Kendal, Cumbria LA8 8LX
01539 736300
www.plumgarths.co.uk
Open 9am–5pm Monday–Saturday.

KING
OF THE
PIPPINS

Westmorland Damsons

Of all the local produce and fine foods associated with Cumbria, damsons are one of the most unexpected, but also one of the most bountiful. Some claim that these small, tart plums were introduced to England by the Romans, while others credit the Crusaders with bringing them from the region around Damascus in modern-day Syria from where they originate.

Since the early 1700s, damsons have grown prolifically throughout the Lyth and Winster valleys to the south-west of Kendal – one of the most tranquil, gentle and least visited parts of Cumbria. Come in the spring and you're greeted by the wondrous sight of clouds of snow-white damson blossom that explode across these soft fells. There's no better time to pull on walking shoes and explore the network of trails that meander through the valleys, leading ramblers past orchards and hedgerows fit to burst with damson flowers.

If you're serious about getting under the skin of this humble fruit, time your visit to coincide with the region's annual Damson Day hosted every April by Low Farm in the Lyth Valley. The purpose of this fun-filled, family-friendly day is to celebrate the history of damsons along with the range of products made from the fruit; plus, it offers a unique opportunity for any visitor to sample a taste of rural Cumbria. The first Damson Day was held in 1997 and since then it has grown to include traditional Cumbrian crafts, such as stone-walling, exhibitions and entertainment from local fiddlers and wind bands.

Damson Day allows local producers to show off their ample ranges of damson wares, their tables groaning under a vast variety of food and drink – damson jam, relish, cheese, beer and home-made damson crumble. And if eating the samples has you wanting more, then watch one of the demonstrations, where you can pick up the secrets of cooking damsons and even buy a damson cookbook.

The damsons grown in the Lyth and Winster valleys are known as Westmorland damsons and exude a strong flavour, which lends itself perfectly to jam-making. Cartloads of the fruit were once hauled south to large jam manufacturers in Lancashire as well as supplying a nearby village jam factory. However, a shortage of sugar and labour during World War II led to this industry's demise. Today, small local businesses, such as Hawkshead Relish (see page 179) who produce a divine damson and port jam, have revitalised the region's jam-making tradition. While on the southern edge of the Winster Valley in Grange-over-Sands, the award-winning Hazelmere Café and Bakery create a mighty tasty damson conserve.

There are few better places to chill on a summer's evening than on the terrace of the Mason's Arms at Strawberry Bank and breathe in sweeping views of the Winster Valley while supping your chosen tipple. A favourite with locals, this pretty pub is also the birthplace of Strawberry Bank Liqueurs whose luscious damson gin, made with fruit from the valley below, can be found on the shelves of

Damson Day
Held every April at Low Farm, Lyth, Kendal, Cumbria LA8 8DJ
www.lythdamsons.org.uk/damsonday

Hazelmere Café and Bakery
1–2 Yewbarrow Terrace, Grange-over-Sands, Cumbria LA11 6ED
015395 32972
www.hazelmerecafe.co.uk
Bakery open daily except Sunday; café open daily.

The Mason's Arms
Strawberry Bank, Cartmel Fell, Grange-over-Sands, Cumbria LA11 6NW
015395 68486
www.masonsarmsstrawberrybank.co.uk

Strawberry Bank Liqueurs
Wood Yeat Barn, Crossthwaite, Kendal, Cumbria LA8 8HX
015395 68812
www.strawberrybankliqueurs.co.uk

Windermere Ice Cream Company
Lake Road, Bowness-on-Windermere, Cumbria
015394 47876
www.scoopchocice.co.uk
Their ice cream van parks daily 11am–5pm at the National Trust car park at Tarn Hows April–end October.

Westmorland Damson Association
Contact Helen Smith on 015395 68698 to buy frozen damsons.

Home Made
Damson Conserve
Extra special jam,
hand made with
damsons from the
Lyth Valley

Extra ...
hand made ...
damsons from
Lyth Valley

"Time your visit to coincide with the region's annual Damson Day hosted every April."

farm shops and food halls throughout Cumbria. And if you want yet more damson delights, check out the damson sourdough bread at the Staff of Life artisan bakery in Kendal (see page 178) and the exceptional damson ripple ice cream from the Windermere Ice Cream Company.

Each Damson Day concludes with the hope that September will yield a fine crop and anyone visiting during the autumn harvest can expect to see piles of the fruit for sale at roadside stalls and in local stores. And it's good to know that those visiting at any other time can still indulge as frozen damsons are available to buy from the Westmorland Damson Association.

Cartmel Sticky Toffee Pudding

The tiny, ancient and picturesque village of Cartmel on the southern outskirts of the Lake District National Park is famous for three things – a 12th-century priory, the smallest National Hunt racecourse in England and being the home of sticky toffee pudding.

Cartmel's devilishly delicious sticky toffee pudding, endorsed by the likes of Nigella Lawson and Antony Worrall Thompson, is a wondrously rich blend of dates, cane sugar and Cumbrian cream, butter and free-range eggs, all topped with a slathering of fine fudgy sauce.

This outstanding pud is a highlight of any sweet-toothed foodie's visit to the Lakes and features on countless menus and the shelves of most farm shops around the region. Dedicated pudding-lovers must make the pilgrimage to Cartmel's charming village shop – the birthplace of this melt-in-the-mouth dessert and treasure trove of other local fine foods.

Cartmel also produces sticky chocolate, sticky banana and sticky ginger desserts, and no visit to the village is complete without a wander around its centuries-old streets and peaceful priory. Best of all, visit on August bank-holiday weekend to enjoy a day at the races topped off with a helping of what many claim is the best sticky toffee pudding in the world.

Cartmel Village Shop 241
Parkgate House, The Square, Cartmel,
Grange-over-Sands, Cumbria LA11 6QB
015395 36280
www.stickytoffeepudding.co.uk
Open 9am–5pm Monday–Saturday and
10.30am–4.30pm Sunday.

Staff of Life Bakery

Anyone serious about bread and the art of baking it should venture away from Kendal's main shopping centre and head down the narrow lane of Berry's Yard. At the end of this centuries-old lane lies the Staff of Life whose hard-working, wood-fired oven has been baking some of the best bread in Cumbria since 1997. Every loaf produced at the Staff of Life is made with love and care, as owner, artisan baker and 'Local Food Hero' Simon Thomas passionately believes in baking by hand and adapting ingredients and methods to suit each batch.

The Staff of Life's moist, organic and Gold Taste Award-winning wholemeal is the bakery's best-selling loaf; but the more adventurous foodie can choose from sun-dried tomato, garlic and Parmesan or rye and pistachio breads. And cake connoisseurs will delight in the morello cherry brownies and the Staff of Life's acclaimed rich, sticky gingerbread.

For those who love to bake as well as taste, Staff of Life run their own day-long bread-making courses. Suitable for all ages and abilities, these courses are an opportunity to don a baker's apron and knead your own apple and sourdough *boule* or any other bread of choice.

Staff of Life 262
2 Berry's Yard, Kendal, Cumbria LA9 4AB
01539 738606
www.artisanbreadmakers.co.uk
Open 8am–5pm Monday–Saturday.
Courses run 10am–4.30pm on Sunday and
cost £60 per person; booking essential.

Hawkshead Relish

The Hawkshead Relish Company 245
The Square, Hawkshead, Cumbria LA22 0NZ
015394 36614
www.hawksheadrelish.com
Open daily 9.30am–5.30pm in summer and
9.30am–5pm in winter.

The quintessential Lakeland town of Hawkshead is home to Wordsworth's former grammar school and the Beatrix Potter Gallery, where many of the author's original illustrations are on display. But this much-loved Lakeland market town also offers foodies 'a bit on the side'. Standing between the town's two centuries-old market squares is a quaint and quirky shop that encourages everyone to 'embellish with relish'.

The Hawkshead Relish Company is celebrated for its imaginative and unusual array of relishes, pickles and preserves, all of which are made by hand using traditional methods in a restored 16th-century cruck barn a mile south of town.

The company's many accolades include 37 Great Taste Awards and their must-visit Hawkshead shop is fit to burst with jars and bottles filled with the likes of apple and lavender jelly, lemon and cardamom chutney, and cranberry vinegar.

Venture to the back of the store where you'll find a large table scattered with open, spoon-filled jars where you can dollop samples of whatever takes your fancy on to crackers and begin the difficult process of deciding just which of these unique, additive-free, taste sensations to take home.

Grasmere Gingerbread

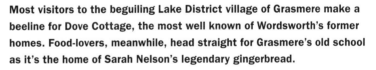

The Grasmere Gingerbread Shop 255
Church Cottage, Grasmere, Ambleside,
Cumbria LA22 9SW
015394 35428
www.grasmeregingerbread.co.uk
Open 9.15am–5.30pm Monday–Saturday
and 12.30–5.30pm Sunday.

Most visitors to the beguiling Lake District village of Grasmere make a beeline for Dove Cottage, the most well known of Wordsworth's former homes. Food-lovers, meanwhile, head straight for Grasmere's old school as it's the home of Sarah Nelson's legendary gingerbread.

After the school was converted into a cottage, in about 1850, Sarah Nelson moved in and began selling her home-baked hearty gingerbread from a tree stump just outside. Fuelled by the traffic of Victorian travellers following in Wordsworth's footsteps, the reputation and popularity of Sarah's spicy half-biscuit half-cake confectionery grew and grew; demand was so great that she later converted her front parlour into a shop.

The secrets of her gingerbread, which is still baked in her old 17th-century cottage, have never been revealed as Sarah's special recipe is stashed in a nearby bank vault. But queues still snake outside her tiny old-fashioned village shop where mop-capped assistants sell what some chefs hail as the best they've ever eaten.

If, after sampling the sticky stuff, you feel you should pay homage to former Grasmere residents, then follow the scent of warm ginger as it wafts from the cottage into the adjacent St Oswald's churchyard, where you'll find the graves of both William Wordsworth and Sarah Nelson.

Staveley Mill Yard

Staveley Mill Yard may not seem like a picture-postcard artisanal set-up, but look past its slightly industrial clutter and you will be surprised to find a clutch of contemporary food outlets. You'll soon be glad you made the effort to explore these old mill buildings on the banks of the River Kent as you tuck into some of the specialities of this home of taste sensations.

In the days when Cumbria was part of Lancashire, this large site was home to Chadwick Mill – one of the county's famous cotton mills. Today the hall that once housed wood-turning lathes has been transformed into Hawkshead Brewery's thoroughly modern beer hall. This much-loved Lake District brewery was established by former BBC foreign correspondent Alex Brodie. Sink into deep sofas while supping some of Hawkshead's fine beers, including the rich and malty porter Brodie's Prime. Tours of the brewery take place on the hour on Saturday afternoons, and massive windows allow visitors in the beer hall a drinker's eye view into the vats below.

If wine is more your tipple, step next door to Organico – the largest organic wine shop in the UK. Organico buys direct from small vineyards around the world but specialises in Italian wine, importing directly from private Tuscan vineyards. The shop's onsite *sommelier* eases the difficult process of choosing from Organico's 250 wines, which include their own-branded Dominico, a Tuscan red named after one of the owner's children. Take your vino of choice upstairs to share in Organico's wine bar while savouring wide views of the surrounding Kentmere Hills.

More? The Artisan Bakery stands next to Organico and obligingly provides the perfect partner to fine wine – fresh bread and, naturally, much more. Here the freshly baked hand-crafted breads include sourdough and rye. More? is also renowned for delicious desserts, and its award-winning muddees – richly moist chocolate brownies topped with a thin crisp crust – are hard to resist.

Lucy Robinson has dedicated the last 20 years to bringing good food to the Lakes and her state-of-the-art cookery school is tucked just behind More?. Her many outlets in Ambleside include a specialist grocer, wine bar and restaurant. Lucy's latest venture, LucyCooks Cookery School, offers a packed programme of full- and half-day cookery courses alongside regular 'Demo and Dine' days. Courses include a Taste of Cumbria, during which local chefs share their secrets of cooking using top-notch regional produce.

If, after a trip around Staveley Mill Yard, your belt is feeling a tad tighter, head out either on foot or by bike (there's a large bike store and cycle hire outfit onsite) into the nearby Kentmere Valley – a glorious, unspoilt pocket of the National Park that most visitors never find.

Staveley Mill Yard
Staveley, Kendal, Cumbria LA8 9LR
01539 821234
www.staveleymillyard.com

Hawkshead Brewery
01539 822644
www.hawksheadbrewery.co.uk
Beer hall open 12–5pm Monday and
Tuesday, 12–6pm Wednesday–Sunday.
Tours at 1pm, 2pm and 3pm on Saturdays.

Organico
01539 822200
www.organi.co.uk
Open daily 10am–6pm.

More? The Artisan Bakery
01539 822297
www.moreartisan.co.uk
Open daily 8am–5pm.

**LucyCooks – the Cookery School
in the Lakes** 261
01539 432288
www.lucycooks.co.uk

Andy and Chrissy Hill

Local food champions Andy and Chrissy Hill claim a family tree whose roots stretch back 700 years into Cumbrian history. Anyone serious about good food and experiencing Lake District hospitality at its best should make a beeline for the Hills' renowned restaurant, the Jumble Room, and their sumptuous B&B, Randy Pike.

The Jumble Room is so popular that visitors often reserve a table before going on to book a room for the night. Realising that people were travelling to eat at the Jumble Room, Andy and Chrissy decided that they would offer visitors their own luxurious, extra-special overnight accommodation, and Randy Pike B&B was born.

No one ever goes hungry at Randy Pike, an old, gentleman's hunting lodge on the outskirts of Ambleside, transformed by Chrissy and Andy into two swish suites, each with its own 'wow' factor. Anyone prone to late-night munchies will delight in Chrissy's boudoir larder tucked away in each suite and filled with fine wine, elderflower pressé, local cheeses and, if you're lucky, a home-made cake. Locally sourced and individually prepared breakfasts are served when you want and either delivered to your room or enjoyed on a private garden terrace overlooking the hills. In the morning, give yourself plenty of time to choose from the sumptuous breakfast menu, which features home-made muffins, *crostini* topped with Hawkshead goat's cheese, a full local breakfast and smoked salmon with scrambled eggs on organic brown toast.

Andy and Chrissy have owned and run the Jumble Room since 1996 and claim it to be not just a restaurant but a state of mind. This intimate, friendly and eclectic establishment displays large oil paintings by local artists and home-made cushions lie scattered around; even the toilet walls are lined with old album covers. The Jumble Room's menu changes every month and features the type of food the Hills love to eat. Organic and locally sourced ingredients are used wherever possible; dishes range from fish and chips with an organic beer batter to warm lobster and fresh salmon terrine wrapped in chive-infused pancakes and served with a champagne and caviar sauce.

Anyone who stays at Randy Pike and also wants to dine at the Jumble Room is offered a complimentary chauffeur service to the restaurant and, unlike many accommodation options in the Lakes, you can stay just one night at any time of the year on any day of the week. Andy and Chrissy believe that if you're only able to spend one night in the Lakes it must be the best possible, and all discerning foodies can rest assured that the Hills will move mountains to ensure your stay is filled with food to remember.

Randy Pike 258
Ambleside, Cumbria LA22 0JP
015394 36088
www.randypike.co.uk

The Jumble Room 256
Langdale Road, Grasmere,
Cumbria LA22 9SU
015394 35188
www.thejumbleroom.co.uk
Open daily (except Tuesdays) 12–3.30pm
and from 6pm until the food runs out.
Booking essential.

Herdwick Sheep

Herdwick sheep are so iconic they have become the Lake District's mascot. Visitors to the region are never far from a branded product featuring a 'Herdy's' cute face. But it's not just for their pretty faces that they're adored; foodies love the unique taste of the meat of this rare breed that is deeply rooted in the landscape it thrives on.

Herdwick are native to the central and western Lake District and this tough breed is hardy enough to survive the region's unforgiving mountain slopes. Herdwick lambs mature slowly on the heather and grasses of these remote fells and as a result their meat has a sweet, slightly gamey flavour that's unlike the taste of any other breed.

Almost all Herdwick herds graze on the Coniston Fells and the prime place to see Herdwick sheep yourself and pick up cuts of its meat is Yew Tree Farm, near Coniston. Once owned by Beatrix Potter, the farm starred as the author's home Hill Top in the film *Miss Potter*. Beatrix herself bred Herdwick sheep and for many years was the president of the breed's association. Miss Potter bequeathed her 15 Lake District farms to the National Trust under the condition that each continued to breed her favourite sheep.

Yew Tree Farm still rears free-range Herdwick on its 600 acres of meadow, pasture and fell. Their meat has been much praised by Hugh Fearnley-Whittingstall, who claims Yew Tree's Herdwick is among the best he has ever eaten. The farm sells its Herdwick lamb, and also its Belted Galloway beef, through its Heritage Meats business: you can buy meat online or directly from the farm, which has changed little since Beatrix Potter's death in 1943.

A visit to Yew Tree Farm is a delight, even for non-meat-eaters. Built in the 17th century, its charming white-washed farmhouse is framed against some of the Lake District's most eye-wateringly beautiful scenery. The adjoining barn features a 'spinning gallery' – a rickety old wooden balcony once used for spinning and working wool. Visitors can tuck into home-made scones the size of the Old Man of Coniston either in the wood-panelled tea rooms, where framed letters to Miss Potter from Wordsworth and Ruskin are on display, or in the farm's gardens, where Herdwick lambs graze. Those wanting to get to grips with the landscape that's been Herdy's home for generations can follow a circular walking trail that takes in Yew Tree Farm and the surrounding Coniston Fells.

Over at Wastwater, in the Wasdale Valley on the western side of the Lake District, you can enjoy Britain's official favourite view while shopping for Herdwick meat at Wasdale Head Hall Farm. This National Trust-owned farm stretches over 2,100 acres at the head of the valley. Here Herdwick graze in the shadow of England's highest peak, Scafell Pike, and cuts of Herdwick lamb and mutton can be purchased directly from the farm or via mail order.

Yew Tree Farm 247
Coniston, Cumbria LA21 8DP
015394 41433
www.yewtree-farm.com
Open daily 11am–4pm Easter–October.
Open 11am–4pm at weekends and in school holidays the rest of the year.

Heritage Meats
015394 41433
www.heritagemeats.co.uk

Wasdale Head Hall Farm 248
Wasdale Head, Seascale,
Cumbria CA20 1EX
019467 26245
www.wasdalefellmeats.co.uk
Open daily 9.30am–6.30pm, but call ahead to be sure.

Yew Tree Farm 253
Rosthwaite, Borrowdale, Keswick,
Cumbria CA12 5XB
017687 77675
www.borrowdaleherdwick.co.uk
The Flock-In tea rooms open 10am–5pm February–October (closed Wednesdays). November closed Tuesdays and Wednesdays.
December open over the Christmas period.

For a range of Herdwick Sheep branded products see:
www.herdy.co.uk

> "Herdwick sheep are hardy enough to survive the region's unforgiving mountain slopes."

Further north near the Honister Pass, a steep and spectacular road that links Buttermere Valley in the west with Borrowdale Valley on the outskirts of Keswick, is another Yew Tree Farm. This one, though, sits on the Borrowdale end of the pass at Rosthwaite near the banks of the River Derwent. The farm's meat is fully traceable from fell to fork and can be bought at the onsite Flock-In tea rooms, or you can arrange for a hamper (containing perhaps a range of cuts, home-made Herdi burgers and Herdwick pasties) to be delivered to your door.

George and Dragon, Clifton

Few establishments have a lower food mileage than the George and Dragon on the southern outskirts of Penrith. This former 18th-century coaching inn, now carefully restored to its rustic glory by local craftsmen, features slate flagstones, stripped wooden tables, archive photos and, in winter, roaring open fires. But what truly sets the George and Dragon apart is the nearby Lowther Estate, which provides much of the produce served in the pub.

The Lowther family have tended the estate under the philosophy of sustainability for over eight centuries and their produce includes high-quality free-range meat as well as seasonal vegetables from their bountiful kitchen gardens.

The George and Dragon's menu changes every month but always includes afternoon cream teas and chef-patron Paul McKinnon's cracking Sunday lunch.

While you're here, why not book a trip into the estate with a local deer stalker or buy a fishing permit and spend the day on the banks of the River Lowther waiting for a brown trout to bite? If you manage to snag a catch, the George and Dragon will even cook it for your dinner.

George and Dragon 260
Clifton, Penrith, Cumbria CA10 2ER
01768 865381
www.georgeanddragonclifton.co.uk
Food served daily 12–2.30pm and
6–9.30pm. Booking advisable at weekends.

Lowther Estate office
01931 712577
Contact for a fishing permit.

The Cottage in the Wood

Whinlatter Forest stretches west from Keswick over a steep pass and is England's only true mountain forest. Food-lovers travel to this dramatic location to feast on stunning views and outstanding cuisine at the Cottage in the Wood. This restaurant with rooms is owned and run by Savoy-trained chef and 'Local Food Hero' Liam Berney who, along with his wife Kath, has created a locally renowned haven of calm and fine dining.

The building, a former 17th-century coaching inn, oozes both simple, traditional charm and luxury. The elegant wooden-floored restaurant boasts tall windows that look out over delicious views of steep tree-shrouded slopes and the distant Skiddaw – the fourth-highest peak in England. A celebrated and regularly changing menu, featuring dishes made from regionally sourced, seasonal produce, such as Galloway beef, Cumbrian ham and west coast crab, perfectly complements the breathtaking scenery.

The Cottage in the Wood 252
Whinlatter Forest, Braithwaite, Near Keswick,
Cumbria CA12 5TW
01768 778409
www.thecottageinthewood.co.uk

For those who choose to stay, a range of deluxe and standard rooms and attic suites await. And the nearby lakes of Bassenthwaite, Derwentwater, Buttermere and Crummock are all begging to be explored after you first fill up on a hearty breakfast of wild forest mushrooms, free-range eggs and sourdough toast.

Quince & Medlar

Cumbrians travel across the county to dine at Quince & Medlar – one of the UK's finest vegetarian restaurants. Housed in a listed building next to Cockermouth's half-ruined castle, Quince & Medlar is owned by Colin and Louise Le Voi who trained at the Michelin-starred Sharrow Bay Hotel on the banks of Ullswater. The couple are part of the 'slow food' movement, which aims to preserve cultural cuisine and counterbalance today's fast-food culture. As such, a meal in their candle-lit oak-panelled dining room is an invitation to relax, enjoy good company and relish superb, meat-free cuisine.

Quince & Medlar 249
13 Castlegate, Cockermouth,
Cumbria CA13 9EU
01900 823579
www.quinceandmedlar.co.uk
Open from 7pm Tuesday–Saturday.
Booking advisable.

Restaurant regulars include many non-vegetarians and all keep coming back for more from the imaginative menu that changes with the seasons. Think fusion of modern British, Mediterranean and cosmopolitan for the cuisine and expect dishes made with local, seasonal and organic produce where possible; a range of organic wines sits alongside. Everything is made on the premises, including the bread and the melt-in-the-mouth chocolates served with coffee.

It's not just the gourmet food that's award winning at Quince & Medlar; the restaurant's toilets receive accolades, too, having twice been recipients of the 'Loo of the Year' award.

Cumbria on a Plate

Few people are as passionate and knowledgeable about Cumbrian food and drink as Annette Gibbons. In 2009 she was awarded an OBE for her services to the food and farming industries in Cumbria. Annette's day-long food safaris around the county transport you directly to the region's producers to discover how food is made and to understand more about the landscape that supports each industry.

Annette Gibbons OBE 250
Cumbria on a Plate, Ostle House, Mawbray,
Maryport, Cumbria CA15 6QS
01900 881356
www.cumbriaonaplate.co.uk
Food safaris cost £120 per person,
which includes all refreshments and a
three-course lunch. Annette will pick up
from anywhere in the county.

No two food safaris are the same, as each is created to suit individual tastes. You can, however, expect to taste food of one type or another all day as Annette drives you in style around a selection of Cumbria's artisan food producers. Each safari typically visits three or four producers, all of which take visitors behind the scenes to reveal how they work and encourage visitors to lend a hand along the way. You could end up making butter, cheese or jam, bottle-feeding lambs in spring or getting close to local deer herds.

Refreshments are supplied throughout the day and lunch is hosted by a regional estate that's rarely open to the public and that creates as much of the three courses from their own produce as possible. By the end of each safari you'll have feasted on authentic Cumbrian flavours and gained an insight into the committed producers who create some of the county's finest foods.

Top Cumbrian Brews

There's no better way to top off a day's walking in the Lakeland fells than sinking a pint of one of Cumbria's world-class real ales. And in this region you'll be spoilt for choice.

The region's largest brewery – Jennings – sits where the River Cocker meets the River Derwent in the heart of the Georgian town of Cockermouth. Jennings has brewed ale since 1828 and the company still uses traditional methods and lakeland water drawn from its own well to create a range of award-winning ales. Jennings' famous regular tipples include Cocker Hoop, Cumberland Ale and Sneck Lifter; plus they brew a range of seasonal beers, such as Redbreast (a Christmas ale) and Fish King (a beer created in honour of Whinlatter Forest Park's Osprey Project). Jennings runs brewery tours twice daily in high season, on which visitors can discover the art of beer-making as well as sample some of Jennings' finest real ales.

Other Cumbrian breweries that run regular tours include the Hawkshead Brewery in Staveley Mill Yard (see page 180) and the Keswick Brewing Company. Keswick also plays host to one of the region's main beer festivals. Held annually in the town's rugby club on the first weekend in June, this two-day-long outdoor event attracts thousands of beer lovers – many in fancy dress – and features a line-up of over 200 different ales all drunk to a soundtrack of live music.

The Boot Beer Festival in the Western Lake District is an altogether smaller and more remote affair. Set in the heart of scenic Eskdale, this family-friendly festival running over a long weekend is hosted by three local pubs – the Brook House Inn, the Boot Inn and the Woolpack Inn. For many the best way to take in the stunning scenery en route to the festival is to travel via the Ravenglass and Eskdale railway (or 'la'al Ratty' as it's affectionately known locally), an old narrow-gauge steam train that regularly trundles from Ravenglass on the west Cumbrian coast deep into Eskdale. From the station, meander up the dale, stopping at whichever of the three inns that takes your fancy to sample a beer or two along the way. You may well stumble upon a curry night, black pudding bonanza or other foodie fest. Many choose to make a weekend of it and stay in one of the pubs or camp in Eskdale – one of the most splendid places to pitch a tent in all the Lakes.

Sample the wares on offer at the Coniston Brewing Company's Black Bull in Coniston, where Donald Campbell lodged during his attempts to break world water speed records on Coniston Water. The pub brews the splendid Bluebird Bitter, named after the boat Donald Campbell crashed and died in on his final record-breaking attempt.

Legend has it that the Drunken Duck Inn near Ambleside derives its name from the time a former landlady found her flock of ducks lying motionless on the road outside the pub. Presuming them dead she plucked the birds ready for

Jennings Brewery 251
Castle Brewery, Cockermouth,
Cumbria CA13 9NE
0845 1297185
www.jenningsbrewery.co.uk
Tours run all year but frequency depends on the time of year. Check website for details.

Keswick Brewing Company 254
The Old Brewery, Brewery Lane,
Keswick, Cumbria CA12 5BY
017687 80700
www.keswickbrewery.co.uk
Tours 1.30pm Wednesday–Friday and 11am Saturday. Booking is essential.

Keswick Beer Festival
Keswick Rugby Club, Davidson Park,
Keswick, Cumbria CA12 5EG
017687 73200
www.keswickbeerfestival.co.uk
Tickets go on sale in December for the June festival.

The Boot Beer Festival
www.bootbeer.co.uk

The Black Bull 246
Coppermines Road, Coniston,
Cumbria LA21 8HL
015394 41335
www.conistonbrewery.com

The Drunken Duck Inn
Barngates, Ambleside, Cumbria LA22 0NG
015394 36347
www.drunkenduckinn.co.uk

The Watermill Inn 257
Ings, Near Windermere, Cumbria LA8 9PY
01539 821309
www.watermillinn.co.uk

the pot, but en route to the oven they mysteriously began to reawaken. Far from deceased, the wayward ducks were merely drunk after supping the contents of a leaking beer barrel. To this day, the Drunken Duck Inn, with its selection of cracking real ales from its onsite Barngates Brewery, remains one of the legendary places in the Lakes to sup a pint.

Serious real ale aficionados undertake a pilgrimage to the Watermill Inn and Brewing Company at Ings on the outskirts of Windermere. Voted by Westmorland CAMRA as 'Pub of the Year' in 2009, the Watermill hand pumps 16 ales, including their award-winning Collie Wobbles – order a pint of lager at your peril.

Bettys Tea Rooms

No discerning tea-lover should pass through the region without stopping at Bettys – Yorkshire's favourite tea rooms, with branches in York, Ilkley, Northallerton, the RHS gardens at Harlow Carr and, famously, Harrogate.

Bettys first opened its Harrogate tea rooms in 1919 with the aim of providing a mix of Yorkshire and continental confectionery served in elegant surroundings. Today the menus still reflect a commitment to Swiss–Yorkshire cooking and its cafés, staffed with white-aproned assistants, ooze an aura of old-fashioned gentility.

A traditional afternoon tea includes the choice of two sandwiches and a selection of miniature cakes and scones smothered in Yorkshire clotted cream. Or choose from the cake menu filled with Yorkshire specialities, such as the large plump fruity scones made with citrus peel, almonds and cherries known as fat rascals, fruit cake served the traditional way with a slice of Wensleydale cheese or melt-in-the-mouth Yorkshire curd tarts. All of these can be washed down with a choice of teas from Bettys own blend to Moroccan mint tisane.

Each branch also has its own shop selling Bettys famous breads, cakes, chocolates and tea, and for those visiting for a special treat, there's a host of Bettys goodies to take home as a memento of the occasion. If you love Bettys bakery then you can learn how to bake the Bettys way at Bettys Cookery School, located next door to its craft bakery in Harrogate; the school runs a regular programme of bread-, cake- and chocolate-making courses.

Further north, Howick Hall on the Northumberland coast is the place to experience an Earl Grey Tea as it was intended to taste and to discover one of the north-east's most magnificent gardens. Former British Prime Minister, Charles Grey, the second Earl Grey, is best remembered for his Great Reform Bill of 1832 as well as for the blend of tea that bears his name.

The Grey family has owned Howick Hall since 1319 and it was here that a Chinese mandarin created the Earl's much-loved tea, flavoured with oil of bergamot, to suit the water at Howick. Charles' wife, Lady Grey, took the Earl's special tea to London from where its popularity spread. Although now drunk across the world, visitors to the Earl Grey tea house at Howick Hall can enjoy a cup of Earl Grey brewed with the waters it was made for.

The Earl Grey tea house is open only to visitors of the Hall's exquisite gardens, so enjoy your afternoon tea after a walk through the estate's acres of woodland or the drifts of snowdrops that smother the grounds in the spring.

Bettys
1 Parliament Street, Harrogate,
North Yorkshire HG1 2QU
01423 814070
www.bettys.co.uk

Howick Hall
Alnwick, Northumberland NE66 3LB
01665 577285
www.howickhallgardens.org.uk
Gardens, arboretum and tea rooms open
early February–mid November;
10.30am–4pm Tuesday–Sunday in winter
and daily 12–6pm in summer.

Leventhorpe Vineyard

It may be hard to believe, but wine has been made from grapes harvested in England's north-east since Roman times. Today, former chemistry teacher George Bowden keeps the tradition alive by producing award-winning wines at Leventhorpe Vineyard near Leeds.

George bought the plot of land where his vines now grow in 1985 after noticing it was free of snow one winter. He realised the aspect and soil of the field were ideal for growing early ripening grape varieties; in fact, Leventhorpe has a microclimate not dissimilar to that of France's Loire Valley.

George uses a mix of traditional and contemporary methods at Leventhorpe with great results: his Seyval Blanc is rated highly by Rick Stein and featured on BBC's *Oz and James Drink to Britain*. Similar to Viognier in style, it is light and delicate – or as James May claims 'crisp, rapier like'. Leventhorpe's other wines include Madeleine Angevine (a crisp white with blackberry overtones), the rich West Riding Red and the sparkling Leventhorpe Brut.

If you don't have time to visit Yorkshire's very own 'Loire', you can find Leventhorpe's wines for sale at the Yorkshire Deli and Shop in Ilkley and at Blacketts of Bamburgh – a restaurant, tea shop and wine store in one.

Leventhorpe Vineyard 279
Bullerthorpe Lane, Woodlesford,
Leeds LS26 8AF
0113 288 9088
Open daily; call ahead to book guided tours
mid July–mid September.

Yorkshire Deli and Shop 276
www.yorkshiredeli.co.uk

Blacketts of Bamburgh 288
01668 214714

The Hairy Fig Delicatessen

In the centre of York is a foodie's Aladdin's cave – the Hairy Fig deli. This cornucopia of fine food stands next to the Merchant Adventurers' Hall on the city's historic Fossgate – a street with a food tradition stretching back to medieval times and still the location of some of York's best restaurants.

This friendly store, crammed floor to ceiling with a wide variety of both local and continental fare, specialises in a range of unusual oils – including truffle – and balsamic vinegars sold on tap (bring your own bottle). Fromage-o-philes will love the cheese selection, which includes the regional favourites Yorkshire Blue and Yorkshire Feta with Nettle. Any of these can be complemented with an array of Italian rustic loaves, supplied by Via Vecchi, a small, specialist bakery on York's famous Shambles. Meat-eaters can pick up locally reared venison, Yorkshire Black Pudding and meat pies bursting at the crust. Drinks on offer include Ampleforth Abbey Cider and beers from Brown Cow Brewery in Selby. And, of course, you can also buy figs.

Ask the staff to make up a platter and then head down Fossgate to The Blue Bell pub where they'll provide the knife and fork and a pint of local ale.

The Hairy Fig 279
39 Fossgate, York YO1 9TF
01904 677074
www.thehairyfig.co.uk
Open 9.30am–6pm Monday–Saturday.

The Blue Bell
53 Fossgate, York YO1 9TF
01904 645904

Swinton Park Cookery School

Swinton Park 273
Masham, Ripon, North Yorkshire HG4 4JH
01765 680900
www.swintonpark.com

If you're looking for a cookery school with clout, look no further. The Swinton Park Cookery School is excellent for two reasons – the award-winning chefs who teach here and the setting, a luxury castle hotel set in a 200-acre estate. The hotel is the ancestral home of the Cunliffe-Lister family and sits deep in the Yorkshire countryside. Its stylish cookery school, housed in converted Georgian stables, is decked out with modern equipment and claims superb views over the surrounding parkland.

Chefs who share their secrets and passion for good food here include Rosemary Shrager, famous for her TV appearances on *Ladette to Lady* and *Soapstar Superchef*, and Robert Taylor, former winner of the Chaine de Rotisseurs Chef of the Year Award. Local food experts also join the teaching ranks, while Susan Cunliffe-Lister throws her tale of restoring the estate's four-acre walled garden (which provides fruits, vegetables and herbs for the courses) into the mix.

Choose from day courses on game food, wild food or cooking for children; speciality courses; wine appreciation lunches and evening curry clubs; or the residential cookery courses, where you can make the most of all the comforts and countryside this lavish hotel has to offer.

The Dales Foodie Festival

The Dales Festival of Food and Drink 271
First May bank-holiday weekend.
www.dalesfestivaloffood.org
One- and three-day tickets can be bought in advance from the Leyburn Tourist Information Centre (01748 828747 or leyburn.tic@richmondshire.gov.uk).

For the discerning food-lover the only time to visit the Yorkshire Dales is the first May bank-holiday weekend, when Leyburn in Wensleydale hosts the Dales Festival of Food and Drink. Part farmers' market part county fair, this regional showcase celebrates food and farming from across the Yorkshire Dales and offers visitors a unique flavour of life in the region, as well as opportunities to sample some of its prime produce.

At the heart of the festival lies the food hall, a large marquee filled with over 80 exhibitors selling a plethora of Yorkshire food – from beef to biscuits, cake to chutney and honey to herbs. More than 30 local microbreweries are represented here and you are encouraged to sample their wares and then vote for your favourite beer of the festival.

Away from the hustle and bustle of the food hall, you can watch top local chefs demonstrate their skills and share their recipes. Visitors can also get up close to local livestock, watch cheese being made, find out how to build a drystone wall and witness ferret racing. And the backing track to all this activity is none other than some of the north's best brass bands.

Real Yorkshire Ales

It's unthinkable for any real ale enthusiast not to visit Masham. This quintessential old Yorkshire market town, nestled deep in the hills of lower Wensleydale, is home to two of the UK's top independent breweries – Theakston's and Black Sheep. Both breweries are legends in the world of real ale, lie within easy walking distance of each other and offer tours of their revamped Victorian breweries.

The Theakston family opened its first brewery in Masham in 1827 and is world famous for its distinctively rich, fruity ale Old Peculier – named after the town's status as a Peculier in medieval times (a town with its own ecclesiastical court). Following a short period of ownership by other breweries, the family bought back Theakston's in 2003 and now produce a range of Legendary Ales, including Theakston XB and Black Bull Bitter. You can see how they make their ale at one of the guided tours of Theakston's tower-style brewhouse, which finish up at the Brewery Tap pub where you can sink a sample or two. The Theakston's Heritage Centre includes a working cooperage where visitors can witness traditional cask-making demonstrations.

Follow the smell of hops to the eastern side of town to visit Masham's other famous brewery – Black Sheep – which was founded in 1991 by Paul Theakston, a fifth-generation member of the Masham brewing dynasty. Black Sheep ale is sold throughout Britain and around the world; and is one of the success stories of British independent brewing. Brewery tours lead visitors through the complete brewing process from the tasting of malts to sealing the final product into wooden casks, and conclude with a pint of one of Black Sheep's award-winning hoppy bitters.

Equally worthy of a visit is York Brewery, located in the shadow of the ancient walls of this historic city. A warm welcome and quaint little bar lies behind the cask-strewn entrance, where you can start the tour with a half-pint sample of ale before heading off around the brewery in the care of exceptionally knowledgeable staff. The ales produced here include the slightly sweet Constantine, which leaves the palate clean and is perfect drinking on a warm day.

York Brewery also own three pubs around the city – the Last Drop Inn on Colliergate, the Three-Legged Mare on High Petergate and the Yorkshire Terrier Inn on Stonegate. Staff at all three pubs can advise on the right ale for you. The Yorkshire Terrier Inn runs regular tasting sessions and houses a York Brewery shop where you can also pick up your favourite ale to take home.

T&R Theakston 274
The Brewery, Masham, Ripon,
North Yorkshire HG4 4YD
01765 680000
www.theakstons.co.uk
Brewery tours daily 11am, 12pm,
2pm and 3pm, plus 4pm in summer.
No children under 10 allowed
on brewery tours.

Black Sheep Brewery 272
Wellgarth, Masham, Ripon,
North Yorkshire HG4 4EN
01765 689227
www.blacksheepbrewery.co.uk
Brewery tours daily 11.30am, 12.30pm,
2pm and 3pm.

York Brewery 280
12 Toft Green, Micklegate, York YO1 6JT
01904 621162
www.yorkbrew.co.uk
Brewery tours 12.30pm, 2pm, 3.30pm and
5pm Monday–Saturday year round and
12.30pm, 2pm, 3.30pm and 5pm Sundays
May–September.

Kenny Atkinson
and Seaham Hall

Since gaining his first Michelin star while working on the Isles of Scilly, Newcastle-born Kenny Atkinson has become one of the bright new lights of British cooking. Now back on home territory as head chef at County Durham's five-star Seaham Hall hotel, Kenny is committed to developing the potential and profile of the north-east as a region of food excellence. Within six months of taking over the culinary helm at Seaham Hall, Kenny bagged another Michelin star and the hotel's restaurant – The White Room – was recognised with a Remy Award as being one of the top 20 restaurants outside of London.

Seaham Hall 281
Lord Byron's Walk, Seaham,
County Durham SR7 7AG
0191 516 1400
www.seaham-hall.co.uk

Awards aside, Kenny is best known by the British public for creating the winning starter on the 2009 series of the BBC's *Great British Menu*. His salad of Aberdeen Angus beef, carrots, horseradish and Shetland Black potato crisps is a perfect example of the modern British cuisine he champions. Modern British cooking takes all the traditional flavours of classic British dishes and adds a new twist, thus giving them a fresh lease of life. And Kenny's formal yet friendly restaurant is the leading place in the north-east to indulge in this exciting cuisine.

Kenny claims the key to good cooking lies with the best ingredients. He champions local producers and his seasonal menus are rich with food sourced from the north-east. Expect to find Northumberland beef and pork, Cheviot lamb and a choice of the most succulent local seafood all transformed into unique dishes that promise an explosion of tastes that are familiar but presented in an entirely new way.

But there's much more to experience at Seaham Hall than Michelin-starred food; the building itself is a wonderfully grand affair with its fair share of stories to tell. Seaham Hall, built in the 18th century on the site of a former medieval manor house, was briefly home to the famous Romantic poet Lord Byron who, in 1815, married Annabella Milbanke, daughter of the Hall's owners. Today guests are invited to enjoy pre-dinner drinks and delicate hors d'oeuvre in the drawing room where Byron and Annabella tied the knot.

In more recent history, the Hall became a military hospital after the outbreak of World War II; since then it has also served as a convalescent home for tuberculosis patients and a nursing home. All those who stayed here surely benefited from the bracing sea air that breezes in across Seaham's nearby wild and wide beach.

It's an altogether different kind of healing that's offered now at one of the UK's foremost spas. Seaham Hall's Serenity Spa wows as well as relaxes and pampers its guests. Huge glass windows flood the spa's large pool with views of the surrounding grounds, and guests can choose to forget the day's stresses

"He champions local producers and his seasonal menus are rich with food sourced from the north-east."

in outdoor hot tubs, a black-granite steam room or a swish hydrotherapy bath. Treatments include an impossible-to-choose-from menu of facials, floats and massages, plus a range of treatments just for men.

If changing from your bathrobe into clothes to take your lunch in The White Room is too much effort, you can choose instead to dine in laid-back luxury at the spa's Ozone restaurant, whose menu is overseen by Kenny and features an unusual range of Pan-Asian cuisine with a western twist.

The combination of Kenny Atkinson's Michelin-starred cuisine, the healing touch of Seaham Hall's Serenity Spa and a stroll along Seaham's windswept beach is one of the most complete luxury experiences the north-east has to offer.

Barny Farmers' Market

The picturesque town of Barnard Castle – Barny, as it's known locally – stands on the fringes of the North Pennines and regularly hosts one of the north-east's best farmers' markets. In the shadow of the great 12th-century castle ruins, Market Place is fit to burst with stalls loaded with local fare on the first Saturday of every month.

Here residents and visitors alike can pick from regional wild and farm foods, such as Broom Mill Farm's hand-reared pork and home-made sausages as well as luxury yogurts from Tree House Creamery in nearby Brignall. But it's the impressive variety, provenance and freshness of vegetables, vegetarian goods and cheeses that have earned Barnard Castle's market the Vegetarian Society's award for best farmers' market for vegetarians.

Barnard Castle's Farmers' Market 270
10am–3pm the first Saturday of the month, on the Cobbles, Market Place, Barnard Castle.

Barnard Castle also ranks in Britain's top 50 historically and architecturally important towns. Spend the afternoon, once the market's packed up, at the magnificent Bowes Museum in the centre of town, which houses one of the most important art collections in the north of England.

Broom Mill Farm
www.broommillfarm.co.uk

Tree House Creamery
www.treehousecreamery.co.uk

Finish off with a stop at the museum's Café Bowes where you can dine on locally produced food such as Teesdale wood pigeon and sample a glass of Leventhorpe's Seyval Blanc (see page 192).

The Bowes Museum
www.thebowesmuseum.org.uk

Colmans of South Shields

The north-east is famous for world-class fish-and-chip shops. But the best of the best is Colmans, which first opened in 1905 in a hut on South Shields' beach. Today the business is housed in a gleaming restaurant and takeaway on the town's Ocean Road and its array of accolades, including being voted the UK's best takeaway and best fish-and-chip shop in England, proves it's much more than your average chippie.

Fourth-generation fryer, owner and 'Local Food Hero' Richard Ord hand-picks the best of the daily catch landed in Sunderland and North Shields from sustainable fishing grounds. On any given day you'll find the usual suspects on the menu along with the not-so-usual turbot, ray, whiting, lemon sole or pollack. Richard fries his fish in free-from-additives vegetable oil (the used oil is turned into bio-fuel) and serves them with thick-cut chips.

Colmans 284
182–186 Ocean Road, South Shields, Tyne and Wear NE33 2JQ
0191 456 1202
www.colmansfishandchips.com
Restaurant open daily 11am–5.45pm, takeaway open daily 11am–6.45pm.

For a taste of tradition, dine in Colman's restaurant whose walls are lined with photographs of the business in bygone days. Better still, pick up a takeaway and walk the short distance to South Shields' beach, where you can sit at the mouth of the Tyne and watch the water traffic slip between the river and the North Sea.

Craster Kippers

Breathe in deeply among Craster's stone cottages and you'll soon catch the scent of the village's pride – traditional kipper smokehouses. In this tiny Northumberland fishing village, Craster's kilns, built from locally quarried stone, were designed to withstand the strong easterly winds. They've smoked local kippers here for generations, but today only one working smokehouse remains, run by the Robsons whose family has been smoking fish here since 1865.

The Robsons embrace traditional methods, resisting the mechanisation of the industry in the post-war years. Current owner Neil Robson, who has worked the smokehouse since his teens, sources plump herring from local waters when in season, soaks them in brine and then cures the fish for up to 16 hours over a careful balance of smouldering whitewood shavings and oak sawdust. The result is a naturally golden, rich, lip-smackingly fine kipper.

Apparently the Queen and her family enjoy Craster kippers for breakfast and they're popular, too, with top chefs from around the country. But the best place to sample these culinary masterpieces is the Craster Fish Restaurant, attached to the smokehouse itself. Here you can savour Craster kippers in their simplest form – on buttered toast with just a dash of Worcestershire Sauce.

L Robson & Sons Ltd and Craster Fish Restaurant 290
Haven Hill, Craster, Alnwick, Northumberland NE66 3TR
01665 516223
www.kipper.co.uk
Open for lunch 12–2pm and for dinner 6.30–8pm Monday–Saturday. Restaurant closes during the winter.

Chain Bridge Honey Farm

Scattered across north Northumberland and the Scottish Borders countryside near Berwick-upon-Tweed are 1,800 colonies of bees belonging to the Chain Bridge Honey Farm. The farm sits on the banks of the River Tweed and takes its name from the nearby Union Chain Bridge – the longest wrought-iron suspension bridge in the world when it opened in 1820.

They've been making honey at Chain Bridge Honey Farm since 1948, and it now produces about 80 tonnes of honey a year from its bees that feast on fields of borage and clover in spring and heather in late summer.

At the farm's visitor centre, you can discover all you ever wanted to know about bees and bee-keeping and get up close to a busy colony located safely behind glass before sampling the honey. Choose between Tweedside Honey, a mild and light set flower honey, and Flower Comb Honey, cut straight from the hive and dripping with floral flavours – or buy both. There are also all kinds of related products for sale including candles, furniture polish and skin creams.

And a must-visit for sweet-tooths awaits at the farm's café – inside a vintage double-decker bus – where you can sample honey flapjacks, honey sponge, heather honey oaties and a delicious heather honey ice cream.

Chain Bridge Honey Farm 285
Horncliffe, Berwick-upon-Tweed, Northumberland TD15 2XT
01289 386362
www.chainbridgehoney.co.uk
Open 9am–5pm Monday–Friday November–March and 10am–5pm daily April–October.

Lindisfarne Mead and Oysters

The tiny tidal island of Lindisfarne is the most instantly recognisable landmark along the Northumberland coast. Most visitors travel to this Holy Island, the cradle of early British Christianity, to tour its famous abbey that dates back to the 7th century or watch birds at Lindisfarne's National Nature Reserve. But for the food-orientated pilgrim two ancient taste experiences – mead and oysters – are also on offer in this Area of Outstanding Natural Beauty.

Where there are monks, there's mead; and the history of this rich honey-based alcoholic drink stretches back to the realms of Norse mythology. Mead was commonly brewed by monks throughout medieval Europe and when, in around AD 634, St Aidan was invited by King Oswald to move his monastery from Iona in Scotland to Lindisfarne, the mead-making tradition travelled with him.

With the monks long gone, mead is now brewed on this island by St Aidan's Winery. At low tide, follow in the footsteps of the faithful and make the centuries-old crossing from mainland to island via the three-mile-long causeway. Once safely across, head to the winery at the centre of Lindisfarne village. Here you can sip free samples of the island's mead and various fruit wines or try the liqueur fudge and a number of other local speciality foods, all of which are on sale.

Mead is known for its aphrodisiac qualities as is Lindisfarne's other taste sensation – oysters. Local legend claims that oyster farming began on the Holy Island in the 14th century when monks stocked the surrounding waters with oysters bought from a Scottish fisherman. Today Christopher and Helen Sutherland grow pacific oysters in Lindisfarne's historic beds and their specialist barge can often be seen plying the mudflats that lie beside the causeway. The Sutherlands allow their oysters to mature for up to four years, which results in an intensely rich flavour, before harvesting a crop of up to 3,000 per week.

Freshly farmed oysters can be bought all year from the Sutherlands' farm in Ross to the south of the Holy Island, where you can also walk along one of the north-east's ruggedly charming beaches. Alternatively, order online and have a parcel of fresh briny-tasting oysters couriered to your door. If sampling oysters the classic way (served raw on a bed of ice) isn't for you, Christopher and Helen provide a range of recipe ideas, including omelettes and slipping one or two into a steak and kidney pie. They also give you instructions on how to safely shuck (open) the oysters.

You can buy Lindisfarne Oysters at fishmongers throughout the area, and award-winning chef Terry Laybourne serves the pick of Lindisfarne's oyster harvest in his stylish Newcastle restaurants – Jesmond Dene House and Café 21.

St Aidan's Winery
Lindisfarne, Northumberland TD15 2RX
01289 389230
www.lindisfarne-mead.co.uk
Open daily 9am–5pm tide depending.
Closed weekends in winter.
Check website for details of tide times.

Lindisfarne Oysters
West House, Ross Farm, Belford,
Northumberland NE70 7EN
01668 213870
www.lindisfarneoysters.co.uk
Open daily; call ahead for directions.

Jesmond Dene House
Jesmond Dene Road,
Newcastle-upon-Tyne NE2 2EY
0191 212 3000
www.jesmonddenehouse.co.uk
Open for lunch 12.30–2pm Monday–Friday,
12–2.30pm Saturday and 12.30–3pm
Sunday; open for dinner 7–9.30pm daily.

Café 21
Trinity Gardens, Quayside,
Newcastle-upon-Tyne NE1 2HH
0191 222 0755
www.cafetwentyone.co.uk
Open 12–2.30pm and 5.30–10.30pm
Monday–Saturday and 12.30–3.30pm
and 6.30–10pm Sunday.

Chester's Gastro Tour

If you like a slab of history served up with some gastronomic gambols then look no further than the Taste of Chester walking tour. Chester's history stretches back to about AD 75 when the Romans built a fort here next to the River Dee. Many visitors come to marvel at its historic buildings, and now you can eat and drink your way along a three-mile-long trail of this walled city, discovering all sorts of tastiest local produce as you go.

Guided tours depart from Chester's Tourist Information Centre, in the Town Hall on Northgate Street, and lead visitors through a series of encounters with contemporary and ancient food experiences alongside the city's history and architecture. Tour stops depend on how busy local stores are, but always include a visit to the Rows – Chester's famous medieval half-timbered buildings whose long, raised galleries today house shops and cafés.

Below ground, the Rows open out into 12th-century crypts built by medieval soldiers wintering in the city. One of these crypts has been a wine store for 150 years and so it makes perfect sense to find a wine merchant there – in this case a branch of the independent Corks Out. At this atmospheric stop, pause beneath the store's ancient vaulted stone ceiling to sample a *soupçon* of fine wine from across the world and around Britain.

On leaving the cellars, the tour often turns from wine to cheese and heads to the above-ground Watergate Deli. Housed within a half-timbered gallery, this foodie's heaven's ample shelves are laden with local cheeses and Cheshire meats, as well as home-made cakes and Cheshire cider vinegar.

Then perhaps you could stop off at one of the city's calmest cafés – the Chester Cathedral Refectory – which in the 13th century was a dining room for local Benedictine monks. The cathedral survived Henry VIII's dissolution by being transformed into a King's School and its refectory claims an unusual stone canopied pulpit as well as a 17th-century tapestry, based on a work by Raphael. And if you like stained-glass windows, then gaze upon the contemporary depiction of the Six Days of Creation.

The tour moves on to the Brewery Tap – a stop much-favoured by real ale drinkers. Run by local brewery Spitting Feathers, the pub is in Gamul House, a Georgian restoration of a medieval great hall. Don't miss the huge fireplace – Charles I is said to have mulled over his fate during the Civil War in front of this beauty. As well as serving its award-winning ales – including Old Wavertonian, a robust stout with strong coffee and chocolate flavours – the Brewery Tap's menus also pack a punch, with fresh, locally sourced food.

Spud U Like might seem like a strange place to stop, but gastro tours often head down the stairs at Chester's Bridge Street branch to view an intact Roman bath

A Taste of Chester [208]
Chester Tourist Information Centre, Town Hall, Northgate Street, Chester CH1 2HJ
01244 402111
www.visitchester.com
Tour runs at 2pm Thursday and Saturday May–September.

Corks Out
21 Watergate Street, Chester CH1 2LB
01244 310455
www.corksout.com

Watergate Deli
53 Watergate Row South, Chester CH1 2LE
01244 323 502

Chester Cathedral Refectory Café
12 Abbey Square, Chester CH1 2HU
01244 500964
www.chestercathedral.com
Open 9.30am–4.30pm Monday–Saturday.

The Brewery Tap
52–54 Lower Bridge Street, Chester CH1 1RU
01244 340999
www.the-tap.co.uk

Three Kings Tea Room
90–92 Lower Bridge Street,
Chester CH1 1RU
01244 317717
Open 10am–5pm Tuesday–Sunday.

and hypocaust (an ancient underfloor heating system). Other tour stops include the Three Kings – a tea shop housed in an old store-room attached to the neighbouring pubs. Here treat yourself to some Chester Cake; in days gone by, this local speciality was made from leftover cakes boiled together and baked under a pastry top. Today's recipe results in a light fruit cake topped with melt-in-the-mouth pastry.

You don't have to join a guided tour to sample the goodie delights of Chester; you can wander around under your own steam with a self-guided version of the tour from the city's Tourist Information Centre. In fact, this tour comes with a booklet of many other taste trails that will lead all lovers of good food and drink on a journey of discovery around the whole of Cheshire.

Nantwich Food & Drink Festival

For three days over the last weekend of September, Nantwich, one of Cheshire's finest old market towns, hosts one of the UK's best celebrations of food and drink – the Nantwich Food and Drink Festival.

Much of the festival takes place on Mill Island where a vast 'gourmet food marquee' takes centre stage. Inside this giant tent are close to 100 stalls laden with a vast array of foods and drinks created by many of the UK's top producers. The Island is also home to a cookery demonstration theatre where celebrity and local chefs rub shoulders and show off their skills.

The festival's free tasting workshops are just the place to learn the right way to sample the foods for sale. Would-be cooks can roll up their sleeves and get cooking at a cookery workshop or learn how to create the perfect mojito at a cocktail workshop.

Over the course of the weekend, the town also hosts a farmers' market and CAMRA beer festival. And if you need to walk off any overindulgence, then follow a guide for a taste of Nantwich's rich history on the daily tours that meander through the town's Tudor-style-building-lined streets.

Nantwich Food and Drink Festival 209
Mill Island, Nantwich, Cheshire
01270 537359
www.nantwichfoodfestival.co.uk
The last weekend of September.

North-west Smokehouses

Smoking food is a centuries-old craft, but no longer are smokehouses content to simply follow tradition and stick with foods such as salmon, haddock, bacon and hams: they're now smoking an array of other products.

The Cheshire Smokehouse near Wilmslow credits its distinct mixture of maple, oak and hickory chippings for the delicate, sweet taste its smoke infuses into its chosen foods. Most of the products for sale in their fine food emporium are smoked on the premises, and the smoked nuts, including cashew, almond and macadamia, are not to be missed.

The Port of Lancaster Smokehouse is just a short walk from Glasson Dock on the banks of the River Lune. Locals hail its smoked Brie as the best smoked cheese in the region. A variety of other cheeses, including Mrs Kirkham's Lancashire (see page 212), along with eels and black puddings, are also smoked here on racks over smouldering oak and beech wood chippings. And you can buy whatever takes your fancy in the shop or online.

Cheshire Smokehouse 211
Vost Farm, Morley Green, Wilmslow,
Cheshire SK9 5NU
01625 548499
www.cheshiresmokehouse.co.uk

Port of Lancaster Smokehouse 233
West Quay, Glasson Dock, Lancaster,
Lancashire LA2 0DB
01524 751493
www.polsco.co.uk

PYO at Kenyon Hall Farm

Kenyon Hall Farm 212
Winwick Lane, Croft, Warrington,
Cheshire WA3 7ED
01925 763161
www.kenyonhall.co.uk
Open daily 9.30am–6pm in season.
Call ahead or check the website to see what
crops are in season.

Picking your own produce is a great British hands-on experience that allows everyone the chance to get up close to the food they eat and the farms that grow it. Cheshire's Kenyon Hall Farm has been run by the same family for over 400 years and is one of the north-west's largest and friendliest pick-your-own farms.

In 1978 the family planted its first two acres of strawberries and today grows 30 acres of fruit and vegetables. You'll find all the seasonal favourites here, such as strawberries, raspberries and rhubarb, as well as more unusual fruits, such as tayberries (a cross between a blackberry and a raspberry) and white- and redcurrants. Vegetable-lovers will enjoy the varied offerings of asparagus, broad beans, sugar snap peas and squash fresh from the Cheshire countryside.

If you're not into PYO, rest assured you can enjoy Kenyon's home-grown produce as ready-picked fruit and veg from the onsite shop, which sells all the farm's produce alongside over 120 different potted herbs, wild flowers and vegetable plants as well as heaps of pumpkins at Halloween.

Make a day of it and bring your own picnic lunch to spread out on one of the tables provided.

Mr Fitzpatrick's Temperance Bar

Mr Fitzpatrick's Temperance Bar 216
5 Bank Street, Rawtenstall, Rossendale,
Lancashire BB4 6QS
01706 231836
www.mrfitzpatricks-cordials.com
Open 9.30am–4.30pm Monday–Wednesday
and 9am–5pm Thursday–Saturday.

In the 19th century, temperance bars were common in Methodist-influenced Lancashire. At this time the temperance movement attracted a large following in the region and its bars, once a regular feature of the high streets in many northern towns, were places where patrons signed a pledge of temperance and abstained from all intoxicating liquors. Today, only one accredited temperance bar remains in the region, Mr Fitzpatrick's in Rawtenstall – ironically housed in a former pub.

Once part of a chain of over 20 temperance bars owned by the Fitzpatrick family, the Rawtenstall bar has been owned and run by Chris Law since 2001. Chris used to visit the bar as a child with his grandfather, who was friends with Malachi Fitzpatrick, the last of the Fitzpatrick family involved in the business.

Today Chris encourages visitors to pull up a seat at his temperance bar and sample the range of old-fashioned cordials he's reintroduced, including black beer and raisin, and award-winning sarsaparilla and blood tonic – a raspberry-tasting drink of rosehips and nettles with claims of helping to ease arthritis. The bar's old shelves are crammed with jars of traditional sweets and the interior offers a nod to a bygone age with vintage signs adorning the walls.

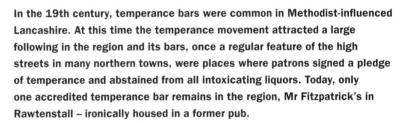

Tatton Park's Housekeeper's Store

The extensive estate of Tatton Park, with its vast gardens, historic buildings and over 1,000 acres of landscaped grounds, is one of the north-west's most impressive attractions. The estate boasts a history dating back to the Bronze Age and was bequeathed to the National Trust in 1958 by the Egerton family, whose ancestors had bought it in the late Tudor period. Tatton's numerous attractions include a remodelled neo-classical mansion house that today showcases important collections of paintings, furniture, books and ceramics. But for a true taste of days gone by, take the atmospheric guided tour with a costumed host through the estate's oldest building – the Old Hall – built at the turn of the 15th and 16th centuries and still lit by tallow candles.

The pride of the park and its pantry is Tatton's 400-head herd of Red and Fallow deer, which you can see roaming freely about the estate exactly as generations have done since 1290. On quiet evenings you might be lucky to spot deer grazing in the grounds around the Old Hall, but if you come in the autumn months you can experience the deer's seasonal rut.

Venison, which is produced from the humane culling of the herd, is sold in the appropriately named Tatton Park's Housekeeper's Store. This cornucopia of fine regional produce is the highlight of any foodie's visit to Tatton, as it stocks the full range of the estate's own produce plus a varied selection of preserves, pickles and chutneys. The Store's cheese counter is renowned for stocking at least one cheese from each country in the UK, but the stars of the show here are the region's specialities. Nibble on some golden organic Brie, infused with the deep aroma of mushrooms and made locally at Oak Dairy in Nantwich or savour some of the rare Heler's Blue Cheshire: both creamy and crumbly, this melt-in-the-mouth cheese is a great choice for sauces.

The Housekeeper's Store also sells meat from Tatton Park's Home Farm. The Egertons began farming in the 1930s, and their estate farm still uses traditional methods and represents the idyll of rural life from that era. At Home Farm, kids can feed goats and hens and meet six rare breeds of pig along with the farm's faithful old donkeys and three gentle-yet-giant Clydesdale horses.

Tatton Park's Housekeeper's Store also hosts regular tasting sessions of their estate produce plus large-scale regional events, including the North West Food Lovers Festival in late October – a three-day celebration of local food. In addition, Apple Day, a popular one with families, is also held in October in the Park's Kitchen Gardens where visitors can sample the fruits grown at Tatton's historic orchards, but if you come in the autumn months you can experience the altogether more boisterous seasonal deer rut.

Tatton Park's Housekeeper's Store 210
Tatton Park, Knutsford, Cheshire WA16 6QN
01625 374435
www.tattonpark.org.uk
Open 10.30am–5pm Tuesday–Sunday
mid March–mid October and 11am–4pm
Tuesday–Sunday mid October–mid March.

North West Food Lovers Festival
01244 350233
www.nwfoodloversfestival.com
Late October.

Nigel Haworth

A passionate champion of both Lancashire's cooking and its local producers, Michelin-starred chef Nigel Haworth has worked to raise the profile and excellence of the county's food for over two decades. Lancashire born and bred, Nigel began his training at a local college in Accrington before heading off to work at top hotels in Scotland and Switzerland. He returned home in the mid 1980s and, disillusioned with Lancashire's food scene, went straight back to college to teach before taking over as head chef at Northcote Manor near Blackburn in the Ribble Valley.

Nigel's dedication to Lancashire food and determination to inject pride and excellence into the region's culinary scene has reaped an impressive array of awards. The many accolades heaped upon him and Northcote include an Egon Ronay Chef of the Year award, *Which Hotel?* Guide's Country Hotel of the Year award as well as the much-coveted Michelin Star.

Once described as 'a true ambassador for the industry', Haworth achieved TV stardom on the 2009 series of *Great British Menu* when his Lancashire hotpot with pickled cabbage was voted in as the winning main course. The recipe for Nigel's celebrated Lonk lamb Lancashire hotpot with organic vegetables is available for everyone via Northcote's website, but the only way to truly appreciate the taste of Lancashire at its best is by dining at Nigel's Northcote Manor restaurant.

Widely recognised as one of the UK's best restaurants outside of London, Northcote changes its menus on a weekly basis in order to ensure that the region's finest local produce is enjoyed at its prime. Although strongly influenced by his Lancashire roots, Nigel's cooking has Swiss undertones in recognition of his training under Natalie Viscardie, one of Switzerland's finest chefs. Vegetarians are exceptionally well catered for at Northcote whether it's via the tasting, à la carte or gourmet menus.

Those dedicated to experiencing the taste of Michelin-starred Lancashire cooking in luxurious style can opt for one of Northcote's gourmet breaks. Former home of a Lancashire textile baron, the Manor is set among extensive landscaped gardens and maintains a homely warmth amid modern luxury. Those who venture beyond the hotel's grounds can explore the nearby wild and rugged Forest of Bowland or spend a day hiking up Lancashire's legendary Pendle Hill – a dark and dramatic peak riddled with walking trails and tales of witchcraft.

Simpler and more affordable, Nigel's chain of Ribble Valley Inns serve creative cuisine made with ingredients sourced from local artisan suppliers. Local ales and fine wine complete the menu at these characterful and charming country pubs.

Northcote Manor 214
Northcote Road, Langho, Blackburn,
Lancashire BB6 8BE
01254 240555
www.northcote.com

The Ribble Valley Inns are:
The Three Fishes 215
Mitton Road, Mitton, Near Whalley,
Lancashire BB7 9PQ
01254 826888
www.thethreefishes.com

The Highwayman Inn 266
Burrow, Kirkby Lonsdale,
Lancashire LA6 2RJ
01254 273338
www.highwaymaninn.co.uk

The Clog and Billycock 213
Billinge End Road, Pleasington,
Blackburn, Lancashire BB2 6QB
01524 201163
www.theclogandbillycock.com

The Bull at Broughton 275
Broughton, Skipton,
North Yorkshire BD23 3AE
01756 792065
www.thebullatbroughton.com

Seaside Ice Cream

For generations visitors have flocked to the seaside towns of the north-west coastline to feast upon scoops and twirls of rich, sticky and consistently delicious ice cream.

Historically, Italian families have been drawn to the region's seaside towns to make and sell their own special ice cream; one such family, the Notariannis, travelled to Blackpool in the early 1900s to set up an ice cream parlour on the town's Central Promenade. Today the third generation of Notariannis sells the family's ice cream from the parlour on Waterloo Road. Here you can devour classic ice cream sundaes, such as knickerbocker glorys, or buy a cone of their original vanilla ice cream to enjoy while strolling along Blackpool's famous prom.

Further north on Morecambe's Marine Parade, Brucciani's ice cream parlour overlooks the vast expanse of Morecambe Bay. This Grade II-listed art deco milk bar is all retro chrome and Formica. Since 1939 visitors to the town have tucked into Brucciani's traditional flavoured gelati in cones, tubs or as classic sundaes.

Further along Morecambe's prom, next to the renovated art deco Midland Hotel, Kate Drummond parks her old-fashioned Sunset Ices van and sells farm-made Wallings Real Dairy Ice Cream, made nearby in Cockerham, along with a healthy serving of seaside nostalgia.

Notarianni's Ice Cream Parlour 232
9–11 Waterloo Road, South Shore, Blackpool,
Lancashire FY4 1AF
www.notarianniicecreamblackpool.co.uk

Brucciani's Ice Cream Parlour 234
217 Marine Road West, Morecambe,
Lancashire LA4 4BU 01524 421386

Sunset Ices 235
www.everyday-is-like-sundae.co.uk

Wallings Real Dairy Ice Cream 236
www.wallingsfarm.co.uk

Potts' Pies

In the north-west, pies claim a near-mythical status and the region is rich with tales of people who have pies sent to them by post or receive dozens as wedding presents. Often served with gravy and mushy peas – or northern caviar – pies are a staple food for locals and tourists alike.

King of Lancashire's renowned pie-makers is Potts' Pies of Lancaster. Hand-made in the company's bakery, the pies stand out for their surprisingly light pastry, freshness and the variety of fillings, including the traditional Lancashire Butter Pie – that's potato and onion pie to non-Lancashire folk.

The company, started by Joe and Vina Potts in 1972, is now owned by the Walsh family and under their guidance Potts now produces 2,000–5,000 pies a week, all made from hand-cut potatoes, the leanest of meats and the tastiest of cheeses.

Despite Potts' Pies now having shops in Morecambe and Bolton-le-Sands as well as Lancaster, you'd do best to sample the pies during half-time at a football match played at the home ground of either Lancaster City or Morecambe Town – the latter claiming that they serve 'the best pies in the Football League'.

Potts' Pies 237
56 Bowerham Road, Lancaster,
Lancashire LA1 4BN
01524 65834
www.pottspies.co.uk

Coffee at J Atkinson & Co

The Georgian streets of central Lancaster are regularly enveloped in the rich, bitter-sweet aroma of roasting coffee, courtesy of one of the nation's top traditional coffee shops – J Atkinson & Co.

Steeped in history, Atkinson's has traded specialist teas and fine coffees from around the world since 1837 and its old-fashioned premises, close to Lancaster's hilltop castle, have been open since 1901.

You'll want to savour every moment of coming here as it's like stepping back in time. Tread on the well-worn wooden floorboards while you watch assistants get 200-year-old tea and coffee canisters down from shelves and use beautifully restored scoops and scales to measure out whatever it is that you desire.

Owner and master roaster Ian Steel is one of the few coffee merchants still to roast coffee onsite using direct flame roasters. The store contains three roasters, including a famous 1945 Uno roaster that sits in the shop's window. The range of teas and coffees on sale is excellent and extensive.

Knowledgeable staff are on hand to help you narrow down the choices to the bean or leaf that suits your taste, and tasting notes are available too. Linger some more to savour one of the best cups of coffee in the whole north-west.

J Atkinson & Co 238
12 China Street, Lancaster,
Lancashire LA1 1EX
01524 65470
www.atkinsonsteaandcoffee.co.uk
Open 8.30am–5.00pm Monday–Saturday.

Morecambe Bay shrimps

When the tide retreats from Morecambe Bay it exposes a vast 120 square miles of sands in this, the north-west's largest bay. And for centuries local fishermen have harvested the abundant seafood living in both the sand and the sea, with the humble shrimp a mainstay of the bay's fishing industry.

Baxter & Sons have peeled and potted Morecambe Bay shrimps by hand since the 1800s and staff at the family's Morecambe factory still follow a generations-old secret recipe that transforms fresh brown shrimps, spices and butter into what Michelin-starred chef Marco Pierre White claims are 'the finest shrimps in the world'.

Visitors can pick up a carton of shrimps at the Baxters' tiny shop off Morecambe's prom. But if your interest is piqued, then book on to a guided walk across the sands at low tide to understand just how special the landscape in this area is.

Cross-sands guides have traditionally come from local fishing families and the current Queen's Guide to the Sands, Cedric Robinson, is no exception. Throughout the summer, Cedric leads groups of walkers across this treacherous and haunting landscape that, hours after you step back on to dry land, is flooded with one of the largest tides in the world.

James Baxter & Sons 239
Thornton Road, Morecambe,
Lancashire LA4 5PB
01524 410910
www.baxterspottedshrimps.co.uk
www.grange-over-sands.com

Note of safety:
The sands are highly dangerous due to the fast moving tides and shifting quicksands and a walk on to them should never be attempted without a trained guide.

Cracking Wensleydale Cheese

England's north-west is stuffed with enough dedicated cheesemakers and cheese shops to please all of the nation's cheese-lovers. The main destination for fromage-o-philes is the Wensleydale Creamery in Hawes, the self-proclaimed home of real Yorkshire Wensleydale cheese.

Hawes is one of Yorkshire's much-loved market towns and a focal point of the Yorkshire Dales National Park as well as a regional hot spot for walkers and day trippers. The town's famed creamery on its south-western outskirts is committed to producing top-quality, authentic Wensleydale cheese from centuries-old recipes using traditional methods.

Wensleydale cheese derives its unique flavour from the milk produced by cows grazing on the dale's ample limestone pastures. The resulting classic white Wensleydale cheese combines a crumbly texture with a mild honeyed taste. Cheese has been made in this stunning dale since the 12th century and was first created by French Cistercian monks who travelled from the Roquefort region to Wensleydale. When the monastery was dissolved in the 16th century local farmers continued the tradition; and today the Wensleydale Creamery is leading a campaign for the area to gain an EU Protected Designation of Origin status for its iconic cheese. This honourable status would ensure that only cheese made in the dale, using local milk, could carry the Wensleydale name.

The cheese from the Wensleydale Creamery has won over 250 awards and the Cheese Experience tour is an integral part of any visit. You'll be led through the entire cheesemaking process from start to finish, and you can top up your newly gained knowledge at the museum in the creamery's visitor centre, which details the history of Wensleydale cheese and its production. The real reason to take the tour, though, is to taste the creamery's famed cheeses, including the mild Real Yorkshire Wensleydale, the drier Mature Wensleydale (a harder, more flavoursome cheese much favoured by cheese connoisseurs) and the veined Blue Wensleydale (similar to Stilton but less salty). The creamery also cold-smokes some of its cheese over oak and hardwood chips to create a golden-brown cheese infused with a mild smoky tang.

No one has done more to promote Wensleydale than those madcap characters Wallace and Gromit: sales of Wensleydale cheeses jumped by 23 per cent following the release of their feature film, *The Curse of the Were-Rabbit*. In fact, the Creamery has honoured this cheese-loving pair in a specially produced Wallace and Gromit Wensleydale – a milder and creamier cheese aimed especially at children. As you'd expect, this and all the creamery's tasty cheeses are for sale in its onsite shop.

The Wensleydale Creamery 269
Gayle Lane, Hawes, North Yorkshire DL8 3RN
01969 667664
www.wensleydale.co.uk
Open 9.30am–5pm Monday–Saturday and 10am–4.30pm Sunday.
The Cheese Experience tour only runs when cheese is being made; phone in advance to check when tours are running.

Churchmouse Cheeses 267
4 Market Street, Kirkby Lonsdale, Cumbria LA6 2AU
01524 273005
www.churchmousecheeses.com
Open 10am–5pm Monday–Friday, 9.30am–5.30pm Saturday and 11.30am–4.30pm Sunday.

Mrs Kirkham's Lancashire Cheese 268
www.mrskirkhams.com

"No one has done more to promote Wensleydale than Wallace and Gromit."

Dedicated cheese-eaters should then head south-west from the Wensleydale Creamery to the small market town of Kirkby Lonsdale. In the heart of the town's jumble of narrow streets and two market squares is Churchmouse Cheeses – a true cheese-lover's heaven. Voted Britain's Best Independent Cheese Shop 2007, Churchmouse Cheeses has filled every inch of its quirky little shop, housed in an 18th-century listed building, with stocks of over 100 varieties of British and continental gourmet cheese.

As well as Wensleydale's finest cheeses, you will find the legendary Mrs Kirkham's Lancashire cheese here too. Chosen by Rick Stein as his preferred Lancashire cheese, Mrs Kirkham's is made in Goosnargh near Preston from the milk of Friesian Holstein cows who graze on pastures washed by salty winds from the Irish Sea. And it's got quite a following – this traditional hand-crafted cheese is sold at the UK's most prestigious farmers' markets as well as in the food halls of Harrods, Selfridges and Harvey Nichols.

Wales

Irish sea

330
329

Conwy
339
340 338
335 337 345
336 344
334
331 333
333 Bangor

Chester
346
341

328

342 343
341 Corwen

Machynlleth
321 327
322
320 326
323 325
324

319
Aberystwyth

314
315
318
312
Cardigan 317
309 313 316
310 311

291
307
306 308
292
301
299 300
298 305
Swansea
302 303
293
294 295 296 304

Cheltenham

Cardiff
297

Foraging and The Foxhunter

In the bucolic nook of Nantyderry, a few miles from Abergavenny, a small group gathers in a restaurant car park. We are booked into the restaurant – the Foxhunter, a handsome gastro-pub where Matt Tebbutt is at the culinary helm – for lunch. Now, though, it is 9.30am and we have our foodie work cut out: in the next few hours we'll be foraging for our meal and bringing back to the kitchen what we've found in the lush surrounding countryside.

The Foxhunter 303
Nantyderry, Abergavenny, Monmouthshire
NP7 9DN
01873 881101
www.thefoxhunter.com
Open Tuesday–Sunday.

Fortunately, we are not alone, but under the guidance and gentle tutelage of expert forager Raoul van den Broucke, a Belgian food entrepreneur and mushroom expert who has sold foraged delicacies to restauranteurs across Europe, and currently supplies a crop of acclaimed local eateries, including the Foxhunter, with his wild, edible finds. He is, you immediately sense, something of a character. Before we head into the hills, he shows us the forager's essential kit: a hat; a basket; a walking stick (mostly, to wipe away cobwebs on autumnal mushroom hunts); a fancy mushroom knife and a handheld portable vacuum cleaner. 'It's not for my car,' he says, as if this would be quite the silliest notion. 'It's for collecting seeds.'

The foraging trips follow routes determined by seasonality, with Raoul taking groups to the best local spots for the time of year. We drive for five minutes, emphatically off the beaten track, then walk along hedgerows which, it turns out, are teeming with wild sorrel and strawberries; Jack-by-the-hedge, with an earthy garlic and mustard flavour; sweet cicely, with its pungent aniseed scent; pennywort, which is like mange tout; wild raspberries; burdock; wood sorrel; bittercress; and about a dozen types of mushroom – from tiny chanterelles and girolles to the allegedly aphrodisiac stinkhorn, rising priapically from the soil and smelling putrid. There are other things we could eat if stranded, but Raoul is highly selective. 'I'm not foraging for survival,' he explains. 'I want very nice food.'

As if to emphasise his point that wild food is everywhere, Raoul suggests we nip into nearby Monmouth, to pick some wild Mirabelle plums he spotted recently while stuck in traffic there. The setting is urban and all the more extraordinary for that; we pick enough to provide for lunch and each take a big bag home (I make jam with mine and it is delectable, and all the better for being free, foraged fodder).

Our work done, we return to the Foxhunter where Matt rustles up a 'wild food' lunch, accenting the menu with our finds. We feast on sautéed duck hearts on toasted brioche with foraged wild garlic root; roast hake served with samphire and girolles, and then poached Mirabelle plum soup with mascarpone cream. It is all divine, and everyone relishes the menu starring the recently picked ingredients in all their zero-food-miles glory.

"In the next few hours we'll be foraging for our meal and bringing back to the kitchen what we've found."

But it's more than that. The walking and talking about food is an immensely relaxing way to work up an appetite, and you are learning more than you realise as Raoul guides you through the local landscape, pointing out what's poisonous and what's irresistible (he knows where to find truffles in Wales but doesn't let on) with charismatic tales and a twinkle in his eye. With the provenance of food a pressing issue for many of us, there is no finer way to address it than finding foodstuffs as you amble through gorgeous countryside and then handing them over to a chef.

While you change out of your walking gear, and swap stories of favourite foraging moments over a glass of something lovely, he'll transform your pickings into a meal that offers a rare, fun and yet meaningful sense of connection with food.

Abergavenny Food Festival

What Edinburgh is to stand-up comedy, and Hay-on-Wye is to books, so the Monmouthshire market town of Abergavenny is to the best of British food. The Abergavenny Food Festival is not simply a mega-celebration, held in September each year and attracting 25,000 visitors over the weekend, but a generous, spirited event that focuses as much on the creativity and conviviality of cooking and eating as the produce itself. Not for nothing is this gourmet fiesta dubbed 'the Glastonbury of food festivals'.

Launched in 1998, with just 30 stalls and 3,000 visitors, the festival has grown to encompass a huge range of elements and activities, all offered in a carnival atmosphere that takes over on the Saturday night, complete with music and spectacular fireworks. During the days, there's the chance to sample food from some of Wales's finest and, in some cases, furthest-flung restaurants, and attend masterclasses given by chefs at the top of their game. Talks feature experts tackling the big foodie issues of the day, while in the big outdoors, visitors can forage or fish locally for their dinner. There are tutored tastings, some lingering over one delectable foodstuff while others take a region, or theme, and explore it through an odyssey of taste. A children's food academy includes lots of fun and inspiring hands-on workshops, and entry to the festival is free to under-16s.

The festival also serves as a reminder of what a gourmet hot spot this part of Wales is, and it's a chance to sample the food and see chefs in action from some of the best local restaurants: from The Bell at Skenfrith – a restaurant blessed with one of the most idyllic settings in the UK, a stunning kitchen garden and stylish rooms to flop in after a fine dinner – to the Michelin-starred Crown at Whitebrook. Local restaurants also offer special menus and events on their own premises to tie in with the festival. In 2009, the Crown's executive chef, James Sommerlin, presented an informal blind-tasting menu at the restaurant; an extra special one-off as he was then the only chef in Wales to hold a Michelin star.

When it began, on a chilly October weekend in 1998 – the move to September was made later in search of better weather – the festival felt very much ahead of its time, raising awareness of and campaigning on issues that were only just emerging for many consumers. Now those same concepts, such as the provenance of food and the vital craft of foodmaking, are much more mainstream. That's thanks, in part, to the work the festival has done year in, year out, with its stellar line-up of guests and always-alluring selection of chefs and restaurants. Best of all is the atmosphere, though, which is sociable and sophisticated, and – like the best meals with friends – all about the joy of sharing with like-minded people.

Abergavenny Food Festival 299
01873 851643
www.abergavennyfoodfestival.com

The Bell at Skenfrith 301
Skenfrith, Monmouthshire NP7 8UH
01600 750235
www.skenfrith.co.uk

The Crown 305
Whitebrook, Near Monmouth,
Monmouthshire NP25 4TX
01600 860254
www.crownatwhitebrook.co.uk

The Chef's Room

There can't be many industrial World Heritage Sites where you can learn to cook with a legend. But in the former mining community of Blaenavon – home to the Big Pit mining museum – you can.

Your teacher is chef Franco Taruschio OBE, who ran the celebrated Walnut Tree restaurant near Abergavenny for 37 years. The restaurant, which showcased Taruschio's native Le Marche cuisine, was so wildly popular that some people were said to have bought holiday homes nearby on the strength of it. It was Elizabeth David's favourite UK restaurant, and accolades don't come much higher than that.

These days, the Walnut Tree is flourishing with Shaun Hill at the helm, and Taruschio has teamed up with food writer and chef Lindy Wildsmith to run the Chef's Room cookery school. Half-day classes include the Gaming Table (autumnal delights and the chance to cook dishes such as quail stuffed with figs), Seafood Demystified (learn to identify, prepare and cook fish, with recipes such as *brodetto* – the classic Italian fish stew) and Wild Mushroom Magic.

The sessions, followed by a delicious lunch with wine, are small, relaxed and suffused with the intense passion Taruschio brings to the kitchen. 'Cook with love, cook with your soul, have fun,' he says. And then he shows you how to do it.

The Chef's Room
Vin Sullivan's, Thomas Gilchrist Industrial Estate, Blaenavon, Gwent NP4 9RL
01989 562353
www.lindywildsmith.co.uk

The Walnut Tree
Llanddewi Skirrid, Abergavenny, Monmouthshire NP7 8AW
01873 852797
www.walnuttreeinn.com

Canteen on Clifton Street

It is the most delicious form of role reversal. Vegetarians, remember all those times in restaurants when you had just one main course to choose from – vegetable lasagne it was for many years, until mushroom risotto took over as the token meat-free option – while fish and meat eaters swooned over the riches on the menu before them? Well now, in Cardiff, thanks to chef-patron Wayne Thomas, a vegetarian for more than 20 years, you can finally trade places. Alongside a range of scrumptious vegetarian and vegan dishes on his menu, which changes every two weeks, there's one slow-cooked meat dish to keep the omnivores happy.

A couple of things you'll need to know: it's a canteen, do don't expect a swanky place; and it's in one of Cardiff's grittier areas. But don't let that put you off because the food, and the mood of the place, is extraordinary: everyone, whatever their dietary habits, needs or intolerances, is well catered for.

Influences are truly global, with accents of Lebanese, Thai, Moroccan, Indian, Italian and French cuisine. This is heart-warming, affordable, vegetarian-friendly gourmet food in a setting that doesn't feel preachy and leaves absolutely everyone feeling gastronomically cherished. That, as any long-suffering vegetarian who likes to eat out will tell you, is quite an achievement.

Canteen on Clifton Street 297
40 Clifton Street, Cardiff CF24 1LF
029 2045 4999
www.canteenoncliftonstreet.com

Haverfordwest Farmers' Market

Haverfordwest Farmers' Market 292
Riverside Quay, Haverfordwest, Dyfed
01437 776168
www.pembrokeshirefarmersmarkets.co.uk

Regularly garlanded with awards, and named best rural or farmers' market in regional and national competitions, Haverfordwest's gathering of local producers on alternate Fridays bustles with energy year round. Its picturesque Pembrokeshire setting guarantees tourist visitors in high summer, but the riverside market – made up of stallholders from within a 40-mile radius – is lively whatever the season, and the Christmas markets are especially atmospheric.

Highlights include thrillingly fresh seafood and cooked whole lobster and crab from Claws Shellfish, run by Christine and Neil Viles. There's fantastic honey from the West Valley Honey Farm and beautifully packaged milk, butter and cream from Bethesda Farm. And at the Cothi Valley Goats stall, you can buy the only halloumi cheese made in Wales. The fine selection of meat producers offer home-cured bacon from Cig Lodor as well as wild boar and prize-winning sausages from Harmony Herd.

The vast majority of stallholders here are primary producers, and every single one is passionate about good food and the vital role it plays in their community. The market is a great first taste of Pembrokeshire and a must-visit if you are nearby on one of the Fridays when it becomes the life and soul of the town.

Morgan's Restaurant

Morgan's Restaurant 291
20 Nun Street, St David's, Dyfed SA62 6NT
01437 720508
www.morgans-restaurant.co.uk

St David's is a diminutive foodie hot spot, with a clutch of smart restaurants, independent cafés and food shops. But the gourmet highlight is Morgan's Restaurant, run by Tara and David Pitman since 2005.

Two things give this place the edge. Firstly, their commitment to sourcing local produce is unusually rigorous: they source absolutely everything they possibly can in Pembrokeshire, and for the odd exotic ingredient, they use only local suppliers. 'It allows me to use some more interesting ingredients, while keeping money in the local economy,' Tara explains. 'I'll go out to local growers and pick what I want. I also gather from the local hedgerows things like pennywort, alexander, nettles, sloes, rowan berries and gorse flowers.'

Then, there's the fish, bought at the Milford Haven fish market, and exceptionally fresh on a daily changing menu. 'On a typical night,' Tara says, 'we offer scallops, mussels, crab, monkfish, bass, John Dory, sewin (sea trout), turbot and hake.'

Tara, a self-taught chef, took over the family cooking in her mid-teens and has never looked back. She has a rare talent for cooking with fish – you'll need to book well in advance in summer – and an impressive determination to do so, brilliantly, with what's right on her doorstep.

Blaengawney Cider

Andy Hallett opens the door at the Caerphilly farmhouse he shares with wife Annie and, despite the astounding views over the Welsh valleys, it's his T-shirt slogan that catches the eye: 'make cider not war,' it suggests. And that's what Hallett now does: making hand-pressed, entirely natural and award-winning cider with his old college friend Stewart Lucas.

Blaengawney Farm 302
Mynydd Maen, Hafodyrynys, Crumlin,
Newport, Gwent NP11 5AY
01495 244691
www.blaengawneycider.co.uk
If you'd like to visit just give them a call.

The duo had always enjoyed drinking cider and making their own as students, but what started out as a hobby soon grew into a successful business. Their ciders have won a clutch of awards at the Welsh National Championships, CAMRA, the Three Counties Championship and the Royal Bath & West Show, where they won the prestigious Pewterer's Cup in 2008.

Blaengawney Cider remains deliberately small scale, though, producing less than 7,000 litres each year. 'We want it to remain a hand-crafted cider,' Hallett explains. 'If you increase things massively, you end up going down the route of additives and preservatives.' He says that last bit with distaste; a clue to how things are done rather differently at Blaengawney.

Cider here is made entirely with apple juice and nothing is added at any stage of the fermentation process. High up in the hills, and with temperatures a few degrees cooler than at sea level, that process is a little slower and longer, which may in part explain the depth of flavour which Hallett refers to as 'Blaengawneyness'. They also use the French tradition of 'keeving' the cider to produce extra natural sweetness. 'It's not a cost-efficient method,' Hallett concedes, 'but it does produce a rich, sweet, thick juice without adding sugar – and that's the one thing we won't do'.

The apples, sourced from local orchards while the Halletts establish their own in the 25-acre grounds, are sorted by hand to check for quality; any rejected fruit is fed to their handful of rare-breed pigs. Then, the apples are put through a press that Andy – an engineer by trade – built himself from an old JCB. After pressing, the cider is then stored in the cider shed over winter in large containers and a range of wooden casks to impart different flavour notes such as whisky or rum.

The ciders are blended into different varieties, balancing out sweetness, sour notes, dryness and tannins to create secret recipes for the three ciders – National Treasure (sweet), True Welshman (medium dry) and Heartbreaker (dry) – and an extremely limited release (150 bottles) of cider champagne. All the bottling and packing for orders is done by hand onsite.

If you want to take your appreciation of cider a little further, Andy runs cider-making days at Blaengawney during the pressing season between September and December. These hands-on days offer small groups of up to four the chance to see how a premium cider is made, and are full of tips for people wanting to try

"The apples are put through a press that Andy built himself from an old JCB."

it at home for themselves. You'll also gain a wealth of knowledge about how and why Andy's cider tastes as good as it does, and he offers brilliant tasting tips to put into practice at home: the crispness of the Heartbreaker cider, Andy tells me, is the perfect partner for Gorwyyd Caerphilly cheese (see page 233). He's right; they go sublimely well together.

The Halletts are ambitious for their farm, with plans to diversify further using the same business model – traditional, small-scale, artisan food production – as the cider. While these plans develop, you can opt to stay in the farmhouse on a self-catering basis and you can buy one of the company's popular 'It's cider o'clock' T-shirts. And at Blaengawney, a relaxed dreamy spot that is guaranteed to bring out lifestyle envy in visitors, it almost always is.

The Gower Peninsula, jutting out into the Bristol Channel to the west of Swansea, isn't the only part of Wales that's home to salt marsh lamb. But it is, arguably, the most beautiful: the Gower, the UK's first designated Area of Outstanding Natural Beauty and a favourite tourist destination for its glorious south coast beaches, is fringed on its quieter north coast by thousands of acres of tidal salt marsh, magically disappearing and reappearing with the tides. The charismatic 13th-century remains of Weobley Castle overlook the marsh, as if keeping watch over the 600 or so lambs below.

The flock, of course, is oblivious to this bewitching landscape but does appreciate its supply of marsh grasses, sorrel, sea lavender, samphire and thrift. So, too, do the farmers behind Gower Salt Marsh Lamb – Colin and Vicky Williams of Summer's Lane Farm and Rowland Pritchard of Weobley Castle Farm – who joined forces in 2004 to produce this seasonal lamb that's so rated by restaurateurs. The trio began with just 50 lambs and awards soon swept in like the tide; in 2009, they won a Gold award in the Guild of Fine Food's Great Taste Awards.

It's a low-key set-up that's as sweet as the meat the salt marshes produce. In the same shop as you buy tickets for the castle, or book mountain-boarding lessons

Gower Salt Marsh Lamb Ltd 293
Weobley Castle Farm, Llarhidian, Gower,
West Glamorgan SA3 1HB
01792 391421
www.gowersaltmarshlamb.co.uk

Palfreys 304
36a Church Road, Newport, Gwent NP19 7EL
01633 259385
www.rkpalfrey.co.uk

Howard Thomas & Son Butchers 295
1–2 Frogmore Avenue, Sketty, Swansea,
West Glamorgan SA2 0UN
01792 204244
www.howardthomasandson.co.uk

Fairyhill 294
www.fairyhill.net

Slice 296
www.sliceswansea.co.uk

Gower Salt Marsh Lamb

"The flock, of course, is oblivious to this bewitching landscape, but does appreciate its supply of marsh grasses."

locally, you can buy steaks, joints, cutlets and burgers, and every purchase comes with a free bunch of samphire from the marsh. Over the phone you can also order whole or half lambs, and these are couriered in wool-lined cardboard chill-boxes.

All the lamb is fully traceable: every animal born on the farms here is slaughtered half a mile away and prepared for sale onsite back at Weobley. 'The food miles involved are almost nil,' says Rowland. But the taste and texture are quite the opposite: tender, yielding (the increased iodine in the lamb's diet apparently breaks down cells), fragrant, buttery and ripe. The company supplies two award-winning local butchers: Palfreys in Newport and Howard Thomas & Son in Swansea.

If you'd rather someone else did the cooking, and would like to try this salt marsh lamb – or other acclaimed peninsula produce, such as Penclawdd cockles – in a restaurant setting, Fairyhill is hard to beat. This elegant 18th-century house sits in a magical setting of 24 acres at the heart of the Gower. Here, the local lamb might be transformed into a ballotine of salt marsh lamb, stuffed with confit tomato and mint, and served with a cawl jus. Swansea's best restaurant opening in years – Slice – run by chefs Helen Farmer and Philip Leach, who live on the Gower, also makes the most of the extraordinary gourmet riches on their doorstep.

Llwynhelyg Farm Shop

It's easy to miss this award-winning farm shop, eight miles from Cardigan on the busy A487. From the outside, where plants are sold next to what appears to be a teensy shop, there's little sense of the treasure trove of fine foods that awaits inside. The only clue to the gourmet delight that is Jenny and Teifi Davies' enterprise (started when they both lost their jobs in 1983 and when milk quotas made dairy farming an unsustainable living) is the steady stream of locals pouring in and out of the place.

Llwynhelyg Farm Shop 312
Sarnau, Ceredigion SA44 6QU
01239 811079
www.llwynhelygfarmshop.co.uk
Open 9am–6pm Monday–Saturday and
9.30am–1pm Sunday. Open later in the
summer and at Christmas.

Inside, it's a foodie's dream, with more than 1,000 products from 120 or so local producers, and 80 per cent of the stock sourced from within Wales. A hand-drawn map on the wall shows exactly where the produce comes from, marking the distances from the shop too – the vast majority of what's sold here originates within 10 miles. Some ingredients, such as herbs and spices, which can't be produced in Wales are stocked from local packaging companies and suppliers.

Highlights include the cheese fridge, crammed with 90 cheeses, 80 of which are Welsh, and portions include affordable slivers that are perfect for a cheese board or picnic. Zingingly fresh produce is restocked daily from local growers, and there's a passion for unusual and heirloom varieties, with 13 British apples stocked in autumn and winter and a stunning range of salad leaves (including selections from the excellent organic Blaencamel Farm nearby) in the summer.

Store-cupboard staples sit alongside dreamy cakes – Jenny makes many of these herself – and preserves, local venison pâté, smoked meats, Carmarthen ham, organic dairy products, Welsh wines, spirits and beers, and flour from the ancient Y Felin watermill a few miles away in St Dogmaels. The shop also offers a hamper service for local holiday cottages.

But what really makes Llwynhelyg Farm Shop stand out is the zeal with which it's run. You can see how much Jenny and Teifi relish their place in the local community, and the role the shop has in sustaining it. There's plenty of cheery banter with customers, and everyone is greeted like an old friend. The Davies were promoting local food many years before it became fashionable, and their shop continues to flourish despite a superstore opening just five minutes' drive away.

The shop, on the edge of Teifi's family farm (which he and Jenny still run) thrives on a sense of place, community and connection with the produce it sells. With a bustling shop, open seven days a week, the hampers business and a farm to work on, it's a wonder they find time to sleep. They both laugh. 'When we do find time,' says Jenny, 'we sleep very well'.

Ty Mawr 10-Mile Menu

It's a tribute to the bountiful natural larder on his doorstep, deep in some of Ceredigion's loveliest countryside, that Ty Mawr's head chef Jeremy Jones is able to do rather more than pay lip service to the current vogue for local produce. So abundant is the local farmland and nearby coast that more than 90 per cent of the ingredients used for the sumptuous dinners at this deeply romantic country house hotel are sourced within 10 miles.

As we stroll through the hotel's own kitchen garden, where figs and melons are ripening, and the sweetest blackcurrants prove irresistible, Jones explains that this sense of connection with food is something he's always known. Both his parents in Swansea, and their relatives next door, had quarter-acre gardens that were given over to home-grown fruit and vegetables. 'If you wanted vegetables for dinner,' he recalls, 'you went into the garden and dug them up.'

Since taking up the job at Ty Mawr, Jones has built strong ties with local producers and is evangelical about the benefits of working so closely with them. 'It's actually cheaper to ship things in from outside,' he says, 'but I'd be a fool to go elsewhere. It's just so much more passionate and pleasurable working with these guys'. To illustrate the point, he describes how he and a supplier worked on the perfect way to cure the bacon served at breakfast in the hotel: 'We devised the recipe between us over six months – you'd never be able to do that with a remote supplier'.

But the commitment to local ingredients runs much deeper than bringing home the deliciously cured bacon. Jones talks through his suppliers, one by one, and the reasons for working with them and his enthusiasm is infectious. He reserves special praise for the fish he sources from Len and Mandy Walters in Cardigan Bay, saying that fish he cooked with in Cornwall and Norfolk was 'not a patch on what I get here'. He also waxes lyrical about Jones, the award-winning butchers in Lampeter (see page 234), for their Welsh Black beef ('the best beef I've ever worked with') and their cuts of rare-breed pork.

The hotel's gracious dining room, all serene blues and double-aspect Georgian windows looking out over the gardens, sets the scene for memorable food. The 10-mile menu, updated every few weeks to ensure seasonality, is studded with local meat and fish: Cardigan Bay crab, roast breast of local duck, Welsh Black beef and local wild rabbit. A main course of roast tenderloin of pork, poached before roasting, is thrillingly flavoursome and cased in lavender and onion forcemeat that gives the dish a distinct aromatic lightness.

A typical high-summer meal begins with a vegetarian starter: an assiette of Ty Mawr tomatoes picked from the gardens here. It's a glamorous, sensual feast. A light, sweet jelly offers a cooling counterpoint to a punchy shot glass of gazpacho and a silky reply to the crunch of bruschetta laden with roasted tomatoes, while a tomato and mozzarella tart is smoulderingly earthy and rich.

Ty Mawr Mansion
Cilcennin, Lampeter, Ceredigion SA48 8DB
01570 470033
www.tymawrmansion.co.uk

Len and Mandy's Fish
The Villa, High Street, St Dogmaels,
Cardigan, Ceredigion SA43 3EF
01239 621043

"The food quite accurately reflects the hotel – a likeable mixture of relaxed and foxy."

The food quite accurately reflects the hotel, which is a likeable mixture of relaxed and foxy (the rooms and sleek bathrooms are vast, and there's also a private cinema for guests) and a favourite with visiting celebrities – Sienna Miller and Keira Knightley stayed here while filming *The Edge of Love* – but it also goes back to Jones' childhood idea of sourcing vegetables. 'We pick produce at 6pm,' Jones says, as he selects leaves from a vast array of cresses in the greenhouse, 'and it's ready at service'. Ten miles, you realise, in this gloriously productive part of rural Wales, is plenty.

Wendy Brandon Preserves

Thank heaven for career changes. Wendy Brandon was once a geography teacher, but since 1985 she has been making some of the finest preserves in Wales; her raspberry jam is to die for. And then there are marmalades, jellies, vinegars, pickles, chutneys, a sugar-free range, mustards, dressings and flavoured oils. It's all high quality, made traditionally and something of a taste revelation if you're used to mass-produced versions.

These days, with more than 180 product lines to make by hand and an order book that includes some of London's finest hotels (The Mandarin Oriental Hyde Park and The Hempel) and shops (Harrods), Brandon employs a team of four, including her son, Ian, at the 250-year-old north Pembrokeshire watermill she lives and cooks in.

You can buy a selection of the range in many good delis and farm shops across Wales, but it's well worth visiting the mill not only to enjoy its picture-postcard setting but also to meet pigs Gertrude and Daisy and the Indian Runner Ducks who pad about the grounds. You can taste and purchase the products here, and get a real sense of just how extensive the ranges are.

Wendy Brandon Handmade Preserves 310
Felin Wen, Boncath, Pembrokeshire
SA37 0JR
01239 841568
www.wendybrandon.co.uk

All Things Sweet at Heavenly

In the handsome, ultra-chic market town of Llandeilo, Tracey and Paul Kindred's chocolate house and ice cream parlour, Heavenly, lives up to its name. A shrine to all things divinely indulgent, this award-winning shop is a cornucopia of irresistible sweet treats.

Highlights include the home-made chocolates and the many forms the milk, dark and white chocolate takes here: stilettos, angels, love spoons, ties and horseshoes. Heavenly also stocks artisan chocolate ranges such as Booja Booja, Rococo and Montezuma alongside a splendid range of nostalgic sweets.

Steer well clear if you're trying to eat healthily because all best intentions will melt away when faced with Heavenly's ice creams, made with organic Welsh milk, cream and, despite the exotic names of some flavours, local ingredients. If you're not tempted by, say, their Banoffee Toffee or Marsala Tiramisu ice creams, both of which won True Taste awards, Heavenly will create any flavour you'd like, savoury or sweet, with 48 hours' notice.

And if you need somewhere to stay while you wait for your bespoke creation, look no further than Fronlas. This sleek organic B&B serves the best local ingredients at breakfast, stocks its bar with Welsh beers, spirits and water, and even offers Heavenly chocolates in your room.

Heavenly 306
London House, Rhosmaen Street,
Llandeilo, Carmarthenshire SA19 6EN
01558 822800
www.heavenlychoc.co.uk

Fronlas 307
7 Thomas Street, Llandeilo, Carmarthenshire
SA19 6LB
01558 824733
www.fronlas.com

The Welsh Cheese Triangle

Trethowans Dairy
Gorwydd Farm, Llanddewi Brefi,
Tregaron, Ceredigion SY25 6NY
www.trethowansdairy.co.uk

Caws Cenarth Cheese
Glyneithinog Farm, Lancych,
Carmarthenshire SA37 0LH
01239 710432
www.cawscenarth.co.uk
It's advisable to phone before visiting.

Teifi Farmhouse Cheese
Glynhynod, Ffostrasol, Llandysul,
Ceredigion SA44 5JY
01239 851528

One of the most cheering food stories in Wales in recent years has been the strong resurgence in traditional techniques of cheesemaking; and Mid Wales is home to some of the finest producers. In fact, there's a triangle – a wobbly triangle, mind, shaped a bit like a roughly cut wedge of Caerphilly – of award-winning cheesemakers nestling between Cardigan and Aberystwyth.

You can't buy direct from Gorwydd Farm, where the highly acclaimed Gorwydd Caerphilly is made, but you can purchase this delectable, lemony cheese from the nearby village shop. Elsewhere it's available from upmarket outlets such as Neal's Yard Dairy (see page 68), Paxton & Whitfield and Waitrose.

Caws Cenarth Cheese, run by the Adams family for more than 40 years, is credited with kick-starting the revival of farmhouse Caerphilly cheese; and their farm is open both for visits and for purchases. Come to watch the cheesemaking process, taste samples and eat in their Café Cwtch.

You can also try-before-you-buy Welsh cheese from family-run Teifi Farmhouse Cheese, which has won an impressive array of awards. Their Celtic Promise has won Supreme Champion at the British Cheese Awards twice, and in 2009 their Saval – a creamy, pungent cider-washed-rind cheese – was awarded the highest accolade: the James Aldridge Memorial Trophy for Best British Raw Milk Cheese.

Ultracomida Über Deli

Ultracomida
31 Pier Street, Aberystwyth, Ceredigion
SY23 2LN
01970 630686
www.ultracomida.co.uk

A word of warning: Ultracomida, the independent chain of delis, will ruin you. You may actually find it hard to shop in any other delicatessens after a visit to their branches in Aberystwyth – where Paul Grimwood and Shumana Palit opened their first shop in 2001 – and Narberth.

You will lust after almost everything on their shelves, which groan under the weight of aromatic cheeses and charcuterie, olive oils, beautifully packaged store-cupboard staples, olives, wine, beers and soft drinks from Wales, France and Spain. Then there's the staff: fantastically helpful, offering tastings until you find what you're after, and brilliantly knowledgeable. It's a right-on kind of place, supporting small-scale and fair-trade producers, but never feels too earnest.

What really distinguishes the shops, though, is a brilliant flexibility. Almost everything can be eaten in or taken out, and through the day there's a rolling menu of delectable things to eat – *huevos a la Flamenca* (Mediterranean vegetables, chorizo and Serrano ham topped with a poached egg) for breakfast, maybe, or a broad bean and dill tortilla at lunch. There are more substantial dishes on offer, too, and the hugely popular tapas, plus an excellent range of wines, with plenty available by the glass.

Welsh Black Beef

You'll see Welsh Black beef on any self-respecting chef's menu in Mid Wales as well as on many a lush, rolling green hillside in the region too. The breed, thought to date from pre-Roman times and famed for its hardy character and stocky, resilient frame, has been undergoing something of a renaissance in recent years and nowhere more so than here. Celebrated for its deep, dense flavour, Welsh Black is said to give Aberdeen Angus a run for its money; actually, in these parts, they tend to put it rather more forcefully than that.

Money is, in fact, part of the ancient breed's colourful history. Drovers would apparently herd their lucrative black cattle from the Welsh Hills to markets in England, but would often be robbed of their market earnings on the way back. The Bank of the Black Ox was founded in 1799 by David Jones, himself a drover, so that money could be safely deposited. That bank later turned into Lloyds Bank, and the black ox became a black horse.

There are some exceptional places in Mid Wales to buy Welsh Black beef, both from butchers and from farms directly. Graig Farm Organics, now run by Jonathan and Sally Rees (formerly of Welsh Farm Organics), is one of the best farms, offering impeccable organic standards, award-winning service and a huge range of other organic produce and products.

You'll notice that in the area butchers' shops tend to feature at least a shelf or two of trophies and rosettes, and for good reason. Especially laden with awards, and famed for their Welsh Black beef, are Dewi Roberts in Llandeilo, Rikki Lloyd in Welshpool, William Lloyd Williams in Machynlleth and Jones in Lampeter. All have a devoted following and are highly regarded by chefs and locals alike. They are also great places to observe the bustle of life in these traditional rural market towns.

It can be fun to buy and cook yourself some Welsh Black beef, chatting to the butcher about the breed and farmer, but one of the finest foodie pleasures in Mid Wales is to eat it simply prepared in a stunning location with someone else doing the cooking. And you don't get many finer pairings than a fillet of Black beef, served with chunky chips, watercress and béarnaise sauce and Aberaeron's cobalt-blue boutique seaside bolthole, the Harbourmaster hotel. The hotel put the area on the map for tourists and made Aberaeron a hip, and rather foodie, destination, with its independent grocers, deli, fish stall and ice cream parlour. Back in the Harbourmaster's restaurant, with a fillet of Black beef in prospect, the past and the present of Mid Wales, both ever so tasty, are happily united.

Graig Farm Organics 318
Dolau, Llandrindod Wells, Powys LD1 5TL
01597 851655
www.graigfarm.co.uk

Dewi Roberts 308
16 Towy Terrace, Llandeilo, Carmarthenshire
SA19 6ST
01558 822566

Rikki Lloyd 327
39 High Street, Welshpool, Powys SY21 7JL
01938 552683
www.rikkilloyd.co.uk

William Lloyd Williams & Son 326
5 Maengwyn Street, Machynlleth,
Powys SY20 8AA
01654 702106
www.wil-lloyd.co.uk

Jones the Butcher 316
4 College Street, Lampeter, Ceredigion
SA48 7DY
01570 422414
www.jonesthebutcher.co.uk

Harbourmaster 314
Pen Cei, Aberaeron, Ceredigion SA46 0BT
01545 570755
www.harbour-master.com

Gareth Johns

For a 'slow food' campaigner, and leader of his local slow food convivium, no less, chef Gareth Johns is surprisingly upbeat about some fast food. The Wynnstay Hotel he co-owns with his brother in Machynlleth – an ancient and historically significant town that was home to the first Welsh Parliament 600 years ago – has twice been voted best pizzeria in the UK by _The Times_.

But this isn't just any pizza restaurant. Like the fine dining menu in the main restaurant at the Wynnstay, the ingredients are strikingly local. The Tricolore uses Welsh goat's cheese, the Marinara is laden with locally landed seafood and the house pizza brings together leeks and locally smoked bacon.

Johns is also a great fan of fish and chips, done well, and recommends the town's award-winning chippie, Hennighan's. 'It's really great fast food, to my mind. And good food shouldn't be the preserve of the well-heeled; it should be for everybody, a fair price for all.'

This touches on one of the three key principles of slow food. 'The watchwords are good, clean and fair,' Johns explains, speaking with such passion that hotel guests linger in the lounge to eavesdrop. 'Food should be good, tasty to eat, and from my point of view, there's an element of traditionality – returning to the old tastes, what are now called rare breeds. It should be clean, produced in a sustainable way, and fair: someone should be able to make a living from food at a fair price.'

There is also, in everything he says, a strong connection with the local landscape and community. 'A restaurant should reflect a sense of place,' he argues. 'We're a Welsh hotel in Wales so we serve an all-Welsh cheeseboard. I love Stilton, Brie and Camembert, but here? Why? Why do you need to bring in cheeses from across the world here when we have superb local cheeses to showcase?'

Although Johns came from a family where communal, sociable meals were the norm, his decision to cook for a living came from a random moment when he was 11. He and his parents were at lunch at a friend's house, and Johns was bored. Scratching around, he found _Great Dishes of the World_ by Robert Carrier and started reading. 'It was a whole new world to me, people talking like this, waxing lyrical about food. I thought right there and then, this is for me.'

That enthusiasm, bolstered by spells of working under the tutelage of great chefs such as Alastair Little, remains obvious as Johns talks about his local suppliers. Across the road from the hotel is his butcher, William Lloyd Williams, whose family have run the shop since 1959. Nothing is sourced further than 20 miles away, and Williams publishes a weekly list of where meat has come from if it's not his own. 'He knows the farmers,' says Johns, 'he can tell you the breed, where it was reared, almost which side of the hill it was on'.

The Wynnstay Hotel 324
Maengwyn Street, Machynlleth,
Powys SY20 8AE
01654 702941
www.wynnstay-hotel.com

Hennighan's Fish and Chips 325
123 Maengwyn Street, Machynlleth,
Powys SY20 8EF
01654 702761
www.hennighans.co.uk

William Lloyd Williams & Son 326
5 Maengwyn Street, Machynlleth,
Powys SY20 8AA
01654 702106
www.wil-lloyd.co.uk

There's a telling quote on the fine dining menu at the Wynnstay Hotel from French chef Michel Bras. It translates as 'He who loses himself in his passion has lost less than he who loses his passion'. The latter, you sense as you watch Johns chatting with suppliers and bewitching his guests with his zeal, is not likely to happen. 'To me,' he says, 'it's just a great pleasure to share with other people, and that's what slow food is about. If I die the cleverest chef in the world and don't pass it all on, then that's knowledge wasted.'

Lake Fishing at Tynycornel

The natural lake of Talyllyn on the south side of lofty Cader Idris (Cadair Idris) could easily qualify for the most beautiful fishing spot in the country. This watery hole was scoured out by a glacier during the last ice age 25,000 years ago and is a glorious sight to behold. The River Dysynni (Afon Dysynni) flows the short distance from the lake through a verdant valley till it meets the sea at Tywyn eight miles away. The lake has wonderful natural stocks of brown trout – it is renowned for gigantic ones – and salmon and sea trout when they 'run' from the sea into the Dysynni and through Talyllyn. Here salmon can be caught on the fly, just as they can be loch fishing in Scotland.

The Tynycornel Hotel sits on the south side of the lake and controls all fishing activities. You can hire a boat here and spend the day gently casting a fly to any rise without getting stuck in a tree – what joy. If you're a novice or just want to learn how best to catch a fish here, then talk to the hotel ghillie, who can advise on the best size and style of fly and the line to use and will even come along if you like.

Should conditions be right and a few tight lines ensue and you land the odd fish, the hotel's kitchen will gladly prepare and cook you a fish supper or pack them so you can take them home. They even go so far as to offer to smoke said fish – either trout or salmon – and then dispatch it to your home address. But if home seems too far away or you just want to stay over and try your hand again tomorrow then book into one of the hotel's 22 rooms, many of which have wonderful views over the lake.

Should your day on the lake be fruitless console yourself with a visit to Gill's Plaice fish shop, enthusiastically run by Gill and her family, in Aberdovey (Aberdyfi), half an hour around the coast. You'll still find fishermen at this seaside resort and former fishing village; several boats still set off in search of lobster, crab and prawns and trawlers harvest prime flatfish. Gill buys as much of the local catch as possible and sources mussels and oysters from the Menai Strait (see page 246). Here you can buy freshly cooked and prepared crab and lobster ready for the table as well as Gill's own smoked trout, salmon and other fish – all of which is top notch and can be bought to take home. In fact, Gill's Plaice supplies many of the local restaurants.

The Penhelig Arms on the seafront has a bar that buzzes all day. Expect to see freshly landed seafood on the specials board in the bar or in the more spacious comfortable restaurant. Freshly dressed crab, grilled plaice, Dover sole and haddock fishcakes tempt many to stop here for a meal.

Tynycornel Hotel 321
Talyllyn, Tywyn, Gwynedd LL36 9AJ
01654 782282
www.tynycornel.co.uk

Gill's Plaice 320
16 Chapel Square, Aberdyfi,
Gwynedd LL35 0LA
01654 767875

Penhelig Arms 322
27–29 Terrace Road, Aberdyfi,
Gwynedd LL35 0LT
01654 767215
www.penheligarms.com

"The natural lake of Talyllyn could easily qualify for the most beautiful fishing spot in the country."

Rhug Estate Farm Shop

When Lord Newborough inherited the Rhug Estate in 1999 he was considered quirky, to say the least, when he announced that he was going to convert the farms to organic status. Now over 5,000 acres of the estate's 12,500 are certified as organic; the remainder being upland and woods used for grazing and shooting.

West of Corwen in the Dee Valley the estate's gentle pastures dip and roll between Llangollen and Lake Bala. You'll find this farm shop as easily as spotting the numerous bison grazing in a nearby field; this small but growing herd is a common sight in these parts. If you want to find out more about these big, black beasts opt for a tour of the estate in a comfy 4x4.

But it's another pedigree that takes pride of place – the Aberdeen Angus herd; apparently the conditions here are perfectly suited to this breed. The cows graze on fields of natural clover and grasses; sharing the same ground with many flocks of free-range chickens and Bronze turkeys for the Christmas market.

The land stretches from the bank of the sylvan Dee way up to the lofty heights of the rugged Berwyn Mountains. Such landscapes offer excellent variety of conditions for grazing sheep. At Rhug, they lamb twice a year in order to give continuity of supply to their restaurant customers. And in a separate part of the estate, Ty Mawr Farm offers superb summer grazing for lambs on the salt marshes. The third part of the estate lies at Peplow in Shropshire, where organic vegetables are grown. Here the farm's herds of Duroc pigs feed eagerly on the fields after the crops have been harvested, devouring the stumps and leftovers with gusto.

But it's at the estate's farm shop that all the produce comes together. The shop boasts state-of-the-art facilities for the correct ageing and professional butchering of the meat. In addition to the joints, chops, steaks, diced and minced meat are home-produced sausages, burgers, bacon, ham, black pudding and pies – all made from the organic meat of the estate. The farm shop casts its net far and wide, taking in organic wine and ales, Welsh farmhouse cheeses, a range of fresh and frozen vegetables and delightful delicatessen products.

In the 'grab and go' burger bar opposite the shop, a stream of people stop for a bacon butty or burger in a bap, with a cup of real coffee or tea. It has become something of a social stop-off for locals and commuters alike. For those in less of a hurry, stay a while at the café, which serves its own organic meat pies, home-cooked beef sandwiches, a hearty bowl of Welsh lamb cawl (broth) and freshly baked apple crumble and Welsh cakes for a relaxed lunch or even afternoon tea.

On the first Sunday of every month you'll find a local farmers' market in the car park at Rhug with over 20 stalls, selling everything from cheese and dairy products to home-made bread and pies.

Rhug Estate Organic Farm Shop 342
Rhug Estate, Corwen,
Denbighshire LL21 0EH
01490 413000
www.rhugorganic.com
Farmers' market 10am–4pm the first Sunday of the month.

TJ Roberts & Son 341
Tryweryn House, 8 Station Road,
Bala, Gwynedd LL23 7NG
01678 520471
www.welshqualitymeat.co.uk

Tyddyn Llan (restaurant with rooms) 343
Llandrillo, Near Corwen,
Denbighshire LL21 0ST
01490 440264
www.tyddynllan.co.uk

J Williams & Co (Glyn Davies) 344
120 Vale Street, Denbigh,
Denbighshire LL16 3BS
01745 812585

Edwards of Conwy 335
18 High Street, Conwy,
Gwynedd LL32 8DE
01492 592443
www.edwardsofconwy.co.uk

Elwy Valley Lamb 345
Rose Hill Cottage, Henllan,
Denbigh, Denbighshire LL16 5BA
01745 813552
www.elwyvalleylamb.co.uk

The meat at the Rhug estate's farm shop is top notch but there are other independent butchers who also specialise in high-quality local meat. TJ Roberts butchers in Bala supply the renowned Tyddyn Llan with excellent local lamb and well-aged beef, plus a range of cooked meats. J Williams in Denbigh is the place for getting your hands on some of the celebrated Elwy Valley Lamb. Daphne Tilley or sons Johnny and David will happily show you around their farms just four miles away. Edwards of Conwy is the best-known independent butcher in North Wales, with a wonderful selection of meat sourced from local sustainable farms. Their range of sausages and pies is simply awesome.

Harvie's Pies

Carol Harvie first made pies when she was asked to provide lunches for shooting parties on the Pentre Hobyn Estate. These little pastry delights went down so well that she rented a small unit to make them on a more commercial basis. The business has grown and Harvie's Pies are now sold at farmers' markets as well as prestigious food halls such as Harrods.

Her pies include classics such as organic beef with ale, and organic beef with Stilton, but also the more unusual, such as the triple award-winning organic pork, prune and calvados pie as well as the Bronze medal winner in the British Pie Awards – smoked haddock and bacon pie. And it's not just savoury pies: Carol also makes a fantastic selection of dessert pies packed with fresh fruit. And what could be better than a tailor-made Harvie's Pies chutney to accompany the melt-in-the-mouth pastry parcels?

If you're in the Nercwys area, follow your nose to Carol's shop, which sells freshly baked pies from the farm. In fact, you can now go full circle and play country squire at Pentre Hobyn Hall with food supplied by Carol and her team of chefs.

Harvie's Pies 346
Waen Farm, Nercwys, Near Mold,
Clwyd CH7 4EW
01352 751285

Conwy Feast

Conwy's own food festival – Conwy Feast – has grown in its first five years to be one of the most exciting foodie events in Wales. The small medieval town of Conwy buzzes with activities in all quarters, but the main focus is down on the quay. Essentially, Conwy Feast is about local sustainable produce that can be bought at any time of the year. It's just one reason why foodies are flocking across the border to get a taste of the action.

Expect to see cooking demonstrations by chefs from North Wales using the produce they feature in their restaurants, as well as some TV chefs. The festival is held annually on the last weekend of October when everything from Welsh lamb and beef, local sausages and autumn vegetables to freshly landed bass, mullet and flounder is in fine form. Favourite stalls include Derimon Smokery, Glasfryn Farm Produce and Billy the Fish in his van with plenty of local fish and his famous push-net shrimps.

And if that's got you planning your foodie fests for next year, start the season off at the Llyn Land and Seafood Festival, run by the Llyn Fishermen's Cooperative, at the end of May. It's just when the first produce – such as lobsters and crab, bass, flatfish and perhaps a few mackerel, Menai oysters and mussels (see page 246) – starts arriving on fishermen's boats.

Conwy Feast 336
Conwy Town Centre, Conwy, Gwynedd
01492 593874
www.conwyfoodfestival.co.uk
Last weekend of October.

Llyn Land and Seafood Festival
www.llynseafoodfestival.org.uk

Anglesey Sea Salt

Even though Wales is surrounded by the sea on three sides, amazingly only 5 per cent of the coastline has been developed. Seawater is a natural asset but it hadn't been exploited till former owners of Anglesey Sea Zoo David and Alison Lea Wilson first tasted the salt that evaporated around the periphery of their fish ponds. Such grains sowed the seeds of an idea.

From their small-scale beginnings, extracting salt using a relatively crude method of evaporation by direct heat, Halen Môn (aka Anglesey Sea Salt) is now produced in a state-of-the-art vacuum to release the salt at a lower temperature. These crystals of pure white are sold worldwide to the catering and retail markets.

You can sample the salt in its natural state or with several different flavourings: spiced, celery, smoked and vanilla. An impressive list of chefs, including none other than Heston Blumenthal at The Fat Duck (see page 114) and Ferran Adria at El Bulli in Spain, now use Halen Môn in their kitchens.

Production is housed next door to the Sea Zoo, which is now owned separately. While you're at Halen Môn tasting the salt, pop next door to those inspirational fish ponds and watch the skates, conger eels, mullet, bass, crabs and lobsters, which is particularly thrilling around the mid-afternoon feeding time.

Halen Môn 331
The Anglesey Sea Salt Company,
Brynsiencyn, Anglesey LL61 6TQ
01248 430871
www.seasalt.co.uk

Anglesey Sea Zoo 332
Brynsiencyn, Anglesey LL61 6TQ
01248 430411
www.angleseyseazoo.co.uk

The Lobster Pot

A few miles along windy roads from the A5 is Church Bay and the hidden gem of The Lobster Pot restaurant. What started as a tea room in the 1950s has gradually taken over the bungalow and, more recently, some small conservatory-style extensions.

Though the décor is basic and unpretentious, the Anglesey sea fare is superb. The freshest lobster, crab and fish is all landed within a few miles. Lobster-lovers can choose from a lobster salad or the classics lobster thermidor or Newburgh; fishy types can ponder over grilled Dover sole, scallops in bacon or baked sea bass.

The lobsters could pretty much waddle their way over from the lobster ponds next door, which supply these alive and kicking crustaceans. Local fishermen sell their catch to the ponds to accumulate quantities for the continental markets. At the ponds, Tristan Wood (whose mother Lindy ran the restaurant for decades) will willingly show you around; you'll see lobsters swimming freely in tanks of all sizes and you'll be amazed at the variation in their dark camouflaged shells. Afterwards, buy a basket of live seafood – lobster, crab, winkles and mussels – and dine like a king at home.

The Lobster Pot 329
Church Bay, Anglesey LL65 4EU
01407 730241
www.lobster-pot.net

Lobster Ponds – Tristan Wood 330
Church Bay, Anglesey LL65 4EU
01407 730588

Hooton's Homegrown

Farm shops that genuinely grow the produce they sell are few and far between. But at Hooton's Homegrown, the name says it all. From an unpretentious prefab-greenhouse alongside the road to Brynsiencyn, the Hooton family grow and sell an amazing array of farm produce; the shop now even has an onsite butchers.

According to Mr Hooton Senior, the soil on their farm is glacial drift and is difficult to work, so everything they grow has to be on a small scale. But these little pockets of good land yield a wide range of fruit and veg. Early crops include asparagus, spring cabbages, leeks and cauliflowers, with courgettes, tomatoes and salads following in the main growing season. Broccoli, beetroot, cabbage and winter roots bring up the rear of the year and fill the shelves in leaner months; but you're sure to find something whenever you visit.

In season, fruit is always plentiful. At one time they grew blackcurrants for Ribena, but now the harvest takes in everything from gooseberries, rhubarb, redcurrants, strawberries, raspberries and blackberries to apples, pears and plums. As you'd expect in a family-run operation, Mrs Hooton makes chutneys, preserves and jams from excess production to ensure there is little waste. She also bakes cakes and makes pies, flans and puddings to serve in the side of the greenhouse that's now transmogrified into a honest-to-goodness café.

The expanded butchery section has an impressive display of the Hooton's own farm meat including Welsh Black beef, pork, lamb and poultry. The standard of butchery and presentation is professional and every cut can be vacuum packed for transportation home and storage. You can buy home-made sausages and burgers or choose from a spread of cuts of meat from belly pork to ribs of beef. But since their stock is their own meat, the choice will depend on what is available from the weekly supply. People travel far for this kind of meat: Chris Chown of Plas Bodegroes in Pwlheli drives here to collect the free-range guinea fowl that features on his award-winning restaurant menu.

Actually, they do stock other produce but it is all local so we forgive them instantly on the trade description front. You'll find wondrous Welsh cheese, such as Gorau Glas blue cheese from Anglesey, and Dragon Salted Welsh Butter from the Llyn Peninsula as well as Anglesey honey. Locals shop weekly at Hooton's and stock their freezers, since the prices, though not at supermarket basic level, are highly competitive; and the quality far exceeds that of any supermarket premium line.

If Anglesey is a tad too far north to venture to, then stop off at Bellis Brothers in Ruthin where they have a range of vegetables and PYO fruit in season. Or wear out the kids while you visit Glasfryn Farm Shop on the Llyn Peninsula north of Pwlheli; their large farm shop sells meat and vegetables, and there's an activity centre too.

Hooton's Homegrown 333
Gwydryn Hir, Brynsiencyn,
Anglesey LL61 6HQ
01248 430344
www.hootonshomegrown.com

Bellis Brothers Farm Shop 347
Wrexham Road Farm, Holt, Near Wrexham,
Powys LL13 9YU
01829 270304
www.bellisbrothers.co.uk

Glasfryn Farm Shop 328
Glasfryn Parc, Y Ffôr, Pwllheli,
Gwynedd LL53 6PG
01766 810044
www.siop-glasfryn.com

Conwy Mussels

As you cross over one of the bridges that spans the Menai Strait (Afon Menai), you'll no doubt be unaware of the dangers, and gastronomic riches, that lurk beneath. This is a curiously treacherous stretch of tidal water. The differing tides at either end result in surging water flushing from one end to the other as the tides ebb and flow. But such turbulent waters are advantageous if you're farming mussels since these molluscs feed on the rich plankton riding the eddies and whirlpools. In fact, the area between Conwy, Bangor and Beaumaris forms the largest fishery for mussels in Britain.

In days gone by, traditional flat-bottomed mussel boats would be filled to the gunwales after a day of hand-raking mussels from the sea bed. Small mussels would be relaid for fattening, while the largest were harvested and sent to the inland markets. A massive mussel sculpture stands on the quay at Conwy as a reminder of the area's traditional industry. And opposite this metallic mollusc is the new home of the Conwy Mussel Company run by Trevor Jones and his small team. The laborious work of hand-dredging is long gone, the modern super-dredgers can do a season's work in a matter of hours.

Nowadays, the relaid mussels fatten on the 'lays' that are easily accessible by boat at low tide and they can be harvested for the market throughout the season. Once gathered they are taken to the quayside purification tanks where they spend a few days before being ready for sale or for transporting to market. You can buy these fresh-from-the-water mussels here by the kilo for throwing together a rustic *moules* dish. You may even find one of the elusive mussel pearls during your cooking; such pearls were in huge demand from costume makers in Victorian times.

Today, the Conwy Mussel Company supplies numerous local hotels and restaurants, as well as sending mussels further afield. If you'd like to taste Conwy mussels but would rather someone else do the prep and cooking, then book a table one evening at Bistro Bach in Conwy. You'll find it up a narrow old lane close to the town centre – it has the look of a church hall from the outside, but the wooden interior, friendly staff and culinary aromas bring a warm ambience. They collect their Conwy mussels daily and cook them in classic *marinière* style.

Equally the all-day food service in Dawson's in the Castle Hotel in the town's High Street guarantees the freshest mussels as well as a host of other locally sourced food cooked by a skilled kitchen team. Dawson's is the hub of the local community, and the bar's bustling all day. The chef is a member of the Welsh Culinary Team and all the menu sings of Cymru. Local crab, Menai bass and oysters, plus Conwy Valley lamb and a host of farmhouse cheeses make this place a great destination.

The western end of the Menai opens out on to a vast area of shore at Brynsiencyn. Here Menai Oysters grows Pacific rock oysters in bags on racks along the low-tide mark. As well as farming oysters, they also harvest the stocks of mussels that

Conwy Mussel Company 337
The Mussel Centre, The Quay,
Conwy, Gwynedd LL32 8BB
01492 592689

Menai Oysters 334
Tal-y-Bont Bach, Llanfiarpwll,
Anglesey LL61 6UU
01248 430878
www.menaioysters.co.uk

Bistro Bach 338
26 Chapel Street, Conwy,
Gwynedd LL32 8BP
01492 596326

Dawson's in the Castle Hotel 339
High Street, Conwy, Gwynedd LL32 8DB
01492 582800
www.castlewales.co.uk

Conwy Brewery 340
Unit 3, Parc Caer Seion, Conwy,
Gwynedd LL32 8FA
01492 585287
www.conwybrewery.co.uk

grow naturally along the shore. At their purification plant, Sean Krijen will show you oysters as fresh, sweet and plump as you are ever likely to see. They can be purchased by the dozen, along with large mussels sold by the kilo.

But seeing as the best things in life are free, you can always have a go at gathering your own mussels at low tide. This stretch of shore does flood incredibly quickly so always keep one eye on the land. Select the largest and cleanest shells, and particularly those growing individually as low down the rocks as possible. Do note that these mussels are unpurified so careful cleaning and cooking are essential. But what could be better than a free supper of delicious Conwy mussels, all washed down with a pint of the local ale from Conwy Brewery? True riches indeed.

Scotland

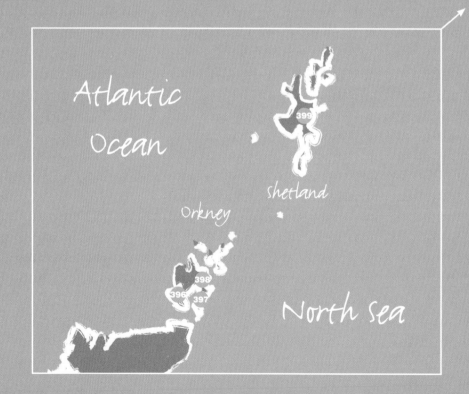

Atlantic Ocean

Outer
Hebrides

383

North Sea

384

Kyle of Lochalsh

387
388

Skye

386

385

393
392
391
394
Inverness

395

390
389

Aberdeen

Fort William

381

382

371

373
372 374 375

Tobermory

376

378
377 379
Callander 380

370

369

368

365
362
363 361
364 366
358 360
359 367
Edinburgh

348

355

354

Glasgow

356 357

349

350

351

Irish Sea

352
353

Dumfries

Scottish Ice Cream

These days, kids chase down the street after the Pied Piper vendors with their annoying jingles, dispensing soft-whipped 99s and lurid ice pops that bear no resemblance to the proper stuff. For ice cream aficionados there should be nothing in the tub or cone that isn't natural, which means cream, milk, sugar and flavourings such as real Bourbon vanilla, fruit or chocolate.

In the heart of the Dumfries and Galloway countryside, with its cracking views of the Solway Firth, is Cream o'Galloway, home to 90 dairy cows that produce organic milk for almost 30 flavours of frozen delights. There's plenty on offer to keep every member of the family happy. 'I scream, you scream, we all scream for ice cream!' goes the song and that's what Cream o'Galloway does exceptionally well, keeping everyone happy with dedicated experiences to these icy delicacies. The dairy runs activities, such as the 'Ice Cream Experience' or the more hands-on 'Ready, Steady, Freeze', where you create your own ice cream from scratch, in any flavour as long as it has a snappy, zappy title.

For those just keen on tucking in, the sundaes in the café are hard to beat. Choose from Saint or Sinner (scoops of raspberry and double choc-chip), or Wickedly Wicked (made with gingerbread and whisky, honey and oatmeal) ice creams, or the belt-busting, to-be-shared Sugar Rush – a double hit of caramel shortbread, double choc-chip and sticky toffee ices, chocolate sauce and choc-chips (not one for kids on a long journey). The good news is that you can work off those newly acquired calories out in the fresh air on the farm's nature trails, or challenge yourself to climb the lookout tower with views across to the Isle of Man.

Heading north towards the east coast is the village of Gullane. Here you'll find Falko Konditormeister (see also page 262) – a German baker who has a penchant for making half-a-dozen flavours of ice cream in the summertime. In a tiny room above the bakery, Falko happily makes small batches of ice cream for his shop. Everything is hand-made and contains no artificial this, that or the other. He makes his custard base from eggs, milk, cream, sugar and several vanilla pods, with the seeds scraped out to fleck the mix. Strawberries and raspberries for the sorbets come from local fruit farms. The caramel ripple is as sinful as it comes.

If you're in Fife, Stewart Tower Dairy creates unusual flavours such as avocado or chocolate and chilli, alongside vanilla, strawberry and chocolate ices.

Whether your Achilles heel is a knickerbocker glory, banana split or just a plain vanilla cone, seek out the real thing and rekindle childhood memories of lazy, hot summers, lounging in the park licking a creamy, flavour-intense ice cream.

Cream o'Galloway Dairy 353
Rainton, Gatehouse of Fleet, Castle Douglas,
Kirkcudbrightshire DG7 2DR
01557 814040
www.creamogalloway.co.uk
Open 10am–5pm 13 March–1 November;
10am–5pm at weekends only for the
rest of year.
Ice Cream Experience at 11.30am and
1.30pm; booking essential (01552 815222).
Ready, Steady, Freeze available Monday–
Thursday during July and August. It costs
£12 for two people or £15 for three people.
Group has to be a minimum of eight; booking
essential (01552 815222).
Farm tours at 2.45pm daily from late March to
beginning of November.

Falko Konditormeister 366
1 Stanley Road, Gullane,
East Lothian EH31 2AD
01620 843168
www.falko.co.uk
Open 8am–5.30pm Wednesday–Saturday
and 11am–5.30pm Sunday. Closed Monday
and Tuesday.

Stewart Tower Dairy 382
Stanley, Perthshire PH1 4PJ
01738 710044
www.stewart-tower.co.uk
Open daily 10am–4.30pm.

Scottish Smokehouses

Think Scotland, think smoked salmon. These thin sheaves of pale pink cold-smoked to tanned hot-smoked juicy fish vary from smokehouse to smokehouse. It's not only salmon that's preserved by smoking either: you will find game, fish, bacon and even goat's cheese. Depending on the type of wood used in the process (each smokery has a favourite), the food takes on different flavours according to how long it lingers amid the aromatic smoke.

Modern-day smokers are often stainless-steel constructions, but some wee places still use wooden sheds; if you fancied doing your own smoking, you could even use an old Reliant Robin. Over in Ayrshire there are two smokehouses not far from each other that have very different ways of smoking their wares, producing some of the best smoked products in the region.

Fencebay Fisheries is owned and run by 'Local Food Hero' Bernard Thain (pictured opposite) and his wife Jill. Once upon a time they had just a trout farm. Then they started smoking fish, built a shop, expanded to include Fins restaurant, and today they run a small farmers' market in one of the outbuildings.

Bernard smokes his fish, cheese and bacon in stainless-steel kilns using beech from trees felled on his land; he says that this lighter smoke gives the fish a sweeter, more delicate flavour than oak smoking. He still takes time out from all his endeavours to fish and creel on his little boat *Pegasus* and you can be sure that whatever he catches will find its way on to the menu in the restaurant.

In contrast, the Smiths at Burns Country Smokehouse have a more eccentric approach to smoking food. Duncan's somewhat Wallace and Gromit contraption is a converted garden shed, with smoke produced by an old Rangemaster. It certainly looks crazy, but he's been smoking food for over 15 years in this way, choosing wood chips from American white oak Bourbon casks to create a sweet and slightly oaky smoke. Not content with creating wonderful smoked fish, he is happy to turn his hand to smoking anything – eel, Brie, duck and chicken breasts and some stunning goat's cheese. All their salmon is sliced by hand, showing the dedication Duncan has for his produce. Venture into the tiny café and sample anything or everything from their range of goodies.

Further south in Dumfries and Galloway, overlooking the Solway Estuary, is Marrbury Smokehouse's shop at Carsluith Castle. Vincent and Ruby Marr catch wild salmon in small sandy pools on the Cree Estuary by hand, using nets and a little boat called a coble. But salmon is just one of many smoky delights to be found – there's Kirkcudbright scallops, mussels and even smoked haggis.

No matter where in Scotland you are, follow your nose and the signs to the local smokery; you are guaranteed to leave with something rather special.

Fencebay Fisheries
Fencebay, Fencefoot Farm, Fairlie, Ayrshire KA29 0EG
01475 568918
www.fencebay.co.uk
Open 9am–5pm Monday–Saturday and 10am–4pm Sunday.
Farmers' market takes place on the last Sunday of the month.

Burns Country Smokehouse
Grange Mains Farmhouse, School Road, Minishant, Ayrshire KA19 8DL
01292 442773
www.burnsmoke.com
Open 10am–5pm Monday–Saturday and 12–5pm Sunday.

Marrbury Smokehouse
Carsluith Castle, Carsluith, Near Newton Stewart, Wigtownshire DG8 7DY
01671 820476
www.visitmarrbury.co.uk
Open daily 10am–6.30pm. Closed Sunday and Monday October–March.

Isle Of Arran Food Trail

Arran is an island of contrasts: white sands, craggy mountains, glittering lochs and panoramic vistas to the Mull of Kintyre; some people even call it 'Scotland in Miniature'. The same could be said about Arran's food, reflecting the diversity of the mainland but confined to an island that is only 25 miles long by about 10 miles wide. The Isle of Arran is literally teeming with local producers from cheesemakers, growers of herbs, vegetables and soft fruits to chocolatiers and bakers who bake oatcakes and fantastic breads.

You're never too far from the sea but there's only one place for fresh fish on the island and that's Creelers' smokehouse, shop and restaurant. Most places are set near the coast, from Lochranza in the north with one of Scotland's youngest whisky distilleries to Kilmoy in the south where you can sample some fine Dunlop cheese. The Blackface sheep grazing on the hills and the more slow-growing Scottish cattle breeds produce the most flavoursome and succulent meat imaginable.

The Isle of Arran Food Trail provides a culinary palette from which you can draw up your own foodie itinerary for exploring some of the most remarkable places, produce and people this island has to offer.

Isle Of Arran Food Trail 350
www.tastetrail.com

Cocoa Black

Culinary Olympian and chocolate maker extraordinaire Ruth Hinks has struck gold with her latest project: to develop a UK centre of excellence for the creation of chocolate and patisserie. And at her Cocoa Black school everyone can indulge their inner artist in all things sticky and gooey.

There's an abundance of classes to suit every ability and craving. Ruth keeps classes small (up to eight) so there's plenty of room to work and talk. She'll enthuse about the origins, history, and processes of chocolate- and patisserie-making and guide you through some tastings before the sticky business of creating your own delectations starts. Once you've mastered the basics, you can always return for one of the two advanced workshops where you can hone your skills by making your own fillings, learn professional moulding techniques and dipping.

If your passion lies on the patisserie side, there's even a class on crafting French-style gateaux with practical exercises in glazing, garnishing and producing the perfectly textured mousse.

Whatever you make you can take home to show off, unless, that is, it gets devoured en route, in which case you'll just have to go back to try your hand on another of Ruth's fun and heavenly courses.

Cocoa Black Chocolate and Patisserie School 356
Unit 7, Southpark Industrial Estate, Peebles, Scottish Borders EH45 9ED
01721 723764
www.cocoablack.co.uk

Earthy Food Market

Serendipity has a lot to answer for at Earthy. This food market is the fortunate outcome of the paths of four passionate people crossing; one a grower, one a marketer, one a horticulturalist and one an organic fruit and veg buyer. All perfectly matched and enthusiastic, they opened a wonderful local produce and organic store on the south side of Edinburgh.

Earthy champions unsung local heroes, such as James the baker whose bread is proved slowly, creating a chewy, crusty loaf that just begs for slabs of unsalted butter. Meats arrive from a few miles outside the city and from around Scotland. Linda Dick's huge 'vicious but delicious' chickens burst with succulence and flavour, easily feeding an extended family and providing enough leftovers for soup.

Working in harmony with the seasons, Earthy produce varies through the year: East Lothian asparagus in spring; lush strawberries, raspberries and the unusual Worcesterberries (a cross between a giant blackcurrant and a gooseberry) in summer; and foraged summer chanterelles. Groaning baskets full of autumnal goodies – apples, plums, squashes and pumpkins – add colour and charm.

Choose your seat depending on your mood: the al fresco café, the communal table upstairs or the slouchy sofa downstairs. The café offers daily-changing salads and sandwiches too. So, do what Chris, Dirk, Patricia and Pete say: 'Dig in'.

Earthy Food Market 358
33–41 Ratcliffe Terrace, Edinburgh EH9 1SX
0131 667 2967
www.earthy.co.uk

East Lothian Mozzarella

For those who have sampled the lactic delights of mozzarella and ricotta in its native home, supermarket equivalents fail to impress. Importer of Italian meats and cheeses Gabriele Caputo was extremely disappointed by the mozzarella brought into the UK, so much so that he tried making his own, initially with little success. But his kitchen-based experiment led to an 18-month search to find a dairy farmer who shared his vision and helped him become one of the few cheesemakers making mozzarella outside of Italy.

Gabriele and his partner, Adriana Alonzi, set up a creamery in the heart of the East Lothian countryside at Yester Mains Farm, producing mozzarella (which they call patcharella) and some of the best ricotta this side of the continent. Using unhomogenised milk from the traditionally raised dairy herd, this young couple are sure to be food heroes of the future. Their methods are traditional (which is rare even in Italy) and, under the guidance of master cheesemaker Michele Paventa, they are producing some utterly sublime cheeses, including *scamorza affumicata* – fantastic with a glass of red wine. But best of all is a bauble of mozzarella filled with cream, whey and mozzarella strips known as *burrata*.

SS dei Naufragati 359
www.ssantissima.co.uk
Edinburgh Farmers' Market takes place every second, third and fourth Saturday.
Glasgow Farmers' Market takes place every first and third Saturday.

Glasgow's Foodie Hub

In the heart of the city's West End and not far from the university is the cosmopolitan, eclectic and fascinating hub of Byres Road, where outstanding specialist delis, glorious greengrocers and buzzing cafés all jostle for attention among the bars, restaurants and more predictable shops.

Any itinerant foodie would be wise to start their pilgrimage at the lower end of the road, towards Partick and the Kelvingrove Art Gallery and Museum, where you'll find the rather retro University Café. Inside you'll be transported magically back to the 1950s – think partitioned booths and Formica tables. Their battered espresso machine is still dispensing great coffee and they concoct fabulous milkshakes.

Further up the street, on the same side, you can't fail to spot Tinderbox with a Vespa scooter in its window. The coffee here is strong; the espresso has the right amount of crema to hold sugar before it slowly sinks into the slightly bitter liquid and offers a real jolt to start the day.

Kember & Jones Fine Food Emporium is just one of the deli-cum-cafés on the street. They have a wondrous collection of superb goodies such as Rococo chocolate, local bacon, Stornoway black pudding and excellent breads. But it's the home baking that is the draw here: savoury tarts are stacked like colourful terracotta tiles; billowing meringues, chocolate cake with summer fruits cascading from the top, scones and all manner of inviting temptations await the intrepid explorer. Unusual dips such as beetroot hummus, vermillion harissa, black-olive tapenade and verdant basil pesto are made in-house. No wonder there is a constant ebb and flow of customers in this delectable little haven.

For fresh fish, Corrigan's display of Scottish scallops, oysters, haddock and salmon as well as the more exotic delights of shark and red snapper on its large marble slab may stop you dead in your tracks. Like many fishmongers, they're also purveyors of game and poultry – the only independent place on Byres Road where you can buy any type of meat at all, and that's a real shame. Right next door is Anderson's with fresh fruit and veg, some organic staples and a broad selection of Scotherbs herbs, which are grown just outside Dundee.

Make a detour for lunch down the cobbled little hideaway that is Ashton Lane, canopied by fairy lights along its length. The renowned Ubiquitous Chip sits here, along with a fair number of other good places to eat and drink.

Heading back on to Byres Road, cross the street to the very sinful 3 Steps to Heaven ice cream parlour. This highly original place will have you choose two flavours of home-made ice cream (the apple pie variety is a favourite, but don't turn your nose up at the native flavours of Irn Bru or fudge-like tablet) along with two toppings and they will mash and bash them together on an iced marble slab, before serving it up with your favourite sauce.

University Café
87 Byres Road, Glasgow G11 5HN
0141 339 5217

Tinderbox
189 Byres Road, Glasgow G12 8SN
0141 339 3108

Kember & Jones Fine Food Emporium
134 Byres Road, Glasgow G12 8TD
0141 337 3851
www.kemberandjones.co.uk

Corrigan's
188 Byres Road, Glasgow G12 8SN
0141 357 2766

Anderson's
190 Byres Road, Glasgow G12 8SN
0141 357 4944

The Ubiquitous Chip
12 Ashton Lane, Glasgow G12 8SJ
0141 334 5007
www.ubiquitouschip.co.uk

3 Steps to Heaven
221 Byres Road, Glasgow G12 8UD
07881 401216
www.3steps2heaven.co.uk

Roots, Fruits & Flowers
351 Byres Road, Glasgow G12 8AU
0141 339 5164
www.rootsfruitsandflowers.com

Heart Buchanan
380 Byres Road, Glasgow G12 8AR
0141 334 7626
www.heartbuchanan.co.uk

Demijohn
382 Byres Road, Glasgow G12 8AR
0141 337 3600
www.demijohn.co.uk

Tchai-Ovna House of Tea
42 Otago Lane, Glasgow G12 8PB
0141 357 4524
www.tchaiovna.com

WEE
CUSTARD
TART
£1.25

ROOTS, FRUITS
& FLOWERS

italian
wild boar
salami

SPANISH
CHORIZO
£1.75 100G

BEECH WOOD
SMOKED HAM

PICK n MIX

Near the end of the road is Roots, Fruits & Flowers. This former butchers has been transformed into a greengrocer's with a small but perfectly formed florist's. They stock an excellent range of local, British and overseas produce, with seasonal fruit and vegetables from Scotland, such as asparagus, tomatoes and soft fruits displayed in boxes like multicoloured marbles. Glasgow-based Tapa Bakehouse supplies the shop with organic breads.

Next, nip over the road to Heart Buchanan's fine food and wine shop for the most gorgeous selection of fresh salads; if you give them some notice they will even make up a picnic for you. Fancy cheating on the dinner party front? Choose from their changing menu of dishes that you can take home to finish off: there's chargrilled chicken with mango and pineapple salsa, or beef meatballs in a tangy tomato sauce, and vegetarian alternatives could be a wild chanterelle risotto or stuffed peppers. Emphasis is placed on the provenance of ingredients, all of which are sourced as locally and as seasonally as possible. They have a diverse selection of wines to boot. Take time out and indulge in one of their deliciously gooey cakes with a cup of tea or a milky latte.

Make your final destination on Byres Road the liquid deli of Demijohn. When the sun shines the huge *damigiana* (Italian for demijohn) filled with organic elderflower, orange or cucumber vodka or gooseberry gin and wild bullace liqueur radiate light like stained glass. Have a wee nip, choose a pretty bottle and they will fill it with your favourite tipple. There's a kaleidoscope of local fruit vinegars and the Perthshire rapeseed oil glows like liquid amber.

Although not on Byres Road, Tchai-Ovna is a tiny tea house a mere 10-minute stroll away and offers a peaceful oasis just above the River Clyde. With over 80 teas to choose from (you can buy to take home too), it may take a while to decide. But there's no rush. Sit and ponder the evocative and imaginative descriptions of the teas, such as Fairy Blood tea made from freshly squeezed fairies from the bottom of the garden. Or Fairy Bounce guaranteed to give your wings a definite lift. Got a hangover? Try Che Ngon So, a popular green tea. Tchai-Ovna is a perfect place to relax after the hurdy-gurdy of the city. The inside is cosy with a 'new age' feel, the staff are informative, friendly and cheery, their vegetarian food is filling and the teas are uplifting. Just the ticket at the end of a busy day.

Edinburgh Farmers' Market

At the base of an extinct volcano and in the shadow of an iconic castle, Edinburgh Farmers' Market is at its bustling best. It really doesn't matter that it's set up on the wide pavement by a multistorey car park because it's the food that's the star here.

The hardy regulars may complain about the wind and rain on *driech* days, but the resilient stallholders simply stamp their feet to keep out the cold and battle with awnings when a sudden gust threatens to carry them off. But when the sun makes an appearance, all is well with the world; smiles replace furrowed brows and banter is lively, raucous and fun.

Not all the products at this weekly market are organic, but almost all of the producers (over 65 in total, but they're not all here on the same Saturday) will be only too pleased to discuss how they grow or rear their produce, how to cook it and how it is made; some even offer free tasters. The majority of the suppliers are small, family-run businesses and they sell what they have ready; everything is seasonal. At the Phantassie stall, you may discover morello cherries (in season), Worcesterberries and a trug of Victoria plums among the familiar carrots, cabbages and potatoes.

This market is the perfect place to buy a picnic lunch, with wonderfully slow-risen sourdough and rye breads from Falko Konditormeister. His *brezeln* (giant pretzels) are addictive and his cakes are heavenly; a December visit also sees his traditional Christmas *stollen*, a sweet bread with dried fruit, almond paste or poppy seeds.

Rachel, from Piperfield Pork, will cut you thick slabs of tasty ham made from Middle White porkers. Just down from her, Muriel has preserves and chutneys to pep up any cold table or sarnie. There are pâtés, cheeses and pies and, when it's a bit nippy, mother and daughter Helen and Sharon, who run the Good Soup Group, serve up fresh, home-made soup free from chemical nasties.

There are some gloriously named spuds to be bought here from Carrolls Heritage Potatoes – such as the red-fleshed Highland Burgundy, the Salad Blue that makes a fantastic pale-purple mash or the waxy Royal Kidney, similar to Jersey Royals, that just cry out for generous knobs of fresh butter.

The market has a whole ark of deliciously local finned, feathered and furred, wild and reared meat and fish. Head to Fletchers of Auchtermuchty (see page 272) and Carmichael's for ethically farmed venison or catch the wild version from Eric at Border County Foods. Ballencrieff and Peelham both have meaty sausages, bacon and free-range porcine cuts; and you can even buy a Tamworth piggy

Edinburgh Farmers' Market 360
Castle Terrace, Edinburgh EH1 2DP
www.edinburghfarmersmarket.com
Every Saturday 9am–2pm.

Phantassie
East Linton, East Lothian EH40 3DF
01620 861531
www.phantassie.co.uk

Falko Konditormeister
185 Bruntsfield Place, Edinburgh EH10 4DG
0131 656 0783

Piperfield Pork
The Dovecote, Lowick, Berwick-upon-Tweed,
Northumberland TD15 2QE
01289 388543
www.piperfield.com

The Good Soup Group
07969 334537
www.thegoodsoupgroup.com

Carrolls Heritage Potatoes
Tiptoe Farm, Cornhill-on-Tweed,
Northumberland TD12 4XD
www.heritage-potatoes.co.uk

Carmichael Estate Farm Meats
Carmichael, Biggar, Lanarkshire ML12 6PG
01899 308336
www.carmichael.co.uk

Border County Foods
The Old Vicarage, Crosby-on-Eden,
Cumbria CA6 4QZ
01228 672020
www.cumberland-sausage.net

Ballencrieff Rare Pedigree Pigs
Ballencrieff Gardens, Longniddry,
East Lothian EH32 0PJ
01875 870551
www.ballencrieffpigs.co.uk

Peelham Farm Produce
Peelham, Foulden,
Berwickshire TD15 1UG
01890 781328
www.peelham.co.uk

> ## "This farmers' market is full of passionate people on both sides of the stalls."

Gartmorn
Gartmorn Farm, Alloa,
Clackmannanshire FK10 3AU
01259 750549
www.gartmornfarm.co.uk

Brewsters
01337 840248

Creelers
Creelers in Edinburgh
3 Hunter Square, Edinburgh EH1 1QW
0131 220 4447
www.creelers.co.uk

J & M Craig
Briarneuk Nursery, Braidwood, Carluke,
Lanarkshire ML8 5NG
01555 850279

Stewart Brewing
42 Dryden Road, Bliston Glen Industrial
Estate, Loanhead, Midlothian EH20 9LZ
0131 440 2442

Cairn O'Mohr Winery
East Inchmichael, Errol, Perthshire PH2 7SP
01821 642781
www.cairnomohr.co.uk

Border Tablet
11 Holmwood Drive, Langholm, Dumfries
and Galloway DG13 0PX
01387 381224
www.sweets-online.co.uk

The Chocolate Tree
5 Mitchells Close, Haddington,
East Lothian EH41 3NB
01620 811102
www.the-chocolate-tree.co.uk

that Peelham will 'grow' for you: you can visit it and when the time comes they will dispatch it and supply you with all the joints from said pig. Be brave and try something new, such as a buffalo or ostrich steak, or start off with their flavour-packed burgers, a gentle introduction to these fine meats. Gartmorn chickens can be huge beasts but they pack big flavours, as their duck breasts do; the legs are excellent value and make great confit. And from chicken to eggs; the best come from Brewsters. Dawn's rare-breed hens lay brown, white, mottled and greeny-blue eggs, much prized by her customers.

As for fish, you will find salmon in all its guises – hot- and cold-smoked, gravadlax, whole or filleted. West Coast scallops and langoustines are reputed to be the best in the world, and both can be found regularly on Creelers' stall at the top end of Castle Terrace, as can the descriptively named 'spoots' or razor clams. These phallic bivalves have the startling habit of squirting water from their bodies, but sliced and flash-fried with herbs and garlic, they make exceptional eating.

From spring to early November you can buy Scottish tomatoes from J & M Craig. These ruby gems are an absolute treat and the queues prove this. From pop-in-the-mouth miniatures to plump plum varieties (a joyous match with East Lothian mozzarella – see page 257 – and some pungent basil), they bring back childhood memories with that distinctive smell of the stalks on warm summer days. Ask for a bag of 'cookers', they're great for soups and sauces. If you like making chutney, you might even be able to get hold of some green toms.

The market offers some cracking beers from Black Isle Brewery (see page 282) and Edinburgh-based Stewart Brewing. You can spot the wonderfully named (say it quickly to get the joke) Cairn O'Mohr fruit wines by their distinctive, wacky labels. Oak leaf wine may sound weird but really is rather good; the Autumn leaf is medium dry, and goes well with lamb; while the Spring leaf is medium sweet; and the Strawberry Fizz is great with summer pudding. Teetotallers rejoice as there are exceptional traditionally pressed, single-variety apple juices or sparkling raspberry and strawberry juices to sip and buy.

Those who have a sweet tooth can feed their cravings with tablet, the grainy Scottish equivalent of fudge, from the Border Tablet stall. And serious chocoholics should head to Ali and Friederike's Chocolate Tree stall; the couple make organic chocolate bars and truffles, all wrapped up in their distinctive Celtic-logo packaging or in pretty, hand-made origami boxes.

Edinburgh Farmers' Market is full of passionate people on both sides of the stalls – people who care about what they produce, what they buy and what they eat. So, grab a cappuccino or espresso from Caitlin in her police box and wander around, deciding what you want to eat for dinner, lunch or, indeed, breakfast.

Monachyle Mhor

You cannot fail to be awe-struck and inspired as you follow the signs in Balquhidder for Monachyle Mhor. The single-track road takes you along the banks of Loch Voil in the heart of the Trossachs National Park, and just when you think you may have taken a wrong turn the marshmallow-pink hotel comes into view, with scenery that makes your jaw drop.

Run by brothers and sister Tom, Dick and Melanie Lewis, Monachyle Mhor sits on the family's 2,000-acre estate, where they farm cattle, sheep, hens and pigs; and you may catch the occasional glimpse of wild deer. The farmhouse, in which the three siblings grew up, is now an award-winning destination with 14 beautifully designed bedrooms. Tom heads the kitchen, cooking food that has been grown or reared on the farm; the bread comes from their own bakery, naturally.

There's more than food on offer here; Tom and his team run courses from drystone walling (dykes in Scotland) to photography for those not heavily into foodie experiences. There's a host of courses and demonstrations available on pretty much anything and everything foodie. Learn how to choose, raise and breed chickens for eggs, make fresh bread, butter and jams or select, prepare and then cook fish. These indoor experiences take place in the dedicated demonstration room above the Lewis' extraordinary fish shop in Callander.

MHORFish is more than a chippie, it's a restaurant and a fishmonger. If you want a takeaway fish supper, you can choose from any fish on the slab; it can be baked, seared, grilled as well as fried. Or take a table and let someone else do the hard work, so you can simply enjoy some of the best seafood Scotland has to offer.

Down the road on the other side of Main Street is another family enterprise – MHORBread. All the bread is made by hand using Scottish-milled flour free from preservatives. Artisan loaves are just as popular as the sliced and unsliced varieties. What's more, they are continuing the tradition of making black buns, bannocks, Scotch pies and perkins, much to the approval of their regular clientele.

You'll find yet another venture at the pretty, blue Library Tea Room in Balquhidder. Inside MHORTea, the ceilings soar and on cooler days, as rain creeps over the loch, log fires are lit to keep out the chill, while warming soup, afternoon tea or home-made scones are served on wonderfully mismatched china. The pastry chefs back at the hotel provide a continuous supply of delicious cakes; choose, if you can, between the sticky carrot or gooey chocolate cheesecake. Bread, of course, is from the Callander bakery and just right for mopping up the last drops of filling soup.

Whether you are spending a night at the hotel, dropping in for a cuppa, grabbing a pie for lunch or buying a piece of fish for supper, appreciation of the quite astonishing attention to detail shown by this Scottish troupe is guaranteed.

Monachyle Mhor Hotel 377
Balquhidder, Lochearnhead,
Perthshire FK19 8PQ
01877 384622
www.mhor.net

MHORTea 378
The Library Tea Room, Balquhidder,
Lochearnhead , Perthshire FK19 8PQ
01877 384622
Open daily Easter–1 October.

MHORBread 379
8 Main Street, Callander, Perthshire FK17 8BB
01877 339518
Open 8.30am–5pm Monday–Saturday
and 9am–5pm Sunday.

MHORFish 380
75–77 Main Street, Callander,
Perthshire FK17 8DX
01877 330213
Open daily 10am–9pm.
Closed Mondays in winter.

"Inside MHORTea on cooler days, as rain creeps over the loch, log fires are lit to keep out the chill."

Stoats Porridge Bars

Tony Stone, the brains behind Stoats, launched the world's first mobile porridge bar back in 2004, serving nourishing, filling organic Scottish oats. The van dispenses steaming cartons of porridge in eight varieties: with local marmalade and whisky, the classic Cranachan (raspberries, cream, toasted oats and honey) or, for the brave, Scots style just with salt.

His distinctive vans can be found at Edinburgh Farmers' Market (see page 262) on most Saturdays and at numerous festivals throughout Scotland. Not content with dishing up to hungry punters, Tony has also made it into *Guinness World Records 2007* for the largest pot of porridge; it weighed a staggering 81.6kg and was stirred anticlockwise (to keep the devil at bay) with a six-foot spurtle.

Stoats Porridge Bars 361
www.stoatsporridgebars.co.uk
Various farmers' markets throughout
Scotland; see website for details.

Stoats also make chunky oat bars packed full of healthy ingredients (apricot and sultana, fig and date or the unusual goji berries and flax seeds). These tasty energy-boosting snacks certainly give you a lift; they've even been supplied to the 45 Royal Marines Commandos out on tour in Afghanistan.

And why the name, Stoats? It's from the Scottish phrase 'It's a stoater!' meaning anything that is exceptional quality. Say nae mare.

Haggis

Any butchers worth their weight in oatmeal have their own closely guarded recipe for the wee beastie known as haggis. You may not recognise a haggis at first glance; they hang in butcher's windows, looking like some kind of medieval weapon. You may even spot signs for freshly shot 'wild haggis'.

The main ingredients of haggis are the same: the offaly bits from sheep or deer, oatmeal, onion, suet and that secret spice blend that is often a family secret; all wrapped up in a sheep's stomach and boiled. It sounds grisly, but it's a remarkable dish. Macsween is the country's biggest commercial manufacturer, but it's the local butchers that make some of the best.

George Bower 362
75 Raeburn Place, Edinburgh EH4 1JG

Normally served with tatties and bashed neeps (that's mashed potatoes and swede) with a wee dram on the side, this national dish is celebrated throughout the world, especially on 25th January – Burns night – the birthday of Scotland's son, poet Robert Burns. It has also courted controversy. In 1977, Robin Dunseath advertised in a Scottish newspaper about the revival of haggis hurling. It was a hoax, but so many people wanted to participate it is now a bona fide event.

Findlay's of Portobello 363
116 Portobello High St, Edinburgh EH15 1AL

Colin D Peat & Son 367
3 Court Street, Haddington,
East Lothian EH41 3JD

WTS Forsyth & Sons 357
21–25 Eastgate, Peebles,
Scottish Borders EH45 8AD

Some have dared to suggest that the haggis may have originated from England. But no matter its provenance, the Scots have made haggis their own.

Puddledub Buffalo

Steve Mitchell is the proud owner of about 400 head of buffalo. Contrary to belief, these are not the kind seen grazing on the plains in iconic westerns; Steve's herd hails from Asia. These gentle giants, with their wide, flattish horns, are more than content to roam the hills of Fife, wallowing in mud and, given half the chance, having the sun-baked clay scratched and rubbed from their bodies by willing visitors.

If you fancy getting up close to these friendly beasts, take one of Steve's 4x4 tours around Puddledub Buffalo Farm; see if you can get them to come over or watch them wallowing happily in muddy pools. And the young calves are just the cutest. Pile on top of that stunning views across the Firth of Forth to Bass Rock and Berwick Law, and that's one grand tour.

But it's not just about watching these placid beasts, this is a working farm after all; Steve also raises Auchertool Angus cattle and Jacob sheep, all of which are destined for the pot just like the buffalo. Steve visits several farmers' markets throughout the east of Scotland to sell his meat but you can also buy it from the family shop in Kennoway.

Puddledub Buffalo Farm 365
Newcottoun, Clentrie Farm,
Auchtertool, Fife KY3 5XG
01592 780087
www.puddledubbuffalo.co.uk

S Mitchell of Puddledub 368
1 Cupar Road, Kennoway, Leven,
Fife KY8 5LR
01333 351245
Open 9am–5pm Monday–Friday
and 9am–2pm Saturday.

Iain Spink's Arbroath Smokies

There is no mistaking when 'Local Food Hero' Iain Spink is in town – if a haze drifting down the street isn't a dead giveaway, then the smokiness on the breeze is.

Being a traditionalist (his way of smoking haddock goes back several centuries), Iain smokes his fish over a half whisky barrel, lined with slate; a blend of beech and oak burns within to produce the heat and smoke. It's an eye-opening experience when charred slats covered with neatly paired, silver, headless haddock or trout are popped into the smoker, covered with hessian, then about 40–60 minutes later, golden smokies emerge from beneath a blanket of swirling smoke.

In the blink of an eye, they can be boned to take home or to be eaten directly from the paper, with fishy juices dripping down your chin. Because of its transportability, Iain can take this rather romantic contraption to many a festival and farmers' market around the east of Scotland. Crowds gather wherever he goes and he will happily chat about his passion for recreating a dying method of preserving fish.

Simple, delicious and utterly sublime, the Arbroath Smokie has to be one of the 50 things a true foodie should try before they die.

Iain Spink 371
01241 860303
www.arbroathsmokies.net

Find Iain at various farmers' markets:
St Andrews (first Saturday of the month).
Dunfermline (second Saturday).
Cupar (third Saturday).
Kirkcaldy (fourth Saturday).

Pillars of Hercules

You can't fail to notice the distinctive green-and-yellow sign on the main road directing discerning locals and foodies alike along the single-track road to this marvellous organically rich farm and shop.

You may wonder what has an all-organic farm in Scotland got to do with the Pillars of Hercules? Well, according to owner and farmer Bruce Bennett, nothing really; it was the name he inherited when he bought the place. There are several possible explanations, but the favourite concerns the stones that once stood next to the house. Story has it that coffins used to rest on said stones on the way to burial; going from the known world into the unknown, perhaps?

On arrival you are greeted with a scene of roaming hens (their eggs are for sale at the shop), scrabbling Bronze turkeys (some 350, all destined for the Christmas table) and working staff (hoeing weeds and shovelling compost on to the seasonal vegetables). There are no chemical influences here, just hard graft to make sure the food is as natural and organic as possible.

Established in 1983, the farm has grown to almost 25 acres and the variety of fruit and veg on offer is remarkable: spring ushers in rhubarb, spinach and broad beans, followed by tender salad leaves, herbs, globe artichokes, cucumbers and soft fruits in the summer; autumn sees squashes alongside apples and plums from the orchard, closely followed by swiss chard, leeks and root veggies in winter. A nice touch is that you can pick your own herbs and edible flowers, cropping what you want and paying by weight.

Within the shop, there are organic groceries to satisfy a world of cuisine from Japan and Thailand to Italy and Greece; everyone is catered for – veggies, vegans and meat-eaters. Bread hails from Tunstall's Organic Bakery in Birnam and you're sure to find a beverage from the extensive selection of beers, wines and soft drinks.

The shop also stocks eco-friendly beauty, cleaning and household products. And then there are the blooms. Floral offerings start around April with blousy tulips, fragrant stocks, alliums, lanky delphiniums and the gossamer varieties like larkspur, nigella, cornflowers and fairy-like gypsophila. Bringing up the rear in October are bold and brassy dahlias. There's also a collection of organic seeds available, so that anyone can try out their green fingers and grow their own.

Everything at the café, like the shop, is organic, suitable for vegetarians and, above all, home-made by the Pillar peeps. Inside is snug, but there is also a vast covered veranda where you can sip a foamy cappuccino and savour a slice of one of the many cakes, including gluten-free and vegan-friendly choices. If the wind picks up, don't head inside; just snuggle up under one of the warm fleece blankets and warm your cockles with a hearty soup. Oh, but when the sun shines it's an idyllic spot, sitting in the orchard as bees bumble from flower to flower.

Pillars of Hercules Farm **369**
Falkland, Cupar, Fife KY15 7AD
01337 857749
Open daily.
Shop 9am–6pm; café 10am–5pm.
www.pillars.co.uk

Tunstall's Organic Bakery 381
Unit 6, Birnam Industrial Estate,
Birnam, Perthshire PH8 0DS
01350 727924

"There are no chemicals...just hard graft to ensure the food is as natural and organic as possible."

Champion of local food and chef Christopher Trotter cooks up a four-course, mainly vegetarian menu here once a month at the aptly named 'Restaurant at the End of the World' (another reference to the Pillars of Hercules). There is no booze licence, so just BYOB. There's no corkage charge either. Bargain.

This child-, dog- and planet-friendly farm should be on everyone's list of must-visit places. It may be off the beaten track, but it is a sanctuary that just takes the sting out of modern-day life. Bruce Bennett and his wife Judy have got it just right.

Fletchers of Auchtermuchty

John and Nichola Fletcher are the pioneers of deer-farming in Britain, having started their own farm over 30 years ago in Fife. They are two of the most passionate, genuine people you could meet, and although Nichola is a skilled jewellery designer, she is also one of the world's foremost authorities on venison. Her husband, John, a vet by training, has set the ground rules for this industry.

Fletchers of Auchtermuchty 370
Reediehill Deer Farm,
Auchtermuchty, Fife KY14 7HS
01337 828369
www.seriouslygoodvenison.co.uk
Shop open daily 8am–6pm.

John's husbandry skills are sought after throughout the world and his affinity with these beautiful creatures is apparent when he talks about them; ask him about Thistle and watch a wistful smile cross his face. John hand-reared this gentle beast when she was rejected by her mother. Whenever he goes into her field, she comes rushing to greet him, making a thrumming sound in pleasure, something John has only experienced with her. This is a working farm after all, so the end result is the meat (excluding Thistle).

The demarcation point for the Fletchers, regarding the deer, is the bullet. According to Nichola, anything before then is John's area of expertise, anything afterwards is hers. This may seem a harsh reality, but in order to eat any meat it has to be dispatched in one way or another. At least the deer at Reediehill don't suffer the stress of being loaded into a trailer to be carted off to the local abattoir, which does affect the meat.

Deer and venison still raise the odd eyebrow, especially when it comes to the culling of wild stags and hinds. Although it would be amazing to see herds roaming free, left unchecked (and with no natural predators) the amount of available food would soon dwindle and they would die of starvation.

Some private estates offer hunting packages to keep deer numbers under control but this isn't without problems; the meat from wild deer can be utterly delicious or totally inedible, depending on the age and health of the animal, and how it has been butchered. There is little consistency for the consumer. Farmed deer, on the other hand, can offer consistently high-quality meat, which is what the Fletchers do as humanely as possible. The deer are no older than 27 months before they are shot in the field (the other deer oblivious to what's happening) and they are skinned before being hung, eliminating any contamination from the pelt.

Through cookery demonstrations, lectures, tutorials and one-to-one sessions, Nichola lays to rest some of the myths and old wives' tales about venison – it doesn't smell off and it isn't tough. She has also written several books including *Ultimate Venison Cookery*, which won her the prestigious Best Single Subject Book in the World at the Gourmand World Cookbook Awards in 2007.

> **"Anything before the bullet is John's area of expertise, anything afterwards is Nichola's."**

But the best way to see how good their venison is, is to try it. The Fletchers first started to popularise their venison in the form of veniburgers, which are still going strong today, along with casserole packs, steaks, venison racks and even haggis and sausages; oh and their wee little pies go down a storm. You can buy Fletchers' venison online or at one of the many farmers' markets they attend, such as Edinburgh, St Andrews and Kirkcaldy. John and Nichola never tire of imparting their knowledge about venison, how to cook it and what it tastes like.

As John Fletcher says, 'There are very few things in life that you can enjoy doing and are also good for you. I can only think of two, and one of those is eating venison'. It makes you wonder whether bitter-sweet, dark chocolate is the second and, if so, whether that makes Fletchers' chilli and chocolate venison sausages some kind of health food.

If you find yourself in Fife, pop over to see the small shop on their farm; you may even be lucky enough to get a glimpse of Thistle.

Oban Chocolate Company

Oban is recognised as the 'Gateway to the Isles' and it's just a few minutes' stroll from the ferry terminal that you'll stumble across the town's wonderful chocolate factory. Situated right on the seafront, the café-shop has humbling views of islands, mountains and boats bobbing on the water that can be lost in a blink of an eye and reappear magically as the weather changes on an angel's breath. Inside, where the muted heather and dusky lavender decor mirrors all the moods that the seasons bring, are some of the best chocolates on the west coast of Scotland.

Oban Chocolate Company 376
34 Corran Esplanade, Oban,
Argyll PA34 5PS
01631 566099
www.obanchocolate.co.uk

Amid the soft centres of rose and violet creams are some more modern and outlandish flavours. Who would have thought that a Marmite ganache surrounded by smooth chocolate could work? Even the most hardened Marmite hater could find a place in their heart for this slightly salty and creamy morsel. Glittering Chilli Chuffles are spiky little beasts, where the heat from the spice is tempered by the dark chocolate. The white version has the added benefit of lime that hula-hoops on your taste buds. But the most sublime and utterly palate-exploding flavour has to be the strawberry and balsamic with its bitter-sweet dark shrouds.

This hedonistic haven is the pride of Helen and Stewart MacKechnie, whose vision now means that they release into the wide world between 7,000 and 8,000 chocolates every week. Anyone can gaze upon the goings-on through the viewing window as creations are blended, whipped, moulded and hand-dipped in molten white, milk and dark gold. So passionate are this couple that they are planning to introduce a children's workshop.

The shop stocks not only truffles and chocolates but also bags of 'Haggis Eggs'; slabs scattered with nuts, fruit and berries that are sold by weight; and giant truffles filled with mini versions. No one is left out from the chocoholic jamboree as there are gluten-free, dairy-free and diabetic-friendly versions too.

With over 40 different types of chocolates, decision-making can be lip-bitingly slow; so while you're pondering, settle into the deep, squishy sofas with one of the decadently smooth hot chocolates and a tasting plate of four or six choccies. Sink back, close your eyes and be transported into a secret realm of pure pleasure as the truffles melt seductively in your mouth.

The chocolatiers create new flavours and combinations on an on-going basis and there is always a 'Chocolate of the Month' featured in the café and shop. If you can't make it to the shop, have no fear – there is a swift online service and the chocolates have a shelf-life of between six and eight weeks, though how long they'll last once you get them is anyone's guess.

Ardnamushrooms

Rob Dunn knows more than a little about mushrooms; to be more specific shiitake, oyster and the pretty but very delicate lion's mane. He grows these edible lovelies on a concoction of oak shavings, hardwood chips, organic bran and gypsum, which is then sterilised so that, when the mushroom spawn is introduced, it's not competing with any other wild spores.

If you are taking the scenic route from Oban and going along the banks of Loch Sunart to Mallaig, you have to go past the turning to Ardnamushrooms just outside Strontian. Rob will be more than happy to show you how he produces the mushroom blocks and the smell is almost intoxicating – a damp forest floor combined with the earthy scent of fungi.

Ardnamushrooms 375
Longrigg Manse, Strontian,
Acharacle, Argyll PH36 4HY
01967 402453
www.ardnamushrooms.co.uk
Open daily 9am–5pm.

You can buy fruiting kits, complete with growing instructions, to take home; there is something pleasing about growing your own shiitake, as they are so expensive to buy. If you don't want to do it yourself, then Rob sells all his produce loose – there's home-smoked shiitake, the feathery, creamy lion's mane as well as the dove-grey oyster mushrooms from his smallholding, and you can also see him at Edinburgh Farmers' Market (see page 262).

Lady Claire Macdonald

One thing you cannot fail to notice about Claire Macdonald is how approachable she is, welcoming guests with a captivating smile, gentle words and an enthusiasm that is infectious.

With a plethora of best-selling books under her apron strings, she is more than eager to share her culinary secrets from the kitchen of her home at Kinloch on the mystical Isle of Skye. If you ask what inspires her, she will reply with humour 'Greed!'. Her passion knows no bounds where seasonal Scottish produce is concerned; it is fundamentally important to her.

Lady Claire Macdonald 386
Kinloch Lodge, Sleat, Isle of Skye IV43 8QY
01471 833333
www.claire-macdonald.com
Cookery courses from £450 (includes three
nights' dinner, light lunch, bed and breakfast).

Claire doesn't preach, she exudes energy and is tireless in imparting what is crucial about using local foods and supporting farmers (she is Patron of Scottish Food Fortnight and the Association of Scottish Farmers' Markets). But cooking is what she loves; feeding people, sharing her ideas, tips and how to avoid pitfalls with her guests through her demonstrations. Those wanting a more practical experience can join Kinloch Lodge's head chef Marcello Tully for two full mornings prepping with him in the kitchen.

If Skye is a tad too far, then simply sign up to Claire's monthly menu club with her foolproof recipes, shopping list and her down-to-earth practical advice.

The Cross at Kingussie

The Cross at Kingussie 389
Tweed Mill Brae, Ardbroilach Road,
Kingussie, Inverness-shire PH21 1LB
01540 661166
www.thecross.co.uk

Food at The Cross is exceptional; chef Becca Henderson has an innate ability to put a cohesive menu together on a daily basis, using local and seasonal ingredients as much as possible. But the truly remarkable draw of this place is David and Katie Young's wine list.

Their well-kept cellar covers Old and New World without any bias and they aren't afraid of offering organic and biodynamic wines either. They have personally tasted and selected all 19 pages (yes, pages) of wines including a rather decadent two-and-a-bit pages of 'stickies' (pudding wines) and ports. Enjoy a glass or two of bubbly on the terrace as you digest this wonderful winey tome.

This little restaurant with rooms, perched above the River Gynack, has to be one of the cosiest, warmest and most welcoming places to stay within the breathtaking beauty of the Cairngorms National Park. The converted tweed mill, run by ex-AA hotel inspector David, is just the place to kick back and relax or, if you prefer, use it as a base to explore the mountains, lochs and rivers.

What draws people back, besides the superb food and the beauty of the area, is David and Katie who embrace everyone like old friends.

Rothiemurchus Estate

Rothiemurchus 390
By Aviemore, Inverness-shire PH22 1QH
01479 812345
www.rothiemurchus.net

Rothiemurchus has to be one of the most remarkable privately owned estates in Scotland; set in 25,000 acres within the Cairngorms National Park, it has some of the oldest uncultivated Caledonian pine woodland in the country. The setting could almost be described as Tolkien-esque, such is the beauty of the region, and it has been in the care of the Grant family for 17 generations, spanning 450 years.

Because of its unique setting, Rothiemurchus is a year-round destination. Come for the ranger-led safaris on foot discovering wild, edible fruits or by Land Rover through the pastures of Highland cattle and deer or perhaps quietly fish the well-stocked lochs. For adrenaline junkies, there's plenty on offer from gorge-walking and swimming to quad-bike trekking and even deer-stalking.

The estate's shop is well stocked with beef from its own Highland cattle, which is butchered onsite, as well as fish from the lochs and rivers. The venison is either wild from the surrounding hills or from the farm. And it's good to see that the local artisan foods sold in the shop also feature on the menu at the café.

There's so much to see you may well need a few days, in which case you can pitch up at the Rothiemurchus campsite.

The Speyside Malt Whisky Trail

In Scottish Gaelic it's *usquebaugh*, to some it's 'the water of life', to others 'The Blood of Scotland' but to most it's plain old whisky. The first noted reference to this renowned drink is an entry in the Exchequer Rolls of 1494: 'Eight bolls of malt to Friar John Cor wherewith to make aqua vitae' and seems to be the earliest record regarding distillation in Scotland.

Today whisky is made across the world, some of these are very good, but they cannot be classed as Scotch whisky; to earn that moniker, the whisky has to spend at least three years in Scotland. There are nearly 100 active distilleries throughout Scotland, and Speyside accounts for almost half of them.

It's amazing that just three ingredients – barley, water and yeast – can be made into an iconic drink recognised throughout the world; and one that varies in flavour from distillery to distillery even if they are made in the same area. Speyside is home to 48 distilleries; some of the biggest names in the industry (Glenfiddich, Macallan and Glenlivet) to little-known distillers such as Benromach (the smallest in Speyside) and Cragganmore.

Unfortunately, not all distilleries are open to the public, but many are. The Malt Whisky Trail guides you to seven working distilleries as well as Speyside Cooperage where they still use traditional methods for making and repairing barrels. Along the trail, you will encounter some jaw-dropping scenery, as it seems many distilleries favour beautiful locations. The iconic pagoda roofs of the peat kilns can be seen peeping out from tree-clad hillsides and the occasional wisp of smoke takes the imagination to past illicit stills.

Cardhu is the only malt distillery to be pioneered by a woman, Helen Cumming, who lived well into her 90s. Now owned by Diageo, it hosts the 'Aromas and Flavours' tour, and, like most distilleries, there is a wee dram to finish, with the added incentive of a discount voucher against a 70cl bottle of malt whisky from the shop. Strathisla is reputed to be the oldest distillery in Speyside, established in 1786; though, as you'd expect, others contest this.

But you don't have to stick rigidly to the trail; there are brown tourist signs throughout the region, pointing you towards any number of distilleries. Time your visit carefully and it may coincide with one of the two Speyside festivals each year: the Spirit of Speyside in spring and the Autumn Whisky Festival, a celebration of Scotland's national drink along with some of the area's wonderful food.

If you want a more intense guided whisky tour, then book a spot on Wild Green Travel's four-day break on Islay. You won't have to worry about driving since you

The Malt Whisky Trail 395
www.maltwhiskytrail.com

Wild Green Travel 364
166 High Street, Royal Mile,
Edinburgh EH1 1QS
0131 478 6500
www.wildgreentravel.com

"Speyside
is home to
almost half
the distilleries
in Scotland."

will be chauffeured around in a supremely comfy Mercedes minibus. And what's more, you get to stay at the beautifully restored Bowmore Distillery cottages. There are only eight distilleries on the island, including the newest, Kilchoman – the first distillery to be built on Islay for 124 years – so you'll easily see them all and get to savour the island's heavily peated drams.

The whisky of Scotland is as diverse, stunning and distinct as any other aspect of the country; from the food and the scenery to the culture and the people. *Sláinte*!

Cruise for Scottish Seafood

All around the Scottish coast a variety of boat trips can take you out to see bird colonies, watch seals or seek dolphins and the occasional whale. But for lovers of all things fishy, Neil MacRae offers a unique experience; he is the only fisherman in Scotland who takes people on a seafood cruise.

Neil MacRae 387
Cruises 07892 772864
Waterside Guesthouse 01599 577230
www.plocktonwaterside.co.uk

The trip starts from either Plockton or Stromeferry, neither of which are far from the Kyle of Lochalsh. Once aboard Neil's wonderfully named little boat *Perfect Day*, it's off into the waters around Kyle or Plockton and into Loch Carron. Neil has a quick smile and even quicker wit. His knowledge of the area stems from years of fishing these abundant waters and his stories may be tall, but you can't help being entertained and endeared to his charm.

Your stomach is sure to be rumbling after a couple of hours on the water and Captain Neil will show how to shuck queenies – small scallops that can be eaten straight from the shell, still quivering and tasting of a mermaid's kiss, sweet and slightly salty. Whipping out a frying pan, he quickly prepares a seafood feast of scallops, langoustine, crab and whatever else he has caught from his other boat *Green Isle*. You will never have eaten crustacea this fresh – from sea to boat to pan to mouth in a matter of hours. Neil is happy for you to bring your own wine should you feel the need, and he will cheerfully provide glasses.

Thrown in for gratis is the marine life. You may be lucky enough to spot the tell-tale signs of porpoise or dolphin dorsal fins, and a break in the surface of the water could indicate the arrival of seals. There's also a whole aviary of seabirds to be spotted, and, of course, there's the grandeur of the scenery that can only be experienced from a boat.

The cruises last between 1½ and 2 hours and can be either in the afternoon or evening, which has the added bonus of spectacular sunsets. Neil runs his cruises throughout the year but they are dependent on weather conditions and he needs 24 hours' notice. The minimum number he takes out is four, but you are more than welcome to double up with any other people booked to the maximum of 12. The *Perfect Day* is fully equipped for everyone's safety. It may not be the prettiest of boats, but the experience of discovering the joys of ultra-fresh seafood with a convivial host more than compensates.

For those who want to spend more time in the area, enjoying Neil's company and eating more of his catch, stay over at the Waterside Guesthouse, which he and his wife Jann run. Their supremely comfortable B&B will pander to your every whim as you relax watching bobbing boats in Plockton Bay.

Black Isle Brewery

There used to be three breweries in Inverness and another in Cromarty. Alas they no longer exist, but David Gladwin, founder and managing director of the Black Isle Brewery, is carrying on the tradition with a twist – Black Isle is the only fully organic brewery in Scotland. Barley for the beer is grown in his fields and although the hops aren't cultivated here, they are fully organic. Pure mountain water wells up from his own borehole and the yeast is held at the national yeast bank (every brewer nurtures their own distinctive culture).

There's a sweet smell of brewing beer as visitors are shown round this dinky brewery (there are plans afoot to extend the premises). With 10 regular beers plus the seasonal St Nicholas' Knicker Dropper Glory, a real winter warmer at 7.5% ABV, and the easy-drinking Yellowhammer at 4.0% ABV, there's a bevvie for every occasion including a rather fine heather honey brew (7.5% ABV) that David recommends with porridge for breakfast.

You can grab a bottle of these fine beers in their distinctive stylised thistle livery throughout Scotland and you'd do well to abide by the Black Isle Brewery's motto 'Save the planet, drink organic'.

Black Isle Brewery 391
Old Allangrange, Munlochy,
Ross-shire IV8 8NZ
01463 811871
www.blackislebrewery.com
Open daily 10am–5pm in summer and
Monday–Saturday in winter.

Wester Hardmuir Fruit Farm

Even on the wettest of days, a constant stream of customers brave the worst of the weather to buy some of the freshest fruit and veg around from James and Sylvia Clarke's farm shop. But when the sun shoulders its golden rays from beneath the clouds, pickers arrive in droves for the glut of fruit that hangs seductively in clusters or droops from singular stems.

There is no mistaking that heady blackcurrant perfume as nimble fingers pluck the plump fruit from the bushes. Raspberries, tayberries and loganberries thrive this far north. Peas and beans taste so much better when freshly picked, but if time is against you just drop into the shop, where everything is harvested fresh that morning. There are strawberries for gluttonous eating or for jam-making and the large gooseberry/blackcurrant cross (known as the Worcesterberry) that makes a fantastic preserve or can be used for staining summer pudding a deep burgundy.

Root vegetables should never be dismissed even in summer; carrots have fine downy roots, while beetroot are small enough to be eaten raw. Leafy, green salad leaves, brassicas, a wide selection of squashes and the king of vegetables, asparagus, are all here in season.

Wester Hardmuir Fruit Farm 394
Auldearn, Nairn IV12 5QG
01309 641259
www.hardmuir.com
Open daily 9am–6pm June–December.

Scottish Cheesemakers

It's difficult to say just how many cheeses are made in Scotland, but with well over 20 independent cheesemakers, there is much more to this lactic staple north of the border than you'd think. Plus, the dairy farms often sit in the most outstanding countryside.

Pam and Nick Rodway of Wester Lawrenceton Farm have been making cheese for over 30 years, but what makes theirs so special is that it's made from raw, unpasteurised milk. Their Sweet Milk Cheese would make a fantastic ploughman's; the cheese that most crofters would have made was just called 'cheese', but the Rodways call it Carola; it's similar in texture to Wensleydale. The best place to try their cheese is at Elgin or Inverness Farmers' Markets.

For a more hands-on approach, head towards the west coast to West Highland Dairy where Kathy and David Bliss run cheesemaking courses – from beginner's to advanced classes. Thankfully, you don't have to get stuck in to taste their cheeses since they have a tiny shop on the farm where they sell about 14 different types – there's a rather fine Highland Blue, various sheep's milk varieties including a well-aged Creag Mhaol and a Fernaig Brie alongside a Highland Brie made from cow's milk.

Wester Lawrenceton Farm 392
Forres, Morayshire IV36 2RH
01309 676566

Elgin Farmers' Market
9am–4pm third Saturday of each month

Inverness Farmers' Market
8.30am–3pm first Saturday of each month

West Highland Dairy 388
Achmore, Stromeferry, Ross-shire IV53 8UW
01599 577203
www.westhighlanddairy.co.uk

Phoenix Community Store

Findhorn Bay greets you with an expanse of calm, glassy water. A roar overhead alerts you to the proximity of RAF Kinloss and it seems a little incongruous to find a spiritual cooperative right next door. As you enter the Findhorn complex, you can be forgiven for thinking that you've come to a static caravan park, but all is not what it seems. What makes this different from other organic shops is that it's owned by a community partnership with hundreds of locals having a share in the business.

Hanging baskets and pots brimming with plants decorate the outside of the shop, which has a wide selection of organic, local, fair trade and artisan produce. There's a fine range of raw-milk cheese and chocolate, a small selection of local meat as well as organic whisky. If you explore this little enclave you are sure to discover the hobbit-like houses made from old whisky mash tuns, and don't miss lunch at the peaceful Blue Angel Café.

This eco-community may have its peace broken by the occasional take-off and landing of the planes next door, but, as one resident commented, 'It makes you appreciate the quiet serenity here.' And who can argue with that?

Phoenix Community Store 393
The Park, Findhorn, Forres,
Morayshire IV36 3TZ
01309 690110
www.phoenixshop.co.uk
Open 10am–6pm Monday–Friday,
10am–5pm Saturday and 11am–5pm
Sunday.

Scotland's Island Gems

Scattered around the Scottish coast, like a bejewelled coronet, are almost 800 islands. They stretch from Arran in the south to some 400 miles north; Unst in the Shetlands is actually closer to Bergen in Norway than the Scottish capital. Not all isles are inhabited, but those that are have an abundance of industrious artisan producers, farmers and fishermen, to say the least.

Far off to the north-west of the mainland, Shetland is a collection of about 100 islands and has an extensive network of foodie producers: Skibhoul Bakery makes oatcakes containing crystal-clear Shetland seawater; and the Valhalla Brewery is the most northerly brewery in the UK. Then, there's the seafood, a veritable treasure trove from Neptune's prolific larder – huge, sweet scallops, shiny blue-black mussels, organic salmon (smoked and unsmoked) through to the humble haddock. Meat is just as important with lamb grazing on the hills and shoreline, giving the flesh its distinctive flavour. As for vegetables, there's more to this land than Shetland Black tatties; in season you'll find salad crops and luscious soft fruits.

The 70-odd islands that make up the band of Orkney look as if they are within spitting distance of John O'Groat's on a map. You'll find local milk, butter and cheese here that tastes like no other; these cows feed on the islands' lush pastures; as for the meat, beef predominates, sold as Orkney Island Gold and Orkney Viking Beef. North Ronaldsay sheep graze entirely on seaweed, imparting a distinctive flavour to their dark flesh. As for drink, there are some rather strong fruit, flower and vegetable wines from the Orkney Wine Company with names such as Strubarb and Gorse. As the majority are sulphur-free the risk of a hangover is reduced, or so they claim. Those who prefer an even stronger tipple should skedaddle over to Highland Park Distillery closely followed by the Orkney Brewery.

Moving further round the coast, we hit the Outer Hebrides – a 130-mile daisy chain of islands that include Lewis, Harris, North Uist, Benbecula, South Uist and Barra. Serious fans of black pudding will no doubt be aware of the Stornoway version, made by Charles MacLeod, and voted by many as being achingly stunning. If you're in this neck of the woods during August, you may be lucky or brave enough to try one of the 2,000 gugas (fat young gannets) that are harvested from the uninhabited Sula Sgeir.

Several of Rick Stein's food heroes hail from North Uist, Benbecula and South Uist, while on Barra you'll find cattle and sheep wandering along the shoreline most likely from Hebridean Beef and Lamb. Here, they dispatch the creatures at the farm's fully licensed abattoir, making for unstressed animals and superlative meat.

The Inner Hebrides hug the mainland from the Isle of Skye, which has more than its fair share of fantastic restaurants – from the Three Chimneys halfway up the island at Colbost to the Duisdale further south on Sleat. Mull's capital – Tobermory

– with its brightly painted main street, has a distillery, the island's only dairy farm, which produces highly regarded cheeses, and even a chocolate factory. Boat over to the tiny windswept Isle of Colonsay where you'll discover some of the best honey you've ever tasted; think, concentrated wild-flower nectar. Gigha has Scotland's only organic halibut farm; give them fair warning and they'll happily send you some of this princely fish smoked, delivered right to your door.

One thing about the Scots, they are a tenacious race. No matter how inhospitable, remote or rugged the islands on which they live, there will always be good food and warming drinks to welcome the weary traveller.

Index

Acknowledgements

Taste Britain

Series Editor	Jonathan Knight
Original Series Concept	Guy Hobbs
Managing Editor	Nikki Sims
Researched and written by	Sandra Fraser, Susan Griffith, Lea Harris, Simon Heptinstall, Katie Jarvis, Jonathan Knight, Jenny Linford, Elisabeth Mahoney, Rosemary Moon, Colin Presdee, Lesley Anne Rose and Emma Sturgess
Design	Kenny Grant
Front Cover Design	Marcus Freeman, Measure Design and Kenny Grant
Proofreaders	Claire Wedderburn Maxwell, Leanne Bryan
Picture Research	Cassidie Alder, Catherine Greenwood
Publishing Assistants	Cassidie Alder, Sophie Dawson, Catherine Greenwood
Marketing	Shelley Bowdler
PR	Carol Farley
Published by	Punk Publishing, 3 The Yard, Pegasus Place, London SE11 5SD
Distributed by	Portfolio Books, 2nd Floor, Westminster House, Kew Road, Richmond TW9 2ND

The publishers and authors have done their best to ensure the accuracy of all information in *Taste Britain*, however, they can accept no responsibility for any injury, loss or inconvenience sustained by anyone as a result of information contained in this book.

Punk Publishing takes its environmental responsibilities seriously. This book has been printed on paper made from renewable sources and we continue to work with our printers to reduce our overall environmental impact.

Picture Credits

Photography by Cassidie Alder, Keith Didcock and Jonathan Knight except as below (all reproduced with kind permission). Key: T – top, B – bottom, M – middle, L – left, R – right. P6 London ©Keiko Oikawa; Southeast ©Thomas Freda; East Anglia ©Simon Crowhurst; P7 Peaks ©JW Mettrick & Son; Lakes ©Caroline Watson, Yew Tree Farm; Northwest ©Tatton Park; South Wales ©Toril Brancher, Highlands ©Bruichladdich; P8/9 ©Graham Jepson; P11 BL ©Simon Crowhurst; P12/13 ©Charles O'Rear/CORBIS; P23 B ©Simon Burt; P31 All ©Martin Ellis; P33 TR ©Kim Million 01392 873778; P35 TL &BL ©Docton Mill Library; P39 TL, BL ©Darts Farm, Topsham, R ©ARTOGRAPHY/A. Tucker; P47 TL & R ©NTPL/David Levenson; P51 B ©Martin Phelps; P53 All ©Jason Ingram; P54/55 ©John Miller/Robert Harding World Imagery/CORBIS; P58 T ©Newsteam/HRP; P63 BL©Helen Miller, www.helenmiller.com, TL, ML & R ©James Bedford; P64 ©Berry Brothers; P65 ©Fortnum and Mason; P67 ©Postcard Teas; P69 Photo supplied by Neal's Yard Dairy. Photographer Ethel Davies; P76 B ©Keiko Oikawa; P77 T ©Sam Thompson www.shrinkpad.com; P79 All ©Thomas Fedra; P81 ©Hogs Back Brewery Ltd; P84 T ©Jerome Dutton at awakeimaging.com, P89 All ©Chris Bardwell; P96/97 ©Mark Bolton/CORBIS; P101 Rob Rees at Stroud Farmers' Market from the book 'The Cotswold Chef – a year in Recipes and Landscapes' available from Darien-Jones Publishing; P110 T ©www.three-choirs-vineyards.co.uk; P111 B ©www.british-asparagus.co.uk; P125 ©By kind permission of Blenheim Palace; P129 Alder Carr; P130 B ©Dave Croker; P131 B ©National Trust; P136 T ©Polly Robinson, Food Safari; P139 TL ©Sue Kington, BL ©Simon Crowhurst, R ©Anne Steel of Maui Waui Design; P141 BL & BR, P149 T, P151 All, P153 BL, P154 B ©Susan Griffith; P145 ©Stilton Cheese Makers' Association; P148 T ©Vicki Marvin at trucreative.co.uk; P155 B ©Philip Hardie; P157 ©Gill Griffiths (www.gills-images.com); P158/159 ©Patrick Ward/CORBIS; P 162 B Peter Goulding; P163 T ©Chatsworth Settlement Trustees/Ryan Browne, B ©Chatsworth Settlement Trustees/Jenny Welch; P167 Chris Saunders; P168 T & P169 T Bryony Bond; P171 Jill Jennings; P173 ©JW Mettrick & Son; P177 Hazlemere Cafe & Bakery/Jonathan Bean Photo; P178 T ©Sticky Toffee Pudding Company, B & P192 B©Lesley Anne Rose; P179 T ©Bennett Design, B ©Dave Wills; P181 T & P189 R ©Dave Buxton, P181 B ©Jonny Moss, Scratch Creative www.scratch-creative.co.uk; P183 BL & TR ©Martin Campbell, TL & BR Annabell Williams; P185 Both ©Caroline Watson, Yew Tree Farm; P186 T ©George & Dragon, B ©Rob Whithrow; P187 B ©Helen Whittaker; P189 TL ©Barngate Brewery/Drunken Duck; P191 BL ©Bettys & Taylors of Harrogate Ltd; 193 T ©Swinton Park, B ©Dales Festival of Food and Drink; P195 ©Andrew Molyneux; P197 All ©John Watson Photography/Von Essen Hotels; P198 T Courtesy of Teeside Marketing and the Barnard Castle Farmers' Market, B ©Colmans of South Shields; P199 T ©Jason Thompson Photography, B ©Chain Bridge Honey Farm; P203 All ©Visit Chester and Cheshire; P204 T Nantwich Festival of Food and Drink/Fido PR, B courtesy of www.tastecheshire.com; P205 T Kenyon Hall Farm, B ©Visit Lancashire; P207 All ©Tatton Park; P210 T© Sunset Ices, B ©Russell Walsh/Potts Pies; P211 T ©J Atkinson and Co Ltd; P213 ©Wensleydale Dairy Products; P214/215 ©Alan Copson/JAI/CORBIS; P221 TR ©Tori Brancher, TL & B ©Nathan Morgan; P222 B ©Paul Tennant; P223 T ©Martin Cavaney, B ©Tara/David Pitman; P226/7 ©Jason Ingram; P247 ©Ken Davies, Conwy Camera Club; P248/249 ©Jim Richardson/CORBIS; P268 ©Visit Scotland/Scottish Viewpoint; P273 R ©John Fletcher of Fletchers of Auchtermuchty; P279 TL ©Visit Scotland/Scottish Viewpoint, R & P283 ©Bruichladdich. Inside Front Cover: T ©Anne Steel of Maui Waui Design, London's Treats ©Helen Miller, www.helenmiller.com, B ©Jason Ingram; Back cover: Farmer's Market ©Sam Thompson www.shrinkpad.com; Inside back cover: Bread ©Jonny Moss, Scratch Creative www.scratch-creative.co.uk; B ©Keiko Oikawa.